ART, DEATH AND LACANIAN PSYCHOANALYSIS

Art, Death and Lacanian Psychoanalysis examines the relationship between art and death from the perspective of Lacanian psychoanalysis. It takes a unique approach to the topic by making explicit reference to the death drive as manifest in theories of art and in artworks.

Freud's treatment of death focuses not on the moment of biological extinction but on the recurrent moments in life which he called "the death drive" or the "compulsion to repeat": the return precisely of what is most unbearable for the subject. Surprisingly, in some of its manifestations, this painful repetition turns out to be invigorating. It is this invigorating repetition that is the main concern of this book, which demonstrates the presence of its manifestations in painting and literature and in the theoretical discourse concerning them from the dawn of Western culture to the present.

After unfolding the psychoanalytical and philosophical underpinnings for the return of the death drive as invigorating repetition in the sphere of the arts, the authors examine various aspects of this repetition through the works of Gerhard Richter, Jeff Wall, and contemporary Israeli artists Deganit Berest and Yitzhak Livneh, as well as through the writings of Virginia Woolf and James Joyce.

First to articulate the stimulating aspect of the death drive in its relation to the arts and the conception of art as a varied repetition beyond a limit, *Art, Death and Lacanian Psychoanalysis* will be indispensable to psychoanalysts, scholars of art theory and aesthetics and those studying at the intersection of art and psychoanalysis.

Efrat Biberman is an Associate Professor at Hamidrasha Faculty of Arts, Beit Berl College, Israel. Her fields of interest are theory and philosophy of art from a Freudian-Lacanian perspective. She is the author of *Visual Text(a)iles: Narrative and Gaze in Painting* (2009, in Hebrew).

Shirley Sharon-Zisser practices psychoanalysis in Tel Aviv, Israel. She is a member of the World Association of Psychoanalysis (AMP) and an Associate Professor of English at Tel Aviv University. Her work focuses on the interrelations between rhetorical theory and Lacanian psychoanalysis. Her publications include *The Risks of Simile in Renaissance Rhetoric* (2001), *Critical Essays on Shakespeare's "A Lover's Complaint": Suffering Ecstasy* (2005, ed.) and *Lacanian Interpretations of Shakespeare* (2009, ed.).

ART, DEATH AND LACANIAN PSYCHOANALYSIS

Efrat Biberman and Shirley Sharon-Zisser

Routledge
Taylor & Francis Group
LONDON AND NEW YORK

First published 2018
by Routledge
2 Park Square, Milton Park, Abingdon, Oxon OX14 4RN

and by Routledge
711 Third Avenue, New York, NY 10017

Routledge is an imprint of the Taylor & Francis Group, an informa business

This book is a translation of a work previously published in Hebrew as *Death Is the Mother of Beauty* by Tel Aviv University Press, 2014. Translation into English by Tamar Gerstenhaber, Keren Shafir, Efrat Biberman and Shirley Sharon-Zisser.

British Library Cataloguing in Publication Data
A catalogue record for this book is available from the British Library

Library of Congress Cataloging in Publication Data
Names: Biberman, Efrat, author. | Sharon-Zisser, Shirley, 1962- author.
Title: Art, death and Lacanian psychoanalysis / Efrat Biberman and Shirley Sharon-Zisser.
Other titles: Maòvet hu imo shel ha-yofi. English
Description: New York, NY : Routledge, [2017] | Includes bibliographical references and index.
Identifiers: LCCN 2017020994| ISBN 9781138044029 (hardback : alk. paper) | ISBN 9781138044043 (pbk. : alk. paper) | ISBN 9781351698535 (epub) | ISBN 9781351698528 (mobipocket/kindle)
Subjects: LCSH: Psychoanalysis. | Art—Psychological aspects. | Death—Psychological aspects.
Classification: LCC BF175 .B17513 2017 | DDC 700/.4548—dc23
LC record available at https://lccn.loc.gov/2017020994

ISBN: 978-1-138-04402-9 (hbk)
ISBN: 978-1-138-04404-3 (pbk)
ISBN: 978-1-315-17266-8 (ebk)

Typeset in Bembo
by Swales & Willis Ltd, Exeter, Devon, UK

CONTENTS

FIGURES

ACKNOWLEDGEMENTS

This book was published with the support of Beit Berl Academic College.

All reasonable effort has been made to identify the copyright holders of the material reproduced in this book. If the authors have inadvertently failed to obtain permission, please contact the publisher so that the necessary arrangements may be made.

Cover image: Yitzhak Livneh, *DS III*, 2005. Oil on canvas, 130 × 120 cm. Reproduced with the kind permission of the artist.

Epigraph featured at the start of the introduction is taken from Wallace Stevens, "Sunday Morning," in *The Collected poems of Wallace Stevens* (New York: Vintage Books, 1990 [1923]). © 1954 by Wallace Stevens and renewed 1982 by Holly Stevens. Used by permission of Alfred A. Knopf, an imprint of the Knopf Doubleday Publishing Group, a division of Penguin Random House LLC. All rights reserved.

Figure I.1: Yitzhak Livneh, *DSIII*, 2005. Image reproduced by courtesy of the artist.

Figure I.2: Yitzhak Livneh, *DS*, 2005. Image reproduced by courtesy of the artist.

Figure I.3: Gerhard Richter, *Tote* (Dead), 1988. © Gerhard Richter images. Image reproduced by courtesy of the artist.

Figure I.4: Jeff Wall, *Dead Troops Talk* (a vision after an ambush of a Red Army patrol near Moqor, Afghanistan, winter 1986), 1992. Transparency in lightbox, 229.0 x 417.0 cm. Image reproduced by courtesy of the artist.

Epigraph featured at the start of chapter one is taken from Jacques Lacan, *The Seminar of Jacques Lacan, Book IX: Identification* (1961–1962), trans. Cormac

Gallagher (unpublished manuscript), lesson of 23 May 1962, p. 269. Reprinted with the kind permission of Cormac Gallagher.

Figure 1.1: Luca Signorelli, *The Resurrection of the Flesh*, 1499–1502. © Opera del Duomo di Orvieto. Image reproduced with kind permission.

Figure 1.2: Luca Signorelli, *The Resurrection of the Flesh*, 1499–1502 (detail). © Opera del Duomo di Orvieto. Image reproduced with kind permission.

Figure 1.3: Sandro Botticelli, *The Birth of Venus*, 1486. © Gallerie degli Uffizi. Image reproduced with kind permission.

Epigraph featured at the start of chapter two is taken from G. W. F. Hegel, *Aesthetics: Lectures on Fine Art*, trans. T. M. Knox (Oxford: Clarendon Press, 1988 [1835]). © 1975 by Oxford University Press. Used by the kind permission of Oxford University Press.

Figure 2.1: Hans Holbein, *The Body of the Dead Christ in the Tomb*, 1521. © Kunstmuseum Basel. Image reproduced with the kind permission of Kunstmuseum Basel.

Epigraph featured at the start of chapter three is taken from Jacques-Alain Miller, "Introduction to Reading Lacan's Seminar on Anxiety", trans. Barbara P. Fulks. *Lacanian Ink* 26 (2005): 6–67. © 2005 by Jacques-Alain Miller. Used by the kind permission of Jacques-Alain Miller.

Figure 3.1: Shosh Kormosh, *Untitled (M19)*, 1991–1993. Image reproduced with the kind permission of the artist's family.

Figure 3.2: Shosh Kormosh, *Untitled (E3)*, 1987–1990. Image reproduced with the kind permission of the artist's family.

Figure 3.3: Annibale Carracci, *Self-Portrait at the Easel*, 1604. © The State Hermitage Museum, St. Petersburg. Image reproduced with the kind permission of the State Hermitage Museum.

Figure 3.4: Caravaggio, *David with the Head of Goliath*, 1609–1610. © Galleria Borghese. Image reproduced with the kind permission of Galleria Borghese.

Figure 3.5: Maurizio Cattelan, *Spermini*, 1997. Painted latex masks, 17.5 × 9 × 10 cm each. Photo Attilio Maranzano. Image reproduced with the kind permission of Maurizio Cattelan's archive.

Epigraph featured at the start of chapter four is taken from Virginia Woolf, *Mrs. Dalloway* (London: Hogarth Press, 1989 [1925]), p. 163. © 1925 by Houghton Mifflin Harcourt Publishing Company, renewed 1953 by Leonad Woolf. Reprinted by permission of Houghton Mifflin Harcourt Publishing Company. All rights reserved.

Epigraph featured at the start of chapter five is taken from a lecture given by Yitzhak Livneh at Gordon Gallery, Tel Aviv, 2006. Used with the kind permission of the artist.

Figure 5.1: Yitzhak Livneh, *Michal I*, 2004. Image reproduced by courtesy of the artist.

Figure 5.2: Yitzhak Livneh, *The Invention of Painting*, 2004. Image reproduced by courtesy of the artist.

Figure 5.3: Yitzhak Livneh, *Goodnight*, 2004. Image reproduced by courtesy of the artist.

Figure 5.4: Yitzhak Livneh, *Astonishment*, 2004. Image reproduced by courtesy of the artist.

Figure 5.5: Yitzhak Livneh, *Medusa*, 2000. Image reproduced by courtesy of the artist.

Figure 5.6: Yitzhak Livneh, *Nude over Mirror*, 2000. Image reproduced by courtesy of the artist.

Figure 5.7: Yitzhak Livneh, *Still Life with Mirror*, 1991. Image reproduced by courtesy of the artist.

Figure 5.8: Yitzhak Livneh, *Broken Mirror V*, 2003. Image reproduced by courtesy of the artist.

Epigraph featured at the start of chapter six is taken from Jacques Derrida, *Copy, Archive, Signature: A Conversation on Photography*, ed. Gerhard Richter (Stanford: Stanford University Press, 2010 [2000]), p. 19. © Stanford University Press. Reprinted with the kind permission of Stanford University Press.

Figure 6.1: Julia Margaret Cameron, *Thomas Carlyle*, 1867. Digital image reproduced by courtesy of the Getty's Open Content Program.

Figure 6.2: Eddie Adams, *South Vietnamese National Police Chief Brig. Nguyen Ngoc Loan Executes a Vietcong Officer with a Single Pistol Shot in the Head*, 1968. © Associated Press. Image reproduced by courtesy of AP Images.

Figure 6.3: Alexander Gardner, *Portrait of Lewis Payne*, 1865. The digital image is in the public domain.

Figure 6.4: Aby Warburg, picture atlas *Mnemosyne*, panel 46, 1928–9. Unknown photographer. © The Warburg Institute. Image reproduced by courtesy of The Warburg Institute.

Figure 6.5: Gerhard Richter, *Newspaper Photos, Atlas Sheet 11*, 1963. © Gerhard Richter Images. Image reproduced by courtesy of the artist.

Figure 6.6: Gerhard Richter, *Tote* (Dead), 1988. © Gerhard Richter Images. Image reproduced by courtesy of the artist.

Figure 6.7: Yitzhak Livneh, *Big Ruin*, 2002. Image reproduced by courtesy of the artist.

Figure 6.8: Deganit Berest, *From the Atlas (The Dead Sea)*, 1976. Image reproduced by courtesy of the artist.

Figure 6.9: Deganit Berest, *M2*, 1992. Image reproduced by courtesy of the artist.

Figure 6.10: Deganit Berest, *Untitled*, 2004. Image reproduced by courtesy of the artist.

Figure 6.11: Deganit Berest, *Icarus*, 2004. Image reproduced by courtesy of the artist.

Figure 6.12: Deganit Berest, from *The Bathers*, 1990. Image reproduced by courtesy of the artist.

Figure 6.13: Deganit Berest, *Swimmer*, 1989. Image reproduced by courtesy of the artist.

Figure 6.14: Deganit Berest, *Swimmer*, 1987. Image reproduced by courtesy of the artist.

Figure 7.1: Yitzhak Livneh, *Untitled*, 1990. Image reproduced by courtesy of the artist.

Figure 7.2: Yitzhak Livneh, *EXIT*, 2007. Image reproduced by courtesy of the artist.

PROLOGUE

Re-hearse

The book before you is concerned with repetition. A fundamental concept of psychoanalysis, Lacan says, for there is no force in human life more fundamental than the compulsion—what Freud calls *Zwang* but Lacan specifies as seduction or fascinated attraction[1]—to summon suffering and destruction in what rhetorician Richard Sherry, when talking about pleonastic repetition, calls *superabundancia*:[2] abundance related to the excess of torture for which the superego does not cease to demand *encore*. This fascinated attraction, Lacan teaches in the last lesson of his seminar on the *Four Fundamental Concepts of Psychoanalysis*, is nothing but compliance with the imperative to sacrifice to what Lacan calls the "dark gods"[3]—those residing on the reverse side of an ideal ego without blemish or hint of castration; residing in what Freud calls the "Id" (*das Es*) as a reservoir of libidinal cathexes that have been abandoned[4] yet always await a recharging as a cruel Other of the phantasm, returning across generations to menace existence itself.

It is this fundamental force that pulsates in William Shakespeare's sonnet 21, conventionally read as Shakespeare's retort to a rival poet:

> So is it not with me as with that Muse,
> Stirr'd by a painted beauty to his verse;
> Who heaven itself for ornament doth use,
> And every fair with his fair doth rehearse;
> Making a couplement of proud compare,
> With sun and moon, with earth and sea's rich gems,
> With April's first-born flowers, and all things rare
> That heaven's air in this huge rondure hems.
> O' let me, true in love, but truly write,
> And then believe me, my love is as fair
> As any mother's child, though not so bright

As those gold candles fix'd in heaven's air:
Let them say more than like of hearsay well;
I will not praise, that purpose not to sell.[5]

To "rehearse" (l. 4) is the Shakespearean name given in this sonnet to the mortifying repetition obeying the imperative of the superego, as seductive as it is diabolical. This is repetition of the order of the "hearsay" (l. 13), of what is heard in what is said, such as the unconscious the analyst listens for. But where the unconscious appears to the analyst's ear as a foreign language heard "at a distance or in a very low voice,"[6] or as Lacan says in the eleventh seminar, in the gaps and cracks, the disappearances and fadings of what is said,[7] what is heard in what is said appears in the sonnet between a "heaven" (l. 3) and an "earth" (l. 6) that are "hemmed" (l. 8) to create what Shakespeare describes as a "huge rondure" (l. 8): a closed spherical shape, visual phenomenalization of the ideal ego, the subject's most archaic and most perfect specular reflection that is also the structural substrate for the ideals to which subjects have never ceased to rally, that is to say, to be seduced to sacrifice themselves and others in perverse feasts of bloodshed that are the wars punctuating history, seduced to a jouissance which almost no one, Lacan teaches, can resist. What is it that occurs when the "re-hearse" takes place in the superegoic shadow of the ideal? In the sonnet, alliteration and assonance, repetition of consonants and of vowel sounds—"heaven" (l. 3), "earth" (l. 6), "rehearse" (l. 4), "heaven's air" (l. 12), "hearsay" (l. 13)—make heard in what is said, make emerge as from nether regions, as from a foreign language heard from afar, a signifier that is not explicitly articulated in the sonnet: "hearse." As in the well-known case of the forgetting of the name Signorelli Freud analyses in *The Psychopathology of Everyday Life*,[8] in the sonnet the unarticulated signifier emerges from a combination of what Lacan calls "metonymic ruins":[9] phonic and graphic remainders of this signifier itself. The signifier "hearse," the sonnet's additional, unspoken signifier, speaks the truth of repetition under the banner of ideals—repetition of the mortifying kind that is a diabolical return of the same. This mortifying and diabolical repetition is the iteration of one note across a diachronic continuum. When such iteration of the One is read synchronically, it is nothing but the One of death as final term.

Yet in Shakespeare's sonnet, as in artistic practice and the reflection upon it that this book examines and that the sonnet synecdochizes, the tautological, homiological One that Sherry (rightly) denominates "*repetitio inutilis*,"[10] repetition that, like jouissance, has no use, no utility, the homiological One whose iteration is as forever self-identical as the glass the alcoholic drinks each time for the first time, anticipates, and as this book argues, is also a condition for, repetition of another order.

For synchronically, the homiological One is nothing but the manifestation of the inanimate state which the drive, Freud teaches, seeks beyond the waves and vaults of its trajectory[11] from one point of an erogenous zone to another, and as such, a terminus; but as such, also a threshold. The sonnet does not reach its term with the first eight lines, an octave whose psychorhetorical structure turns it into a poetic hearse in which fragments of letters and sounds do not cease to repeat themselves as products of the disintegration of what is "hemmed" within the subjective hearse any ideal becomes. Its retroaction is the emergence of a sestet whose focus is the possibility to "truly write" (l. 9); to write not as "that Muse" (l. 1) described in the octave; to write what is not the hermetic, "hemmed" structure of a hearse that is the echo chamber for a single note but in the structure of an open-ended chain such as is manifest in the poem's first line, "So is it not with me as with that Muse" (l. 1), concatenating similaic copulas that are various ("So," "as") with nonspecific pronouns ("me," "that Muse"), the first of which, whose logical place would be before the copula initiating the line, is missing. Octave and sestet are bound by a rhetorical hinge comprising two signifiers, "O' let" (l. 9), the first of them, the apostrophaic copula "O'," a grapheme tracing the borders of a rim, the second not only the inaugural syllable of the signifier "letter" whose agency in the unconscious is decisive, but at once a verb indicating a possibility and a noun denoting what obstructs. Poetically positioned beyond a textual terminus (of the octave), the hinge conjoining obstruction and apo(s)trophaic border made of letters and rhetorical forms operates apotropaically, operates, that is, as what causes destiny—in this case, what appeared as the insistence of a mortifying homiological repetition—to turn (from Greek *trepein*) differently. Rhetoric's name for what turns differently is "trope," an operation of style that, unlike elocution's other programmatic operation, figure, is not only ornamental supplement but an alteration of sense. One example of this is *antanaclasis*,[12] the replication of a word so that it signifies otherwise. Antanaclasis is never iterative and hence never of the order of the automatism of the death drive. It is the logic of the structure of such transformative tropaic repetition beyond the closure of a hem or end that is at work in the invigorating repetitions of art beyond the terminations declared from its inception which the following pages unfold. Another rhetorical name for such invigorating antanaclastic repetition is *antistasis*:[13] what stands in opposition to the stasis such as Freud exposes as the ultimate aim of the death drive. Such invigorating repetition is not of the order of the One, of the order of the hearse emerging from hemmed and harmonic coupling Shakespeare calls "couplements of proud compare" (l. 5), but of the order of a couplement or combinatory that would be, the sonnet's closing line homophonically suggests, "not to se(a)l" (l. 14). Such an antistatic combinatory that does not seal and does not hem structures the sestet's second sentence, ". . . my love is *as* fair / *As* any mother's child" (ll. 10–11, our emphasis) just as it structures the sonnet's first line, "So is it not with me *as* with that Muse" (l. 1, our emphasis). Couplements are combinatories into less than seamless self-identity of signifiers whose content is less than definite and hence might be of the order not of the automaton but of the *tyche*,[14] of what unforeseeably emerges to cut the insistence of the mortifying insistence of the same, of what the speaker apo(s)trophaically gestures toward in the sestet's opening line: "O' let me true in love but truly write" (l. 9).

Beyond the art of the "hearsay" (l. 13), the knowledge such as the analyst's to locate what is heard in what is said, there is the art of the "truly write" (l. 9), the art of a writing that is not of the order of the "say more" (l. 13), the saying in excess that is hence a saying that mor-tifies. This is a writing that does not respond to an imperative to sacrifice because it is grounded in desire, emerging from the empty place marked by the limits of the O, in the cause as lost but as precisely for that reason operative. What returns, is repeated, in an art of "truly write" emerging from the empty place of the cause is not the litter of decomposing letters produced by the emphatic sealing of poetic lines into a "huge rondure . . . hem[med]" (l. 8) but the less than definite, unhemmed components of a similaic chain such as constitutes not only the sonnet's first and eleventh lines but also the title of Shakespeare's pastoral, *As You Like It*, that also gives voice to a desire. Such is the psychorhetorical structure of a repetition subtended by desire, what we have called in the pages that follow an "invigorating repetition," for which the mortifying manifestation of repetition is in effect a dialectical condition.

In the life of each subject, mortifying repetition presents itself as the recurrence precisely of what is most unpleasurable. In the life of civilization, one of its manifestations is the perennial presence of war. Such mortifying repetition manifests in a will to destroy. Freud writes in a correspondence with Albert Einstein: "War is in the crassest opposition to the psychical attitude imposed on us by the process of civilisation,"[15] yet is inextricably "alloy[ed]" with this attitude whose work is the work of representation and whose symptoms include aesthetic production, and indeed, at times is "what enables it."[16] The death drive as mortifying repetition, that is, functions as the backdrop and condition for the emergence of Eros, one of whose manifestations in culture is the invigorating repetitions we isolate in the arts. It makes possible the emergence of what in Lacan's terms is the effect generated by a desire that treads beyond the pleasure principle, the effect of beauty such as the splendor of Antigone the chorus speaks of in Sophocles's play,[17] to which we shall, in what follows, return.

Death, then, "is the mother of beauty," as Wallace Stevens writes in "Sunday Morning":

> Death is the mother of beauty; hence from her,
> Alone, shall come fulfilment to our dreams
> And our desires. Although she strews the leaves
> Of sure obliteration on our paths,
> The path sick sorrow took, the many paths
> Where triumph rang its brassy phrase, or love
> Whispered a little out of tenderness,
> She makes the willow shiver in the sun
> For maidens who were wont to sit and gaze
> Upon the grass, relinquished to their feet.
> She causes boys to pile new plums and pears
> On disregarded plate. The maidens taste
> And stray impassioned in the littering leaves.[18]

Death is the mother of beauty, Wallace Stevens enables us to say; it is within its "bosom," within the constraints of a mortifying repetition, that the beauty that insists as art is "devise[d]" and made to emerge (VI. ll. 13–16). It is to the exploration of the structural foundations of this insistence that we dedicate this book.

Notes

1 Jacques Lacan, *The Seminar of Jacques Lacan, Book XI: The Four Fundamental Concepts of Psychoanalysis*, trans. Alan Sheridan (New York: W.W. Norton, 1998 [1964]), p. 259.
2 Richard Sherry, *A Treatise of Schemes and Tropes*, ed. Herbert W. Hilderbrandt (Gainesville, FL: Scholars' Facsimiles and Reprints, 1961 [1550]), p. 25.
3 Lacan, *Seminar XI*, p. 259.
4 Sigmund Freud, "The Ego and the Id," in *The Standard Edition of the Complete Psychological Works of Sigmund Freud, Vol. XIX*, trans. and ed. James Strachey (London: Hogarth Press, 2001 [1923]), pp. 12–66.
5 William Shakespeare, "Sonnet 21," in *The Sonnets*, ed. Katherine Duncan-Jones (London: Arden, 2010 [1609]), p. 41. All further references to the sonnet are to this edition by line number and will be incorporated in the text.
6 Sigmund Freud, "Remarks on the Theory and Practice of Dream-Interpretation," in *The Standard Edition of the Complete Psychological Works of Sigmund Freud, Vol. XIX*, trans. and ed. James Strachey (London: Hogarth Press, 2001 [1922]), p. 110.
7 See Lacan, *Seminar XI*, pp. 17–28.
8 Sigmund Freud, "The Psychopathology of Everyday Life," in *The Standard Edition of the Complete Psychological Works of Sigmund Freud, Vol. VI*, trans. and ed. James Strachey (London: Hogarth Press, 2001 [1901]), pp. 1–7.
9 Jacques Lacan, *The Seminar of Jacques Lacan, Book V: The Formations of the Unconscious* (1957–1958), trans. Cormac Gallagher (unpublished manuscript), lesson of 13 November 1957, p. 28.
10 Sherry, *Treatise of Schemes and Tropes*, p. 25.
11 Sigmund Freud, "Beyond the Pleasure Principle," in *The Standard Edition of the Complete Psychological Works of Sigmund Freud, Vol. XVIII*, trans. and ed. James Strachey (London: Hogarth Press, 2001 [1920]), p. 38.
12 See Henry Peacham, *The Garden of Eloquence* (London: I. Jackson, 1593), p. 56.
13 See Richard A. Lanham, *A Handlist of Rhetorical Terms* (Berkeley: University of California Press, 1991).
14 For the extended theorization of the categories of *tyche* and *automaton*, appropriated from Aristotle, see Lacan, *Seminar XI*, pp. 53–64.
15 Sigmund Freud, "Why War?" in *The Standard Edition of the Complete Psychological Works of Sigmund Freud, Vol. XXII*, trans. and ed. James Strachey (London: Hogarth Press, 2001 [1932]), p. 215.
16 Ibid., p. 209.
17 For Lacan's analysis of "The Splendor of Antigone," see Jacques Lacan, *The Seminar of Jacques Lacan, Book VII: The Ethics of Psychoanalysis*, trans. Dennis Porter (New York: W. W. Norton, 1986 [1959–1960]), pp. 243–256. The analysis is discussed in detail in chapters two and six of this book.
18 Wallace Stevens, "Sunday Morning," in *The Collected Poems of Wallace Stevens* (New York: Vintage Books, 1990 [1923]), p. 69, ll. 48–60.

INTRODUCTION

> Death is the mother of beauty; hence from her,
> Alone, shall come fulfilment to our dreams
> And our desires.
>
> —*Wallace Stevens, 1990 [1923], "Sunday Morning"*

In 2005, Israeli artist Yitzhak Livneh painted a series based on photographs of German marble sculptures, sculptures of dead soldiers dating back to the eighteenth century. The sculptures of the soldiers' heads, which had been placed as a memorial in the upper part of the building housing the Berlin History Museum, were fastened to a wall as an architectural detail. The sculptures realistically portray the very last moments before death, the facial expression which freezes as life departs. Although the sculpted soldiers are not identified by name, the series of sculptures exemplifies various particularities of the last moment of life: gaping mouth, drooping eyelids or wide-open eyes. In Livneh's paintings the sculptures become large-scale portraits consisting of monochromatic stains; the image, emerging from amorphous puddles of paint, becomes almost abstract. The gaping mouths and closed eyes grant the portrayed soldiers an unclear appearance; the processes of enlargement and abstraction render them sexless. The soldiers' expressions range from great suffering to ecstatic chant, from the semblance of a last cry of a departing soul to that of a voice vivacious, loud and clear.

An eerie atmosphere pervades these paintings, upon their rich colorfulness and horrifying source, underscoring the impossible moment they are supposed to portray. The strangeness and terror the paintings evoke blend with their beauty, a beauty manifest in the quick brush strokes and the lightness with which the image emerges onto the canvas. The last gaze of a life becomes the first gaze of a portrait. The moment of transition from the end of life to the

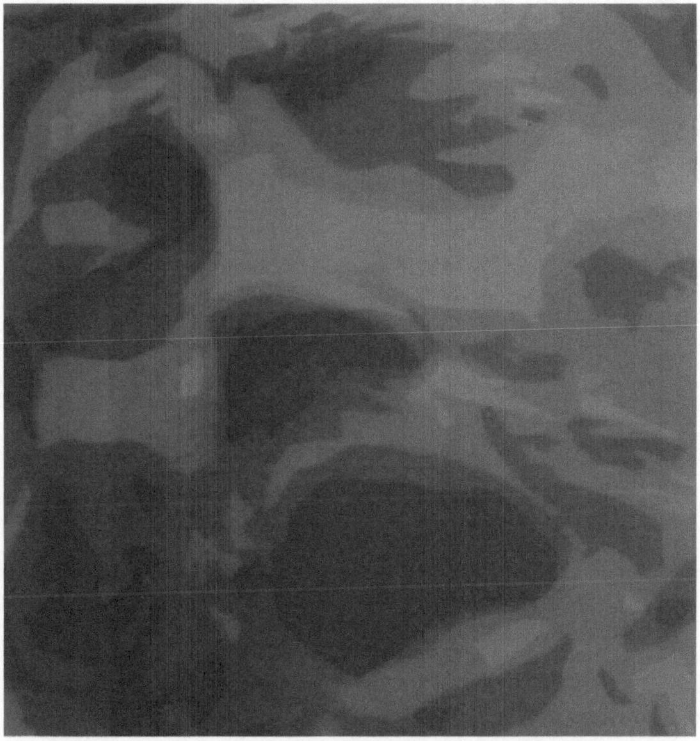

FIGURE I.1 Yitzhak Livneh, *DSIII*, 2005. Image reproduced by courtesy of the artist.

birth of painting vacillates between these two possibilities of the gaze and is hence suspended.

Livneh's images of dying and singing soldiers allude to numerous precedents in twentieth-century art. In the context of the major issue discussed in this book, we wish to point out two of them: Gerard Richter's painting series *October 1978* of 1988 and Jeff Wall's photograph *Dead Troops Talk* of 1992. Richter's paintings refer to the suicide of the imprisoned members of the Baader-Meinhof Group. Several of the paintings, such as the profile of the dead Ulrike Meinhof, brought down from the noose on which she hung herself, feature images of dead bodies, blurred in Richter's photo-painting style. The composition varies from one painting in the series to another. As is the case with Livneh's portraits, Richter's paintings portray a last moment, and they too implicitly address the issues of the impossibility to portray this moment and of painting's ways of contending with this impossibility. In *Dead Troops Talk*, Wall, using a wartime press photo showing the results of an ambush, stages dead soldiers, bleeding makeup colors, talking to one another. Like Livneh, Wall treats the dramatization of the portrayed event, the very fact of the event's being a representation, and the proximity as well as the gap between pathos and the grotesque.

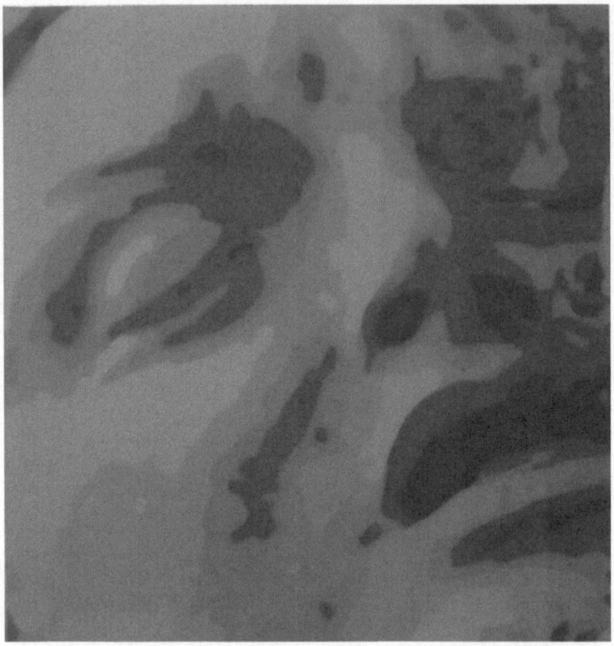

FIGURE I.2 Yitzhak Livneh, *DS*, 2005. Image reproduced by courtesy of the artist.

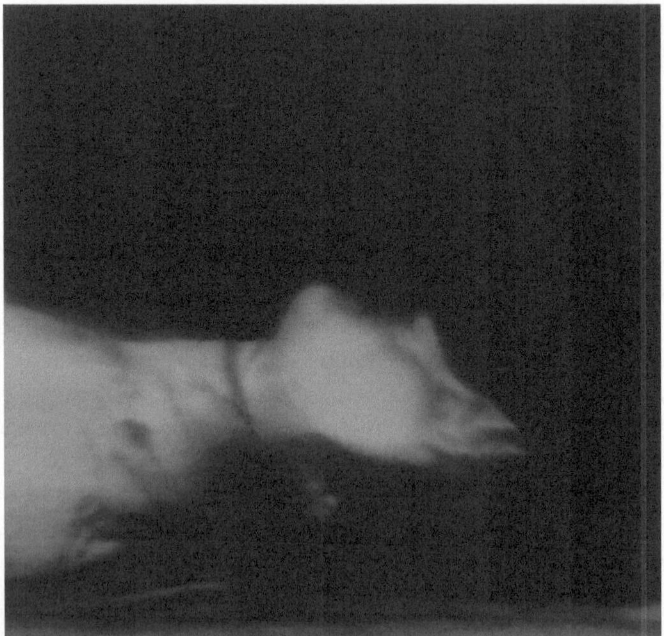

FIGURE I.3 Gerhard Richter, *Tote* (Dead), 1988. © Gerhard Richter images. Image reproduced by courtesy of the artist.

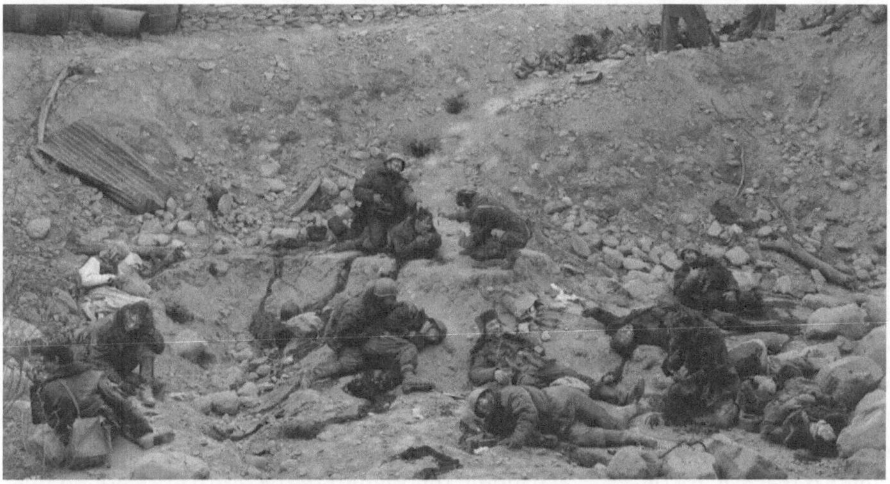

FIGURE I.4 Jeff Wall. *Dead Troops Talk* (a vision after an ambush of a Red Army patrol, near Moqor, Afghanistan, winter 1986), 1992. Transparency in lightbox, 229.0 x 417.0 cm. Image reproduced by courtesy of the artist.

These artworks by Livneh, Richter and Wall, which place death at their forefront, strangely link the issue of death with the artistic medium in which it is presentified. In these works, that is, content and means of representation are intertwined. Livneh's soldier-singers are stamped in color stains close in tonality, values proper to abstract painting thus substituting the horror of their death scene. Richter's paintings dissolve into a fog, eliciting a wish to see better while careful not to make clear and sharp vision possible. The makeup-covered wounds of Wall's chattering soldiers signal the possibility of their being but painted figures and reference the theoretical question of the relation between photography and death. Death appears in the image itself as well as in the meta-image, that is, in the thought about its status as image. It is the camera's mortification of the image that makes its freezing and fossilizing possible, rendering it an eternal object of recurrent observation.

In the three above examples, drawn from contemporary art, the representation of death is inextricably intertwined with the modes of image production. Is the recurrence of this intertwining in contemporary art a chance occurrence, the result of historical contingency, or does it rather point to a fundamental structure? And if there is a fundamental structure to be extricated from this recurrence, what might it teach us about a question that has preoccupied the philosophy of art from its inception, the question of the relation between the making of art and death?

This book examines the relation between art and death not as a theme represented in artworks but as a structure, from the vantage point of Lacanian psychoanalysis, built upon its Freudian roots.[1] We propose to explain and qualify this structure by means of a major concept in psychoanalysis, one closely linked with the death drive: the compulsion to repeat.[2] We find the compulsion to repeat on three levels which we trace in the sphere of art from its inception to its contemporary manifestations: that of works of art, visual and literary, themselves; that of interpretations of works of art; and that of theorizations of art. That we locate a compulsion to repeat on all three of these levels of the manifestations of art in culture does not mean that we regard the artworks, analyses of artworks, or theorizations of art as illustrations or examples for a theoretical discourse. We do not, that is, approach the phenomena we analyze on all three of these levels as objects to which we apply a knowledge or theory already known to psychoanalysis, which would make our study a simple instance of what François Regnault calls an "*experimentum mentis*," the abstract mental exercise which "takes place in what we ordinarily call applied psychoanalysis, which is in fact for Lacan theoretical psychoanalysis."[3] Rather, we follow Lacan's dictum regarding literature in "*Lituraterre*," according to which psychoanalysis does not approach literature to discover what it already knows, but to extract new knowledge regarding the enigmas that are its concern,[4] expanding this dictum to the visual arts. We do not, that is, apply psychoanalysis to our examples from the sphere of art on all three levels, but apply these examples to psychoanalysis.[5] In this sense, our position with respect to the artworks, the interpretations of artworks, and the theoretical discussions of art and death or the death of art we consider is akin to the position of the analyst with respect to a clinical case in its singularity. It is from the singularity of the cases examined, that is, the way in which every one of them exceeds the structure it exemplifies (in this case, the structure of an invigorating repetition following an alleged end) that we reach the conclusions presented in this book. In this sense, the artworks, interpretations of artworks and theoretical discussions of art and death or the death of art on the basis of which we reach our conclusions and extract new knowledge would be in Regnault's terms instances not of an *experimentum mentis* but of an *experimentum crucis*, experiments crucial because of what they prove,[6] but because the only true crucial experiment for psychoanalysis is the experience of the subject in an analysis, they cannot be such.[7] Perhaps the most precise way to locate their status, then, would be as cases which do not exemplify a psychoanalytic category but embody it. At the same time, as singular cases, they are, like every clinical case in psychoanalysis, paradoxically excluded from the very category they embody.

The connection between art and death is ubiquitously present in the long history of art, the philosophy of art, and the theory of art. According to Pliny the Elder, the Roman author of the first century A.D., painting was invented by a young woman who traced the shadow of the beloved from whom she was about to part forever. It was thus that the birth of painting was first linked with the loss of a nonretrievable object. The idea of a relation between the making of art and loss remained central in Western culture. Over the past two hundred years, from the time Georg Friedrich Hegel proclaimed the death of art and into our own times, philosophers and theorists of art have been preoccupied not only with art as a medium for documenting death but also with the death of painting or the end of art in general. As the abovementioned artworks by Livneh, Richter and Wall demonstrate, the interlinking of art and death is manifest not only on the level of thought and theory but also on the level of practice: in manifold artistic works in which death is present not only as theme, but in the modes of production of the image.

From whence the persistent linkage between art, death and finitude, both on the level of theory and on the level of artistic practice? Even from critical perspectives of the late twentieth century, art does seem to be a field of creation and reinvention. Why, then, is it constantly linked with death? How does what psychoanalytic discourse claims has no representation in the unconscious become a major pole of interest in artistic work which aims, at least ostensibly, at representation? In what follows, we would like to propose that psychoanalytic theory makes it possible to address these questions in a productive way.

The connection between art and death is multifaceted. The field of art evidently makes it possible to represent death as theme. This is attested to, for instance, by paintings that make death a primary subject matter: paintings of the crucifixion, the resurrection, *vanitas* paintings, paintings of autopsies and more. But artistic practice also involves the possibility of going beyond death by inventing a mode of representing the unrepresentable. Furthermore, artistic production by its very nature is challenged by the possibilities of its exhaustion, that is to say, of its reaching an end beyond which there is nothing. Yet, as the chapters of this book seek to demonstrate, the end point of seeming annihilation is a necessary condition of a repetition subsisting beyond it. It is this repetition that constitutes the presence of the death drive in culture. It is by means of this presence that art charges what was at first a traumatic event with the force of life. Hence, as this book claims, the death drive is manifest in art as a force that is not mortifying; not as what causes suffering but as what can extricate from it; as a force that is invigorating and revitalizing.

The chapters of this book consider various manifestations of the invigorating presence of the death drive in the sphere of art as predicated on a structure of seeming annihilation and a repetition persisting beyond it. The first chapter lays the theoretical foundation for interrogating art's connection to death and finitude by discussing the concept of the death drive in the teachings of Freud and Lacan. The chapter considers the death drive and the repetition compulsion from Freud's writings of the early twentieth century, most markedly "Beyond the Pleasure Principle" of 1920 to the late teaching of Jacques Lacan. This discussion suggests that in the manifestations of the death drive in the field of art, death constitutes not nullity nor destruction, but a condition for a repetition subsisting beyond it.

The various manifestations of the death drive in culture are not limited to the sphere of artistic practice but also percolate into the theoretical discourse concerning art. The second chapter presents different theories in Western culture which link art, death and finality. The chapter begins with an analysis of the myth of the invention of painting and of other moments linking art and death in the writings of Pliny the Elder. We then consider later theoretical formulations of the connection between art and death as these appear in Leon Battista Alberti's writings on geometrical perspective and in their contemporary interpretations. Later in the chapter, we show how the manifestation of the death drive in culture rises to a higher power. It takes the form not only of a thinking linking art and death but of the discussion of the very end of art, which of course continues to exist, and in a way that this very discussion brings into relief. We locate the source for the discourse on the end of art mainly in Hegel's aesthetics, emphasizing its intensive treatment of death and finality in relation to art. Following a detailed analysis of the Hegelian idea of the end of art, we show the different ways in which this idea resonates in the philosophy of art written in the twentieth century.

Subsequent chapters of the book examine various manifestations of the death drive in culture by analyzing paradigmatic cases from artistic practice, each of them revealing a different facet of the manifestation of repetition in art as a revitalizing repetition.

Chapter three discusses autobiographic representation in the visual field. In this chapter, we examine several self-portraits in which the artist chose to represent himself as a dead body or as a body part torn off and discarded, as a remainder ejected from the sphere of life. Engaging the work of Paul de Man that regards autobiography as effacement, we discuss these strange representations as modes of representing the nonrepresentable. Most significantly, however, these examples of self-representation as an object cut off from the body make it possible to conceptualize the work of art itself as a body part to be lost, as an artist's way of observing himself as foreign to himself. The self-portrait is, then, an object that is cut off from the body and that continues to exist as a physical remainder beyond the artist's biological demise, in a twilight zone between death and life.

Chapter four too considers self-representation, but this time in another artistic medium, that of literature that is autobiographical, though in a way different from usual conceptions in literary criticism. The literary autobiographies of James Joyce and Virginia Woolf enable us to distinguish between autobiographical writing narrating events from the artist's life and autobiographical writing of a different order, one that deconstructs sense in language. In the cases of Joyce and Woolf, texts depicting the course of their lives are actually the ones that have less to do with the inscription of life. In psychoanalytical terms, such autobiographical writing, a registration of conscious memories, veils not only unconscious memory traces but also death, which, as Freud explains in "The Unconscious" of 1915, being an abstraction of negative content, has no unconscious correlate—that is, no representation in the unconscious.[8] Death is present in the writings of James and Woolf not as conscious inscription but materially, in the repetition of graphic, phonic and rhetorical devices. Unlike in painted self-representations, in literary autobiography repetition appears only in a particular dimension of the artistic work: its style.

Chapter five focuses on the recurrence of the death drive in culture by means of artistic style, taking as its focus paintings by Yitzhak Livneh. In this case, the death drive is manifest not in material but in structural aspects of style. We extract two such structures from Livneh's paintings: witticism as theorized by Freud, and the use of framing as stylistic dominant. Witticisms, Freud shows, are often based on the condensation of signifiers. In many paintings by Livneh, one of these signifiers is the image of a skull, while the other is a sports ball. Death, Freud taught, cannot be repressed because it is not registered in the unconscious. In Livneh's paintings death is indeed not seen, but is nevertheless present as an effect of the condensation of signifying images. This condensation gives rise to a visual hybrid evoking laughter because of the defamiliarization it involves. The hybrid image, the product of condensation, no longer signifies in itself, but indexes something beyond signification. In the second stylistic structure characteristic of Livneh, the use of frames, the return of death through style emerges as an effect of use of infinite regression or *mise en abyme*. We identify this structure in a series of painted portraits of women consisting of a series of concentric frames: the woman's lips frame an oral cavity represented by a dark stain at the center of the painting. This frame is placed within the frame of the painted woman's face. The woman's hair functions as a third frame, and all three frames are held within the confines of the canvas. In these paintings, we claim, Livneh interrogates and represents what is beyond representation, that is, beyond the pleasure principle.

In addition to manifestations of the death drive in culture which are medium-specific, or which traverse artistic media, there are such manifestations subsisting between two media, whose conjunction creates an artistic medium in its own right. Chapter six considers such a medium—photo-painting, painting based on and referring to photography, yet grounded in conceptions of painting. We propose to examine the presence of death in each of the visual media constituting photo-painting by means of a distinction between two fundamentally different categories: of the veil and of the hole. We examine photo-painting via works by Gerhard Richter, Deganit Berest and Yitzhak Livneh, showing how mediumal repetition itself is what makes it possible for something to flicker between the different media. For it is precisely in between the death of painting and the death of photography that the artistic act emerges.

In the epilogue we revisit paintings by Livneh. We consider two seemingly unrelated series of paintings, created almost two decades apart: mirror paintings from the 1990s and the *EXIT* paintings of the early twenty-first century. Though death is ostensibly present in these paintings only on an associative level, the two series crystallize the conceptual move we trace throughout the book: they exemplify the possibility of reaching the limit of painting and even going beyond it. Reaching this limit results not in a loss but in the possibility, for the painter, to continue reinventing himself, and the art of painting.

Notes

1 Throughout the book, we use the term "death drive" in the sense of an end that is not final, that does not herald annihilation, but is a pause following which something insists on reappearing.

2 For Freud, the repetition compulsion is rooted in a primal trauma that remains unconscious. This trauma returns in an event that recurs in the subject's life, an event that, even if ostensibly contingent, the subject is in effect compelled to repeat because of the satisfaction involved in it. Freud's conclusion in "Beyond the Pleasure Principle" is that

the satisfaction from suffering is none other than the death drive. What is at stake is not the death wish of an individual but the subject's aspiration to die after his own fashion. See Sigmund Freud, "Beyond the Pleasure Principle," in *The Standard Edition of the Complete Psychological Works of Sigmund Freud, Vol. XVIII*, trans. and ed. James Strachey (London: Hogarth Press, 1955 [1920]), pp. 7–23.

3 François Regnault, "Lacan and Experience," in *Lacan and the Human Sciences*, ed. Alexandre Leupin (Lincoln: University of Nebraska Press, 1991), p. 45.

4 Jacques Lacan, *The Seminar of Jacques Lacan, Book XVIII: On a Discourse That Might Not Be a Semblance* (1970–1971), trans. Cormac Gallagher (unpublished manuscript), lesson of 12 May 1971.

5 Regnault, "Lacan and Experience," p. 55.

6 Ibid., p. 46.

7 Ibid., pp. 44, 54.

8 Sigmund Freud, "The Unconscious," in *The Standard Edition of the Complete Psychological Works of Sigmund Freud, Vol. XIV*, trans. and ed. James Strachey (London: Hogarth Press, 1957 [1915]), pp. 166–204.

1

BEYOND THE ART PRINCIPLE

> [E]ven if we were not mortal,
> even if we had the promise of eternal life,
> the question still remains open whether this "eternal life" [. . .]
> is not conceivable as a form of eternally dying.
>
> *—Jacques Lacan, May 23, 1962, p. 269*

More than a hundred years after Livneh's singing soldiers met their end on the battlefield, other soldiers who had survived horrors returned home, physically intact yet wounded psychically. It was none other than Freud who was asked to give his expert opinion on how best to treat these shell-shocked soldiers. Freud's encounter with the soldiers who returned from the trenches of the First World War generated several studies he published in 1919–1920. What astounded Freud in the phenomenon of shell-shock was the manner in which the traumatic event would be repeated again and again in the dreams and hallucinations of the suffering patient. This occurred although in terms of Freud's view of the operation of the pleasure principle and of the dream as a fulfillment of a wish, the repetition of the anxiety-provoking event seemed unreasonable.[1] Freud reached the conclusion that the pleasure principle, which he had heretofore viewed as the driving force in human life, was not the only principle at work in the psychic apparatus. Another principle existed, functioning beyond the pleasure principle and embodying what Freud then found to be the very essence of the drive, the death drive. For Freud, and for Lacan who followed in his footsteps, the death drive is not an individual's wish for annihilation but the repetition of a traumatic event in varying permutations. This principle functions within the psychic apparatus as a system of representations in their relation to a satisfaction that cannot be represented. Freud called this principle the compulsion to repeat.

Until his theorization of the death drive, Freud assumed it was the pleasure principle that was the major principle operative in the psychic apparatus, an apparatus whose aim is to reduce excitation to a minimum and to function homeostatically. The pleasure principle as Freud conceived it is in effect a corollary of the tendency toward stability. Any eschewal of stability or deviation from it leads to the inverse of pleasure.[2] What then caused those shell-shocked soldiers who returned from the battlefields struck by trauma to repeatedly reproduce the horrors they encountered in their dreams? While trying to explain this paradoxical phenomenon, Freud recounts an anecdote of his infant grandson playing a game of disappearance and return with a wooden reel of string while his mother is briefly away from home. Freud inquires as to why the scene which the child repeatedly reenacts through the game is not the happy scene of the mother's return but the presumably much more distressing instance of her disappearance, embodied by the vanishing reel. How might one explain, Freud asks, the relation between the compulsion to repeat such an unpleasurable disappearance and the pleasure principle?[3]

Freud's conclusion was that the compulsion to repeat constitutes not an opposition to the pleasure principle but an aberration from it. At this juncture, Freud looks to the natural sciences and the conjecture that all organic matter ultimately strives not only to develop and progress but even more so to return to an ancient state of preexistence. The aim of all organic matter, Freud writes,

> must be an *old* state of things, an initial state from which the living entity has at one time or other departed and to which it is striving to return by the circuitous paths along which its development leads. If we are to take it as a truth that knows no exception that everything living dies for *internal* reasons—becomes inorganic once again—then we shall be compelled to say that "*the aim of all life is death.*"[4]

How might this thesis be reconciled with the myriad instances indicating that the aim of any organism is its self-preservation? Freud argues that the living organism does seek to die, but above all, it seeks to die in its own fashion.[5] For Freud, what transforms a life from mere biological existence to a subjective and unique mode of being, characterized by an inimitable style which includes the style of demise, is repetition, which more often than not is the repetition precisely of what causes suffering. This repetition straddles the subject's life. It transforms this life from a straight line between the points of birth and death (in which case all trajectories of human life would be identical) into a singularly circuitous path. The operation of the death drive as repetition thus makes each and every life trajectory not only singular but winding, meandering as it repeats, and as such, longer than what would have been the direct progression of the biological organism from birth to death.

The monotonous repetition of what is most unbearable, however, is not the only form of repetition in human life. This kind of repetition, what Freud called the compulsion to repeat, is manifest in the subject's recurrent encounters with difficult or painful events which have an unconscious connection with primordial trauma.

Although such encounters are ostensibly imposed on the subject, it is the subject himself who facilitates their repetition and return, deriving satisfaction from the suffering they incur. Lacan calls this satisfaction in suffering enjoyment or *jouissance*. Psychoanalysis, however, makes it possible to think of another form of repetition which is of an entirely different nature. What this form of repetition involves is not the precise iteration of primordial trauma but its replication with a difference, one that transforms the trauma, attenuating its mortifying power. Such repetition is not necessarily charged with a high quantum of suffering. Far from being opposed to life, it invigorates and may be experienced as a *joie de vivre*. In psychoanalytic terms, this form of repetition involves desire (*désir*), which may be defined as a lack functioning as a motivating cause in human life. This form of repetition too can constitute the subject's singular meandering path to die, as Freud put it, in his own fashion, beyond trauma, deferring and exceeding what would otherwise have been the short and direct path to biological extinction.

Within Freud's work, the discussion of the category of the double in the 1919 essay on "The Uncanny," published one year before "Beyond the Pleasure Principle" where Freud first theorized the death drive, exemplifies the second, invigorating form of repetition. In "The Uncanny," Freud considers the tendency to repeat, in the lives of children and in the course of psychoanalytic treatment, as indicative of an innate and fundamental quality of the drives.[6] Freud finds one manifestation of this tendency in the motif of the double, to which Otto Rank devoted an extensive study. The double, Freud writes, citing Rank, "was originally an insurance against the destruction of the ego, an 'energetic denial of the power of death.'" The "'immortal' soul," Freud continues,

> was the first "double" of the body. This invention of doubling as preservation against extinction has its counterpart in the language of dreams, which is fond of representing castration by a doubling or multiplication of a genital symbol. The same desire led the Ancient Egyptians to develop the art of making images of the dead in lasting materials.[7]

Freud, then, links the phenomenon of the double with the subject's response to death and specifies it as a repetition. The confrontation with the utter and horrifying absence associated with death, he suggests, leads to the seemingly contrary emphasis on what is present, which is then subjected to a doubling and repetition which might keep the horror masked. This Freudian theorization of the tendency to double and repeat in the face of "the power of death" can help explain not only the ubiquitous cultural phenomenon of reifying the dead but also, not least, the preoccupation with the relation between death and representation in the theory of art starting with the writings of Pliny the Elder and Leon Battista Alberti.

Later in "The Uncanny," Freud notes that the phenomenon of repetition, whose source he locates in the drives, is predominant in the unconscious to such an extent that it can override the pleasure principle. When writing "The Uncanny," Freud had yet to theorize the compulsion to repeat upon its implication with the structure of the drive. Even then, however, he recognized repetition's involving acquiescence to what exceeds the pleasure principle. A year later, Freud published "Beyond the Pleasure Principle," in which he explicitly equates the compulsion to repeat, which in "The Uncanny" he had associated with "preservation against extinction," with what he calls the death drive.[8]

What this means is that the death drive as Freud theorizes it is an impelling force, an element inextricable from life itself. It is distinct from the actual death of an individual, which has no representation in the unconscious. In "The Uncanny," Freud writes: "It is true that the statement 'All men are mortal' is paraded in text-books of logic as an example of a general proposition; but no human being really grasps it, and our unconscious has as little use now as it ever had for the idea of its own mortality."[9] What is of much use for the unconscious, however, is the death drive in its manifestation as what impels a repetition that preserves and protects rather than destroys, such as Freud had spoken of when revisiting the phenomenon of the double in "The Uncanny."

Lacan, who reads Freud rigorously while refuting traditional interpretations of his writings, pauses upon this second manifestation of the death drive as repetition, which we would like to isolate as paradigmatic to the field of the arts. "Life is the totality of the forces which resist death," Lacan writes, quoting the great eighteenth-century French physiologist and anatomist François Bichat.[10] If there is anything quintessential to psychoanalytic experience, says Lacan, it is the Freudian formulation of the vortex of death to whose edges life clings so as not to fall into it. Lacan then goes on to differentiate between death and the inanimate.[11] In other words, as Bichat had already made clear, death does not mean the absence of life. The death drive is to a great extent a driving force of life itself, which gushes all the more against death. Thus, in a paradoxical manner, the vortex of death is a condition for life in its capacity as limit, in view of which life gushes forth all the more forcefully.

As Lacan explains, Freud conceived of the pleasure principle in economic terms, as a principle seeking to regulate psychic energy (libido). Situated at the threshold of the psychic apparatus, the pleasure principle is triggered whenever this apparatus encounters stimuli. Its function is to reduce these stimuli to a minimum so as to maintain pleasure, that is to say, to keep the apparatus at the lowest possible level of excitation. But what exactly, Lacan asks, is this reduction of excitation to a minimum? Is it bringing the apparatus to an equilibrium, or is it, rather, the restriction of its activity to an absolute minimum, that is to say, to the point of its own extinction? Lacan recalls at this point that for Freud in "Beyond the Pleasure Principle," something other than the homeostatic pleasure principle operates within the psychic apparatus, and its name is the death drive. Lacan explains that the death drive is not a wish for annihilation but an inherent component of human experience. In effect, Lacan indicates, it was from the very beginning of his work that Freud discerned that the subject does not operate according to the pleasure principle alone. Indeed, the symptom which brings a subject to analysis is precisely what is unpleasurable and a cause of much suffering, and yet what the subject nevertheless finds himself compelled to repeat. The human being, in other words, is very far from consenting to the pleasure principle's attempt to attenuate every stimulus which is so high as to induce unpleasure. As Freud discerned in "Beyond the Pleasure Principle," Lacan continues, alongside the pleasure principle, another principle is operative in the psychic apparatus, one which draws the libido toward a state of absolute stasis such as characterizes the inanimate. What is at stake in this principle in the pleasure principle's beyond, however, is not finding the shortest and most direct route to the cessation of individual life. It is, rather, the conveying of libido whose ultimate goal is the return to the inanimate through the pathways of life while relentlessly repeating an archaic trauma. The human being, then, operates in ways that cannot be exhaustively explained by the pleasure principle. What accounts for the regular course of a life is the principle of the insistence to reach death in a particular and inimitable manner which involves the repetition of what hurts. The path of repetition, then, is foundational to the unfolding of life as human life.[12]

To explain the function of the death drive in the very pulsation of life, Lacan turns to two laws of thermodynamics: the law of conservation of energy and the principle of entropy. The law of conservation of energy entails the assumption that the product of any action is a remainder of what was already there. The principle of entropy, however, indicates that every action involves some form of loss. What this means in terms of the subject is that what returns as a symptom during the course of a life is the remainder of a traumatic encounter. This remainder persists and recurs because it is grounded in a representation of the traumatic event which is unconscious, that is to say, preserved as a memory which is not consciously known. Yet the condition for unconscious representation is loss. It is thus that the principle of entropy appears in human life. Like the remainder of a trauma that once was, the loss of satisfaction involves suffering, a seeming disruption to the functioning of the apparatus to which it is nevertheless essential.

The disruption built into the human subject as integral to its functioning, Lacan teaches, has to do with the repetition inherent in the very structure of language. What the subject repeats is not his successes, as might be expected were we to read the pleasure principle in the simplest sense, but precisely his mistakes. Such is repetition as it appears in the human sphere, and as Lacan's reading of the story Freud's grandson and his wooden reel shows, in his early teaching Lacan reads it as pertaining to the symbolic, that is, to representation and thus to language. Repetition in human life, then, has to do with the status of language as the discourse of the Other. The Other is not another person who can be a rival or a locus of identification, but an Other *for the subject*, for instance, the father figure. To the extent that the father functions as an Other for a particular son, the son inherits the father's mistakes in the form of unconscious representations he is then destined to repeat while knowing nothing about this. Unless an analysis intervenes, the son himself will pass on the unconscious registrations of his father's mistakes. What this means is that far from being a mere reservoir of known words, language is the field into which the subject as speaking being is cast. The son who repeats the mistakes of his father repeats what he heard from his father or about his father; he repeats the way in which these mistakes were registered in the discourse he heard in one way or another as a child. The child, that is, takes part in life by means of language, which is none other than unconscious representations which recur.

Such is the significance of repetition in "Beyond the Pleasure Principle": it launches the psychic apparatus beyond the biological mechanism of equilibrium and harmony. It is what makes the death drive as compulsion to repeat inextricable from life, indeed a very condition for a subjective engagement with it.[13]

It is in this vein that Lacan asserts that when the subject's unconscious is not present, that is, when only the conscious system manifests itself, the death drive is in abeyance, or in Lacan's words, functions as a "death mask" for the symbolic.[14] When the unconscious is in operation, the death drive too lives. In speaking of the death drive as the symbolic's mask, Lacan emphasizes the split between a subject of the unconscious and conscious life. Conscious life may be understood as a view of the world in empirical terms, wherein the course of life is perceived as a self-evident sequence of events unrelated to the history of the subject. The unconscious is the chain of signifiers pertaining to the chapter of the subject's history about which the subject knows very little or nothing. It is there that the death drive works ceaselessly, manifesting itself as repetitions in the subject's life which are nothing but his particular mode of relating to the world, of being alive.

The connection Lacan draws between the death drive and the unconscious as a chain of representations, that is to say, as symbolic, is evident also in his 1953 article "The Function and Field of Speech and Language in Psychoanalysis." The notion of the "death drive," Lacan writes, involves a basic irony as it conjoins two seemingly contradictory terms: the drive, which in its common acceptation has to do with the accomplishment of a life function, and death, which appears first of all as the destruction of life.[15]

The notion of "life," too, however, is far from univocal. Life may be conceived of as a resistance against death—as death's diametric opposite. At the same time, life may be viewed as it is in Freud's early writings, as the striving of the psychic apparatus toward equilibrium and the constant maintaining of the lowest possible level of stimulus. Both life and death, that is, are operative at the very heart of phenomena people associate with life.[16] In subjective life their compounding manifests itself in the death drive as repetition. Lacan writes:

> the death [drive] essentially express[es] the limit of the historical function of the subject. This limit is death—not as an eventual coming-to-term of the life of the individual, nor as the empirical certainty of the subject.[17]

Death as limit is, rather, as Lacan puts it in Heideggerian terms, "that 'possibility which is one's ownmost, unconditional, unsupersedable, certain and as such indeterminable.'"[18] Lacan differentiates here between death as the historical limit of life and death as what is "ownmost" to the subject. This is the death drive as an insistent repetition of what is unique, which is not always a mode of enjoyment in suffering. What emerges from this repetition is the singularity of the subject, and it is marked by a peculiar temporality. Lacan points out that the past involved in the death drive is neither a physical past that has come to an end, nor an epic time preserved in memory, nor even a historical past holding the promise of a future. It is, rather "the past which reveals itself reversed in repetition."[19] It is as an effect of this past revealed in and as repetition that the deeds of an individual no longer alive can continue to appear, as in the instance of the son who repeats the mistakes of his father.

The subject does not cease to repeat in ciphered form unconscious representations transmitted to or inscribed in him. These recurrently appear in the choices of his love life, in his dreams, in the symptoms which cause his suffering and in what appears on the stage of transference in the clinic. The representations in question are those that are inscribed in the unconscious as a result of contingent traumatic encounters with objects of the drive and then function as unary traits, signifiers which have no sense in themselves but in relation to which the signifying chain of the unconscious is established. Lacan designates the unary trait "S1" and emphasizes that it is none other than a "mark toward death."[20] Were it not for the operation of this mark toward death, however, nothing whatsoever would receive any sense. The function of the unconscious signifying chain and of the phantasm with which the subject interprets what he encounters in the course of his life is to make predications on the unary trait, inscription of a traumatic encounter, to endow it with sense.

The unary trait, primary inscription in the unconscious, implicates death not only because it emerges in psychic life as a repeated satisfaction that hurts which is none other than the death drive but because its very constitution involves a mortification. The symbol, Lacan says, "manifests itself first of all as the murder of the thing."[21] For representation to emerge, something must be killed, no longer be, or as Freud puts it, must be lost. The condition for unconscious representation, Freud writes in his 1925 article on "Negation," is that things have been lost which once brought real satisfaction.[22] This is why, as Lacan puts it, the word is "a presence made of absence."[23] Representation, that is, necessitates the absence, loss, death of a real satisfaction, such as Freud's grandson does not cease to repeat as he throws away the reel of string he makes reappear, equipping Freud with an example for what he would theorize as the death drive.

Both Freud and Lacan, then, delineate a double relation between representation and death. Death, the death of the thing that had brought primordial satisfaction, which is none other than the thing's expulsion from representation, is a necessary condition for representation in the unconscious, a product of the judgment of the pleasure principle. This does not mean, however, that representation involves a loss of all drive satisfaction. Indeed, satisfaction insists within representation, as the repetition of unary traits in the phenomena that Freud locates beyond the pleasure principle. It is this repetition of a satisfaction that animates representation, makes it into more than an automated output of words.

What this means is that the death drive is not simply the satisfaction of the suffering registered in the unary trait Lacan calls jouissance; it also involves what animates, what is on the side of what Lacan theorized as desire. Lacan infers the category of desire from Freud's notion of the libido present only by virtue of its effects. In Lacan's reading of Freud, desire is "the relation of being to lack." The lack at stake is not the lack of any concrete object but the lack of being that is the very condition of the subject. This lack is "beyond anything that can represent it." It cannot be represented, which is precisely why any form of representation preserves and vehicles it. It is only ever represented, Lacan says, "as a reflection on a veil."[24]

Desire, then, is not a desire for anything namable, and it is precisely as such that it is inherent to the very foundation of life. What this means is that the human subject is not simply a positive being but a being whose positivity is contingent upon a constitutive lack. What animates this being, its desire, is nothing but the pursuit of the lack which appears but as a reflection on a veil. The desire fundamental to any human experience, then, is a consequence of the constitution of the subject as a lack in being. Conversely, the subject comes into being as a function of lack. This is precisely what the self-conscious being transparent to itself that is assumed by philosophy will never know, seeing itself as it does as an object among other objects, not recognizing what is lacking in any being. [25]

The centrality of lack to the constitution of desire too is evident in Freud's anecdote of his grandson playing with the reel of string, since at the heart of the game, the subject seizes himself at the very moment of his absence. This is precisely the moment in which desire is constituted, and it is constituted in relation to a phantasm. The child playing with the reel of string is registered in his own phantasm. The phantasm supports his desire and is linked from the outset with the lack that is both cause and result of the representation of the absent mother. What this means is that desire can become manifest only at the joint of speech, where representation or symbolization is present.

The experience of an analysis is an attempt to give place to the subject's desire. The very act of speaking in the analytic situation causes the subject to forge a new presence in the world: a presence of desire. At the same time, speech in analysis perforates and empties out the presence it itself creates. This is because desire is never the desire for what is articulated, always the desire for something else. Once desire is spoken, it becomes something other than the uttered word, which as mentioned earlier, kills the thing for which it stands.[26] Desire as a desire for something that is always other is also what lies at the core of repetition's invigorating aspect, since it is desire which has the ability to transform the monotonous reiteration of a trauma into a repetition of an entirely different order

The invigorating repetition Freud and Lacan point to emerges in the field of sexuality as well as in the field of representation. What suggests this is a distinction Lacan makes in his twelfth seminar between two facets of sexuality: the sexual act and the propagation of future generations. The link between propagation and sexual copulation is not necessary but contingent: some species procreate by means of asexual reproduction; in the human sphere, copulation has to do less with reproduction than with rejuvenation. It is precisely as such that it has a fundamental and complex relation to death. The tremor permeating the human sexual act, Lacan says, is nothing but a sign of death, because this act is an instance not of biological reproduction but of a struggle against extinction.[27] The propagation of the species, then, is a possible effect of the sexual act but certainly neither its cause nor its purpose. Sexual encounters in the human sphere are repeated acts of defiance in the face of death. Manifestations of a subjective recognition of death, sexual encounters do not cease to seek to eschew it. Once again, death appears not as the decimation or annulment of life but as the motivating force of an invigorating repetition.

Invigorating repetition emerges, that is, as an effect of the traversal of a real threshold such as the recognition of death. This is precisely why it is located beyond the pleasure principle. In his seventh seminar on the ethics of psychoanalysis, Lacan turns to Sophocles's *Antigone* to demonstrate the operation of what lies beyond the pleasure principle.[28] It is in the context of this analysis that he invokes a category permeating the philosophy of art from its inception: beauty.

In his analysis of the play, Lacan considers the consequences of going beyond the possibility of representation, beyond the symbolic. Antigone transgresses the symbolic, manifest in the play as the laws made by Creon. For Lacan Antigone's refusal to comply with the law of the state is a definitive example of a subject following her particular desire beyond the pleasure principle even at the price of life itself. Toward the end of the play Antigone finds herself between symbolic death, the death sentence Creon imposes upon her, and the real death of her body. The portion of the play between these two deaths functions as an in-between zone which Lacan parallels to a crystal refracting rays of light. Just as a beam's passage through the medium of crystal causes the light to refract and luminesce, so too the traversal of the zone between two deaths by means of Antigone's desire has the effect of splendor. It is this effect of splendor and not any quality attributed to the protagonist, Lacan teaches, that is the beauty of Antigone.

Lacan in seminar seven, then, links beauty as it emerges from a work of art to two facets of death: real and symbolic. He takes this link one step further in his seminar of the following year, whose topic is transference. In this seminar too, Lacan speaks of real death as biological expiration, the severing of an individual life. Symbolic death, however, is here not death as decreed by law but the cessation of life so that it might continue to be preserved and transmitted as memory, and its example is Socrates's choice to accept the verdict of his trial.[29] This commemoration is inherent to art, as in its deviation from the movement of life it preserves what is otherwise destined for annihilation within this very movement. Both in seminar seven and in seminar eight, then, Lacan isolates an aesthetic effect in the transition between two deaths (symbolic and real in the first instance, real and symbolic in the second). In the first instance, the effect in question is beauty as a splendor refracted by the traversal of the harrowing zone between decreed and actual extinction by the vector of an invincible desire. What is at stake in the second is commemoration. In both instances, the deconstruction of death into its real and symbolic components allows Lacan to situate death as a necessary condition for the creation of art and as cause of art's effects. Art becomes what subsists beyond the double annihilation of death as symbolic as well as real and thanks to this double annihilation itself.

The psychoanalytical thinking of death as an annihilation that cannot be registered which functions as a condition of the artwork existing beyond it as repetition is present as early as Freud's *The Psychopathology of Everyday Life*, to which Lacan returns in his fifth seminar, *The Formations of the Unconscious*. In his book, Freud demonstrates the functioning of the unconscious via the analysis of an anecdote where the name of the artist Luca Signorelli, the painter of the fresco *The Resurrection of the Flesh* in the Orvieto cathedral, slips his memory.[30] Instead of the artist's name, Freud remembers the names of other artists, Botticelli and Boltraffio, but Freud knows they are not the artist in question.

In an attempt to decipher the forgetting of the artist's name, Freud reconstructs the associative sequence which unfolded in the conversation during which the forgetting occurred. He remembers that he spoke of the customs of the Turks living in Bosnia and Herzegovina and had argued that these people tend to have the greatest confidence in their doctors. When a doctor tells them that there is no hope of a certain patient's recovery, they immediately answer, "'Sir [*Herr* in German and *Signore* in Italian], what is there to be said? If he could be saved, I know you would have saved him.'"[31] Freud further recalls that while he was saying these things, he recalled another story about the very same Turks, but refrained from

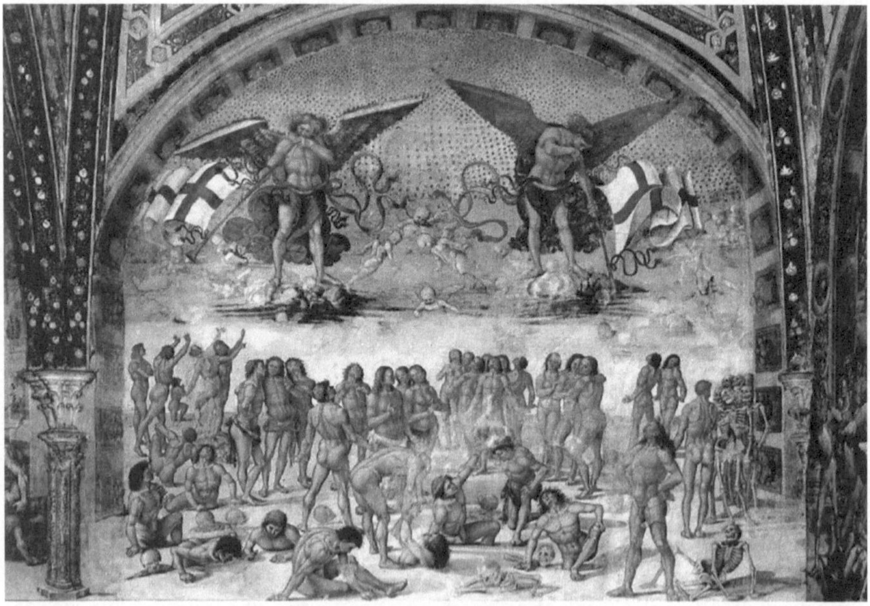

FIGURE 1.1 Luca Signorelli, *The Resurrection of the Flesh*, 1499–1502. © Opera del Duomo di Orvieto. Image reproduced with kind permission.

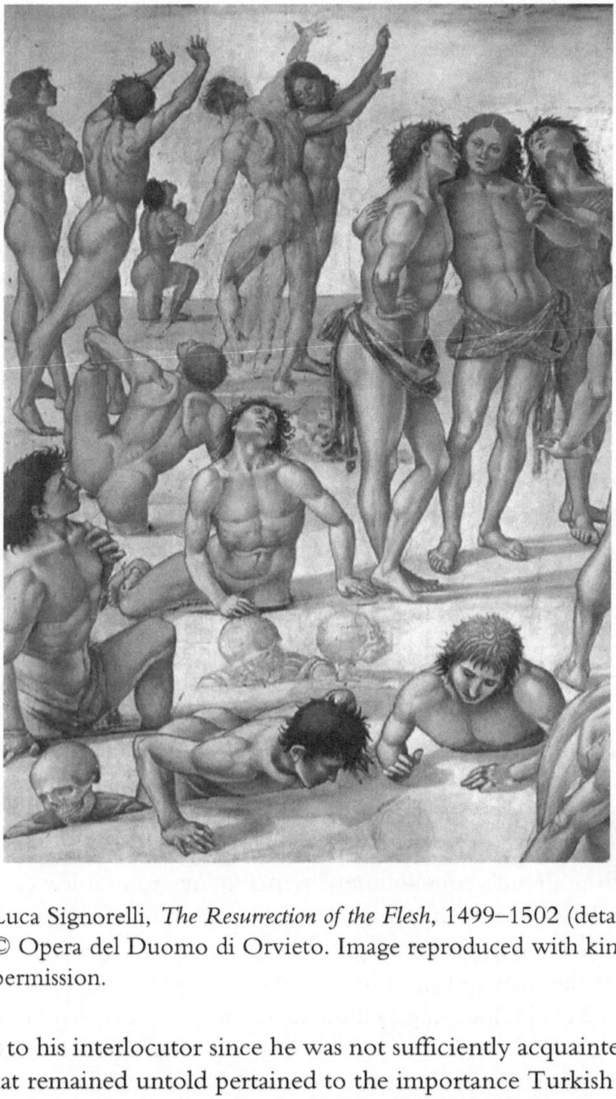

FIGURE 1.2 Luca Signorelli, *The Resurrection of the Flesh*, 1499–1502 (detail). © Opera del Duomo di Orvieto. Image reproduced with kind permission.

conveying it to his interlocutor since he was not sufficiently acquainted with him. The story that remained untold pertained to the importance Turkish men accord to sexual potency, to the extent that without it they deem life to be of no value. At this juncture Freud discovers that the forgetting of the name "Signorelli" initially had to do not with the name of the fresco's artist, but with another event which occurred around the same time but which Freud had attempted to push away from consciousness. The event in question concerned a patient of Freud's who had committed suicide due to difficulties in sexual functioning. The terrible news of his patient's tragic fate had reached Freud during his stay in Trafoi, a short time before the conversation in which he forgot the painter's name took place.

What Freud discovers in the course of his reconstruction of the forgetting of a name in view of a sequence of events in his life is that neither the forgetting of the name "Signorelli" nor the substitutes for this name which emerged in his consciousness were incidental and that the forgotten name and its substitutes were connected by copious associative links. Freud's patient had committed suicide due to impotence, which the Turks in Bosnia and Herzegovina too viewed as reason to give up on life. The bitter news reached Freud during his stay in Trafoi, a place whose name phonically and anagrammatically resonates with one of the substitute names, Boltraffio, and so on and so forth. Fragments of words representing the event Freud had tried to push away from his consciousness emerged all along the path of his forgetting, resonating this troubling event, which functioned as a hole they veiled. The circumstances of his patient's death constituted an unbearable encounter for Freud, and in the course of the effort to forget it he also forgot an innocuous detail (the name "Signorelli") which ostensibly had nothing to do with it. Only once the word fragments serving as substitutes for the repressed event retroactively came together did the event of the patient's suicide about which Freud did not want to know reemerge for him.

Lacan returns to Freud's discussion of the forgetting of the artist's name in his 1957 seminar on the formations of the unconscious.[32] Lacan shows that the forgetting of the signifier "Signorelli," ostensibly unrelated to the event that had been repressed, tore open a hole in representation where metonymically connected words swirled and broke, their shattering generating fragments starting from which it was possible to reconstruct the repressed event as a hole in reality. The absent name "Signorelli" was first replaced with "*Signore*," the Italian designation for "master," which in this case was the absolute master, death. In German, "master" is "***Herr***," which phonically resonates with "**Her**zegovina," whose Turkish inhabitants view impotence as a sufficient reason to abandon life, as do those of "**Bo**snia," whose name phonically resonates with the substitute names "**Bo**tticelli" and "**Bo**ltraffio" which arise in Freud's mind. These fragments surge up once the name "Signorelli" is torn away from Freud's consciousness, as metonymic ruins it leaves in its wake.

Lacan recalls something more from Freud's account of forgetting the name "Signorelli." Freud recounts how during the incident of forgetting, he could vividly remember the image of the Orvieto fresco depicting the resurrection of the dead.[33] What he could not bring to mind in any way was the inverse of the image, the name "Signorelli" which was metonymically connected to the unbearable thought of the patient's suicide. It is here that the relation between death and the work of art becomes clear. The point of departure for reconstructing a metonymic chain of signifiers clustered around a repressed memory trace must be an empty space which would allow substitutions to unfold. In the case Freud recounts, this empty space is the absence of the name "Signorelli" from Freud's mind. What appears in its stead is a vivid visual image. What is significant, however, is not that this image is of a work of art but that it is a representation which veils the hole of a death the subject cannot bear. What this means is that the nonrepresentability of death functions as a condition for the emergence of representation such as is foundational to art.

The specificity of the artwork in question in Freud's story of his forgetting of the name "Signorelli" is nevertheless instructive for the theorization of the relation of art and death. In their dazzling psychoanalytical accounts of this story, both Freud and Lacan do not relate to the particular image of the Orvieto fresco that emerges in its course. One of the paintings in this fresco depicts a fantastical spectacle of the resurrection of the dead. In it, the body of the resurrected is whole and untainted once again, unblemished by age or sickness. This is the image Freud remembers instead of the name "Signorelli." This image, which neither Freud nor Lacan comment on, may help further explain why Freud thought of "Botticelli" as one of the substitutes for the forgotten name. Botticelli is most often associated with his *Birth of Venus*, wherein Venus rises from the foam of the waves in a vertical movement resembling that of the resurrected in the Orvieto fresco, or with *Primavera*, a painting celebrating the spring associated with birth and growth—and ostensibly opposed to any thought of death.

As both Freud and Lacan explain, Freud could not remember the name "Signorelli" because of its relation to the signifier "death." What he had no difficulty remembering in great detail was the image of the fresco Signorelli painted, and one reason for this is the fresco's depiction of the process opposite to dying: the emergence of life from death. The substitution of the name "Botticelli" for the name Freud could not recall links this image with the Botticellian image of the rise of Venus from the waves, another pictorial occurrence of the vector of the emergence of life, and with the *Primavera*'s thematic depiction of the regeneration of life. These Botticellian images too, then, become veils, artistic veils, by means of which what Freud cannot allow himself to know as he tries to remember the name "Signorelli" may nevertheless be thought.

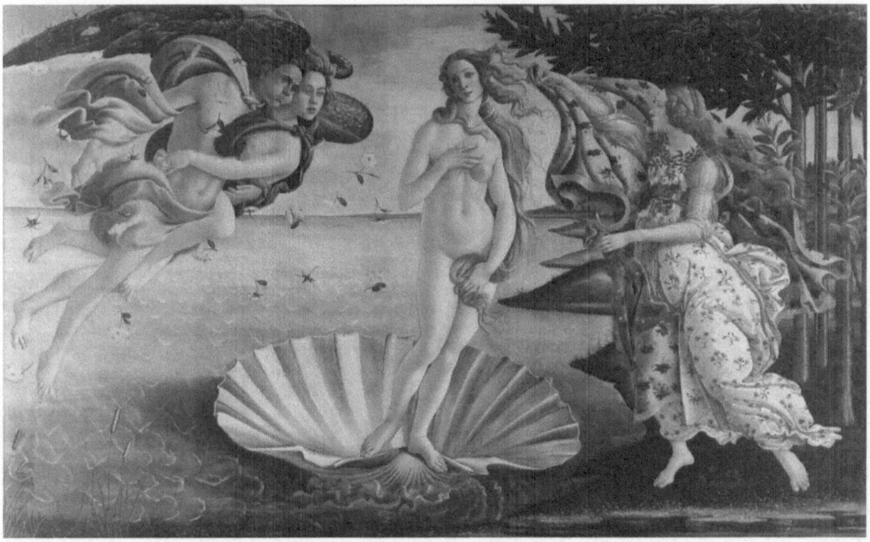

FIGURE 1.3 Sandro Botticelli, *The Birth of Venus*, 1486. © Gallerie degli Uffizi. Image reproduced with kind permission.

Freud and Lacan's analyses of the Signorelli story indicate quite clearly that the word and image from which the work of art is woven cannot represent death, which pertains to the order of what is not representable that Lacan calls the real. Death is quite unrepresentable, Lacan says in one of his later seminars; no one knows what it is. Its designation in language, the signifier "death," is but a dazzling glimmer revealing nothing of its referent.[34] What Lacan says of the signifier "death" is applicable to the content of an artwork composed of words or images. What the Signorelli story also teaches, however, is that certain dimensions of representation (in this instance the metonymic fragments) allow something of the unpresentable to return in disguise, and not in the register of sense or content.

Lacan's late teaching, which emphasizes the category of the real and includes a detailed examination of the artwork of James Joyce, makes it possible to say something more about this dimension of art. The work of art is not only a texture of words or images. A visual artwork or a literary text includes a dimension supplementary to sense, image or content. This dimension, which can never be absorbed into thematics or iconography, is the register of style. Meaningless in itself, style thus is able to manifest what is unrepresentable as content, including the unrepresentable of death. It is the dimension of the artwork in which the death drive as invigorating repetition, as a variation implicating beauty, can be made to emerge.

In his twenty-third seminar, Lacan shows how in his last artwork, *Finnegans Wake*, James Joyce creates a literary object which is almost pure style, forged from fragmented shards of the English language deconstructed to the level of the letter which are woven together into largely felicitous syntactic structures. This object, almost completely outside of sense, allows Joyce to act in relation to those dimensions of human experience which are not registered in the unconscious, one of which is death. Lacan shows that the very act of creating this object allowed Joyce to live a jouissance outside of sense that Lacan terms "Other jouissance"[35] over the course of the decade in which he worked on *Finnegans Wake*. Once this object was released into the world, becoming, as Joyce predicted, a focus of indefatigable hermeneutic efforts, *Finnegans Wake* became an object registering Joyce's relation to his own death. The hermeneutic-academic occupation with Joyce's writings misses what the writing of *Finnegans Wake* was in Joyce's own life. The very refusal of the academic preoccupation with Joyce to wake from its infinite but futile hermeneutic efforts is precisely what enables a wake—that Irish ritual for the dead, which is part lamentation, part feast—to take place around the object of pure style Joyce created. This hermeneutic wake, which Joyce predicted would continue for three centuries, functions as a preservative of Joyce's conditions of enjoyment. It does not cease to allow these conditions to be repeated beyond his biological death. The repetition at stake in the case of Joyce's late art is not the reiteration of what is most traumatic, for instance, of what lies at the origin of the failure of the paternal function in Joyce's life which Lacan points to. Quite to the contrary, as Lacan shows, Joyce puts the products of the failure in the paternal function to use. He deploys the outcomes of the deconstruction of the imaginary and symbolic caused by the failure of the paternal function so as to produce unique styles of writing he does not cease to employ in his art. Death, then, is indeed registered in *Finnegans Wake*, but this is not in the book's title, which refers to a ritual of mourning, but in the book's functioning as an object of pure style. The resistance of this object to sense engenders innumerable interpretive efforts which can nevertheless never be a deciphering. What they ultimately amount to is the performance of a ritual for the dead, an act of embalming the particles of jouissance from which Joyce wove his last great text. This ritual perpetuates Joyce's mode of jouissance, that is to say, the repetitive action of his death drive, beyond his biological death, which cannot be represented in the text.

What then can psychoanalysis in its relation to death, particularly in its development of the notion of the death drive, teach us about the relationship between art and death? What psychoanalysis shows is that aside from annihilation or ruin, anticipated death may function as a threshold for an invigorating repetition. This conclusion makes it possible to explain two widely prevalent phenomena in the sphere of art through the ages: the preoccupation of art with death and the preoccupation of the discourse on art with the end of art. If repetition in psychoanalysis is not only the monotonous repetition of satisfaction in suffering but may become an invigorating repetition, bound up with desire, whose very condition is death as limit, it becomes possible to explain why, despite recurrent declarations of its demise, art and the discourse concerning it continue to exist all the more forcefully. Indeed, the discourse on the end of art and the art which persists in the face of this discourse may be said to be manifestations of the death drive in culture, beyond the pleasure principle. As Freud demonstrates in his paper on drives and their vicissitudes, every drive, which Freud would later show is ultimately the death drive, operates as a phoenix rising from its ashes, beginning again at the very moment of its destruction. Every drive, that is, is destined to a repetition. Repetition, however, does not necessarily spell sameness. It can involve variation. As the following chapter will show, the phenomena of repetition that appear in the sphere of art and the discourse concerning art are primarily of this order of a repetition that varies. These include the various theories of the end of art. The purpose of presenting these theories in the following chapter is not to expand the theoretical framework of this book beyond psychoanalysis. It is, rather, an attempt to demonstrate by means of psychoanalysis how the various discourses concerning death in art and the death of art are none other than a manifestation of the death drive in culture.

Notes

1 Sigmund Freud, "Beyond the Pleasure Principle," in *The Standard Edition of the Complete Psychological Works of Sigmund Freud, Volume XVIII*, trans. and ed. James Strachey (London: Hogarth Press, 1955 [1920]), pp. 1–64.
2 Ibid., pp. 8–9.
3 Ibid., p. 20.
4 Ibid., p. 38.
5 Ibid., p. 39.
6 Sigmund Freud, "The Uncanny," in *The Standard Edition of the Complete Psychological Works of Sigmund Freud, Vol. XVII*, trans. and ed. James Strachey (London: Hogarth Press, 1955 [1919]), pp. 217–56.

7 Ibid., p. 235.
8 Freud, "Beyond the Pleasure Principle."
9 Freud, "The Uncanny," p. 242.
10 Jacques Lacan, *The Seminar of Jacques Lacan, Book IX: Identification* (1961–1962), trans. Cormac Gallagher (unpublished manuscript), lesson of 23 May 1962.
11 Ibid.
12 Jacques Lacan, *The Seminar of Jacques Lacan, Book II: The Ego in Freud's Theory and in the Technique of Psychoanalysis*, trans. Sylvana Tomaselli (New York: W. W. Norton, 1988 [1954–1955]), p. 81.
13 Ibid., p. 90.
14 Ibid., p. 326.
15 Jacques Lacan, "The Function and Field of Speech and Language in Psychoanalysis," in *Écrits: A Selection*, trans. Alan Sheridan (New York: W. W. Norton, 1977 [1953]), p. 101.
16 Ibid., p. 102.
17 Ibid., p. 103. The word that appears in the French text is "*pulsion*," the equivalent for what in Freud's text is "*Trieb.*" Despite Freud's clear distinction between "Trieb" and "Instinkt," his English translator, James Strachey, chose to translate both as "instinct." Lacan's English translators preserved Strachey's terminology.
18 Ibid.
19 Ibid., p. 103.
20 Jacques Lacan, *The Seminar of Jacques Lacan, Book XVII: The Other Side of Psychoanalysis*, trans. Russel Grigg (New York: W. W. Norton, 2007 [1969–1970]), p. 177.
21 Lacan, "The Function and Field of Speech and Language in Psychoanalysis," p. 104.
22 Sigmund Freud, "Negation," in *The Standard Edition of the Complete Psychological Works of Sigmund Freud, Vol. XIX*, trans. and ed. James Strachey (London: Hogarth Press, 1955 [1925]), p. 238.
23 Lacan, "The Function and Field of Speech and Language in Psychoanalysis," p. 65.
24 Lacan, *Seminar II*, p. 223.
25 Ibid., p. 224.
26 Ibid., p. 229.
27 Jacques Lacan, *The Seminar of Jacques Lacan, Book XII: Crucial Problems of Psychoanalysis* (1964–1965), trans. Cormac Gallagher (unpublished manuscript), lesson of 12 May 1965.
28 Jacques Lacan, *The Seminar of Jacques Lacan, Book VII: The Ethics of Psychoanalysis*, trans. Dennis Porter (New York: W. W. Norton, 1986 [1959–1960]).
29 Jacques Lacan, *The Seminar of Jacques Lacan, Book VIII: Transference*, trans. Bruce Fink (Cambridge: Polity Press, 2015 [1960–1961]), pp. 1–48.
30 Sigmund Freud, "The Forgetting of Proper Names," in *The Standard Edition of the Complete Psychological Works of Sigmund Freud, Volume VI*, trans. and ed. James Strachey (London: Hogarth Press, 1960 [1901]), pp. 1–7.
31 Freud, "The Forgetting of Proper Names," p. 3.
32 Jacques Lacan, *The Seminar of Jacques Lacan, Book V: Formations of the Unconscious* (1957–1958), trans. Cormac Gallagher (unpublished manuscript), lessons of 13 November 1957 and 20 November 1957.
33 Ibid., p. 46.
34 Jacques Lacan, *The Seminar of Jacques Lacan, Book XXII: RSI* (1974–1975), trans. Jack Stone (unpublished manuscript), lesson of 8 April 1975.
35 Jacques Lacan, *The Seminar of Jacques Lacan, Book XX: Encore*, trans. Bruce Fink (New York: W. W. Norton), p. 74.

2

WHAT NEVER STOPS DYING

The beauty of art is beauty born
of the spirit and born again

—G. W. F. Hegel, 1988 [1835], p. 2

During the last moments she spends with her beloved who is about to depart far away, never to return to her again, the daughter of Corinthian potter Butades asks her beloved to stand against a wall lit by a lamp so that she might trace the outlines of the shadow his body throws upon it.[1] Immersed in the pain and sorrow of their impending separation, the girl does not realize she has just invented not only painting, but also the myth of its invention, and the complex link between the work of art, loss, death and finality. For according to a myth told by Pliny the Elder and repeated in various versions in the theory and practice of art, painting originates in an attempt to preserve an object on the brink of vanishing. Though Pliny points to other possible inventors of the art of painting, it is the myth of the art's invention by the daughter of Butades which has been the subject of numerous pictorial renderings in the course of art history. But whether the inventor of painting was Egyptian or Corinthian, what remains clear in Pliny's text is that the first painting was the product of tracing the outline of a human shadow on a wall, and that the potter's daughter was the first to make use of painting as the basis for casting a relief (of the face of her lost lover).[2] Other passages concerning painting in Pliny's *Natural History* too touch upon the link between painting and death. For instance, when he praises Apelles as one of the greatest Greek painters, Pliny states Apelles's portraits were so perfect they could predict the life expectancy of the person painted. Apelles's spectacular paintings, Pliny writes, included portraits of people during their last moments, much like the soldiers Livneh would paint millennia later.

In these passages, Pliny the Elder seems to relate to the very act of painting as a signifying act whose substituting a representation for a thing accounts for its eternalizing power, which stands in an inverse ratio to death and finality. However, when painting substitutes for an object, anticipated loss becomes the very guarantee of its quality, measured, for instance, in its ability to predict the time left till the object's demise. The relation between death and painting is thus more than causal. The two are structurally intertwined in a less than stable manner attested to by the variety of paintings depicting Butades's daughter and her lover. In these paintings the girl is so utterly absorbed in the image she is sketching that she never once looks at the beloved she does not want to lose yet abandons while painting.[3] Thus the act of painting, seemingly designed to alleviate the pain of impeding separation, is precisely what also anticipates it. In other words, Butades's daughter not only invents painting and its relation to death but also indicates the structural necessity of this relation. Henceforth, manifestations of painting will repeat a moment necessitating a separation. Painting in Western culture is thus perceived as an act whose origin is a moment of loss and whose future is a series of repetitions. Western theories of painting reiterate, in various manners and formulations, the connection implicit in Pliny's text between the invention of painting and death as cause of a chain of repetitions. Almost two thousand years after Pliny, Freud would formulate precisely this structure of loss and repetition as the substrate of the death drive.

Between Pliny and Freud, approximately one thousand and four hundred years after Pliny's *Natural History*, Leon Battista Alberti composed his treatise *On Painting*. Although Alberti protests that unlike a storyteller such as Pliny, a theorist like himself has no need to resort to myth to account for the invention of painting, he does, when speaking of the origin of this art, allude to the myth of Narcissus. "Since painting is already the flower of every art," Alberti writes, "the story of Narcissus is most to the point. What else can you call painting but a similar embracing with art of what is presented on the surface of the water in the fountain?"[4] Seemingly using this myth metaphorically, Alberti in effect inverts it. Whereas in the original myth it is Narcissus who is captivated by his charming reflection, Alberti describes him as able to captivate it. This ability is precisely what ruins him: his embracing of what is presented on the surface of the water leads to his death.

The relation of painting to death emerges, albeit differently, a few paragraphs earlier in Alberti's text, when he writes that

> painting contains a divine force which not only makes absent men present, as friendship is said to do, but moreover makes the dead seem almost alive. Even after many centuries they are recognized with great pleasure and with great admiration for the painter.[5]

Painting, that is, endows its topics with eternal life; but as the reference to Narcissus suggests, should a mortal completely immerse himself in the image it offers, this eternizing image might consume him. Later, Alberti connects painting's ability to memorialize the face of the dead with its power to stir belief in the gods, as it

> shaped the gods who were adored by the nations. It certainly was their greatest gift to mortals, for painting is most useful to that piety which joins us to the gods and keeps our souls full of religion.[6]

These statements concerning the relation of painting and death may seem unrelated to the overall purpose of Alberti's project: providing a theoretical and scientific formulation of the proper way to paint. Indeed, Alberti himself confesses they are incidental to his argument. But Alberti does grant death and absence a pivotal role in his first formulations of the laws of perspective, even if he does not explicitly state this. The vanishing point, after all, is nothing but a point of absence into which all straight lines in the painting converge; it marks infinity as impossible to represent. As Norman Bryson argues following Lacan, the vanishing point does represent the unrepresentable: the fading of the subject.[7] In Alberti's formulation, the picture plane is produced when the subject is located between two symmetrical inverted pyramids. One is the pyramid of vision, precisely tracing the way in which the painter sees his object and the painter's distance from this object. The other is the visual pyramid, the way in which the pyramid of vision is manifest on the surface of painting. The two pyramids are identical but inverse. The apex of the pyramid of vision is in the eye of the painting's observer, while the apex of the opposite pyramid ostensibly indicates the gaze of another observer, located in the depths of the painting and directed at its observer.[8] Bryson writes:

> The single vanishing point marks the installation within the painting of a principal of radical alterity, since its gaze returns that of the viewer as its own object: someone is looking at my looking: a gaze whose position I can never occupy, and whose vista I can imagine only by reversing my own, by inverting the perspective before me, and by imagining my own gaze as the new, palindromic point of disappearance on the horizon. [9]

Even if Bryson does not indicate a direct link between painting and death, his argument does make it possible to consider the significance of the vanishing point not only as a fading into the horizon, but also as the fading of the subject himself, who turns from embodied being into abstract presence.[10] The act of vanishing that serves as a condition for art that is present in Pliny's text narratively and mythically reappears in Alberti's text geometrically, via the pivotal role of the vanishing point.

Alberti's declared purpose in *On Painting* is to articulate a theory of painting for painters, but another dimension emerges in the course of the treatise. Painting, for Alberti, has to do with more than seeing and representing accurately. When sight is translated into perspective painting, it comes to include something more, something which transcends the dichotomy between presence and absence, life and death, and which maintains a dialectical relation with painting.[11] After all, perspective painting's greatest advantages, such as its pivotal vanishing point, are immanently linked to absence, which is in effect what breathes life into pigments and stretched canvas. The very mortifying presence encoded in painting is what enlivens it, just as the anticipated loss of the beloved is what propels the potter's daughter to paint.

The elaborations of Alberti and Pliny the Elder constitute the foundation for the thinking of art in Western culture in its relation to death and finitude as what is predicated on a loss and continues to exist beyond this loss precisely by never ceasing to repeat it. Structurally similar elaborations recur in texts on art by key thinkers of the twentieth century. For instance, in her book *Black Sun: Depression and Melancholia*, Julia Kristeva claims:

> The imaginative capability of Western man, which is fulfilled within Christianity, is the ability to transfer meaning to the very place where it was lost in death and non-meaning. This is a survival of idealization—the imaginary constitutes a miracle, but it is at the same time its shattering: a self-illusion, nothing but dreams and words, words, words . . . It affirms the almightiness of temporary subjectivity—the one that knows enough to speak until death comes.[12]

Ultimately nonmeaning, Kristeva argues, death allows only for imaginary representation, which can take one of two forms: portrayals of the pathos of natural death, a possibility realized by Gothic art, or elevated and colorful depictions of death such as appear in Italian Renaissance painting, rendering death sublime by means of their harmonic compositions and luminous color schemes. Holbein's painting seems to point at another way of inscribing death in art, located at the very epicenter of the impossibility to represent. The singularity of Holbein's achievement in *The Body of the Dead Christ in the Tomb* lies in his refusal to undertake either of the two forms for the imaginary representation of death in Western art. His painting devoid both of Gothic pathos and of Renaissance splendor, Holbein remains at the very heart of a severance. His minimalism allows for a rare and perhaps unique mode of representation, metaphoric of the schism between life and death, meaning and nonmeaning.[13]

Kristeva's argument seems to emphasize the necessarily partial manner in which death may be represented in art, pointing to Holbein's case as an exception. Yet this argument in effect repeats the structure already apparent in the writings of Pliny the Elder and Alberti. For what it implies is that a difficulty to represent rooted in what Kristeva calls "non-meaning" functions precisely as the cause for the repeated attempt to tackle the representation of death.

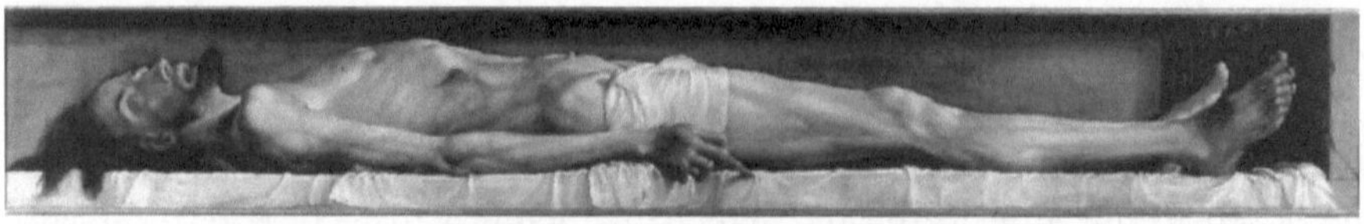

FIGURE 2.1 Hans Holbein, *The Body of the Dead Christ in the Tomb*, 1521. © Kunstmuseum Basel. Image reproduced with the kind permission of Kunstmuseum Basel.

If for Kristeva in her analysis of Holbein death propels the production of art because of the challenge it poses to representation, George Bataille's treatment of cave paintings paves the way for the localization of death as representation's very condition. In *The Tears of Eros*, Bataille meditates about consciousness of death and eroticism, claiming it is this consciousness that distinguishes man from animals.[14] Bataille's point of departure is the erect male organs featuring in cave paintings, such as an obscure image from the caves of Lascaux depicting a man falling in front of a dying bison. Having surveyed some unsatisfactory interpretations of that image, Bataille concludes it is to be understood differently, as testament to death's inherent relation to the erotic. Yet in what way, he asks, may death be perceived as related not to the extinction of life but to an exuberant manifestation of its perpetuation?[15] Apes, known for their intense sensuality, Bataille explains, nevertheless know nothing of the erotic since they lack any awareness of death. Humans, by contrast, are conscious of both death and sexuality, as the use of the expression "little death" to mark the climactic moment of sexual intercourse demonstrates well.[16] Similarly, while sexual behavior in animals is an instinctual response, human beings "discerned the meaning that this response had for them."[17] It is hence in the human sphere that copulation takes place for pleasure and not for procreation alone, and that it comes to be associated with sexual passion.[18]

Lacan's later commentaries on the Lascaux paintings bear out Bataille's thesis concerning the immanence of death to the erotic, taking it further in a way that clarifies the immanence of both to the creation of art. In his seminar of 1971–1972, Lacan remarks that in the course of becoming a hunter who takes the lives of animals, man not only became conscious of the possibility that he too might die, but consequently also to love what he killed.[19] Killing the thing one loves, Lacan adds, is common to the first hunters and to the mythical sons of the totemic father in Freud's *Totem and Taboo*. "The hunter loves his game, just as the sons, in the event described as primordial in Freudian mythology . . . killed their father . . . because they loved him." It is the traces of those archaic killers of what they love, Lacan argues, that are found on the walls of the Lascaux caves.[20] As for Bataille in *The Tears of Eros*, then, for Lacan the Lascaux cave paintings are testaments to the uniquely human phenomenon of the consciousness of death as inherently connected with love, that in Bataille's case takes the specific form of eroticism. What Lacan stresses in an earlier account, however, is the signifying status of the cave paintings. Although we will never be able to hear the voice of the painting cave man, Lacan says, we can rest assured he was a speaking being.[21] Like the shadows in Plato's cave, the Lascaux paintings are a closed system of signifiers without external referent. They function, that is, as a signifying chain, are of the order of what structures the unconscious, where each signifier represents a subject for another signifier and functions as a screen or veil which is synecdochic or representative of signifiers that are further repressed. The paintings on the walls of the Lascaux caves, then, have the status of what Freud theorized as a *Vorstellungsrepräsentanz*, a representative of representation. They demonstrate the function in human life of the screen, the exhibition of an image not so as to point to a referent but so as to veil. These striking cave paintings, then, attest to the existence of a being not only conscious of its death, which becomes related to its sexual function, but signifying. The production of art, once again, is linked to death, but this is death as distinctively human, different from mere slaughter, bound up with the generation of signification. Death in Lacan's analyses of the Lascaux paintings is not the cause of a difficulty to represent engendering attempts to surmount it. Resulting from love (rather than, as for Bataille, engendering the erotic), death in the human sphere is also what generates its own trace and the signifying battery that screens it, of which the Lascaux paintings are paradigmatic.

The age-old conceptualization of art as caused by a loss it repeats reappears in twentieth-century theories of photography. Some theorists of photography like Philippe Dubois even directly allude to the myth of the invention of painting by Butades's daughter, since the manner in which she makes use of light and the projection of an object on a surface have to do also with what would become salient features of the art of photography.[22] But one need not reach as far back as Butades to link this artistic medium with death and loss. Several modern theories of photography regard this art as a presentification of absence, a testimony of what once was and is no more. Tacitly implied in Walter Benjamin's *A Short History of Photography* of 1931,[23] the view of photography as predicated on loss is overtly stated in Roland Barthes's *Camera Lucida: Reflections on Photography* of 1980.[24]

Benjamin implicitly points to the link between photography and death, for instance when analyzing Eugène Atget's humanless photographs, or when, in his later essay "The Work of Art in the Age of Mechanical Reproduction," he presents the photographs of portraits of deceased loved ones as a phenomenon unique to the photographic medium which preserves the ritualistic value of the work of art.[25] In Barthes's book, which revolves around his search for a photograph preserving something of his dead mother, the relation between photography and death is explicitly addressed throughout.

In an essay from the late 1970s, Thierry de Duve points to another aspect of this relation. De Duve distinguishes between two photographic practices: snapshot and time exposure. The conception of temporality emerging from each of these practices, he shows, connects both to different facets of death.[26] In *L'acte photographique*, Philippe Dubois too argues for an inherent link between photography and death. Photography is inherently "tanathographic," Dubois says, that is to say, a way of inscribing death.[27] Photographic technique as Dubois describes it rips a moment from the sequence of time and freezes it in the timeless dimension of the image, hence reproducing the structure of the transition from life to death. In all of these theories of photography, death is immanent to the photographic image, regardless of the contents of this image. Insisting on the constitutive connection between art and death, these theories are iterations of what has not ceased to repeat itself in art theory since the myth of Butades's daughter.

For all their immense differences, theories of art from Pliny to de Duve, spanning two millennia, all point to the immanence of death and loss in the object of art. The beloved's approaching loss is what propels Butades's daughter to the work of painting. Transposed onto the plane of representation, this loss reappears as painting's vanishing point, ceaselessly disappearing on the horizon, never to be reached. This is a blind point for the subject, marking a gaze whose position he can never occupy, to use Bryson's words.[28] Kristeva's treatment of Holbein makes a single painting deviating from competing paradigms of representation speak at once for the nonrepresentability of death and for its constitutive role in propelling new modes of artistic representation. De Duve isolates the particular way in which an artistic medium of representation, photography, cannot fail to designate death either because, as snapshot, it steals the life it freezes or because, as time exposure, it moves away from the event that precipitated it.

Loss, vanishing, severance, suspension—such is the variety of terms used to articulate the relation between art and death in the discourse of art, whether it appears in the naïve guise of a myth or takes the form of a sophisticated semiotic theory. What the theories of art putting these terms into play indicate is that death is not only a theme in art but a fundamental element built into the very nature of the art object, a hole which makes the art object possible and reverberates in it. From the point of view of psychoanalysis, these theories constitute a symptomatic repetition of a primal trauma of loss in culture, of which the myth of Butades's daughter is simultaneously the first veiling and the first repetition.

Art as philo(soph)y[29]

At a certain point in history, most clearly identifiable in Hegelian philosophy, a structural change occurs in the manner in which the death drive returns in culture and the philosophy of art. Hegel and the thinkers who follow in his footsteps no longer discuss death in art but rather the death *of* art. What this means is that from Hegel's *Aesthetics* onward, the manifestation of repetition (the death drive) in culture is raised to a higher power. If until Hegel, both death and the existence of the work of art as its repetition and beyond appear on the level of theory, starting with Hegel's aesthetics a split occurs between the level of theory, which is concerned with a loss it calls "the end of art," and the level of artistic practice where art continues to exist beyond this loss.

From the point of view of psychoanalysis, what is at stake in the structural shift manifest in Hegel's *Aesthetics* is yet another form of repetition. Lacan's theorization of the status of the analysand's speech in the clinic constitutes a properly psychoanalytical formulation of a structural change such as is involved in Hegel's conceptualization of the end of art in relation to earlier conceptualizations of death in art:[30]

> It is in as much as the relations in which he is caught up are themselves brought to the level of symbolism, that the subject questions himself about himself. For him, when it occurs it is as a problem in the second degree on the plane of the symbolic assumption of his destiny . . . . this is the essentially analytic level.[31]

A subject's speech in analysis, then, may first involve his account of what befalls him or is done to him, but at another stage of the analysis the subject may question himself about the way in which he is implicated in what happens in his life. What appears first as account or complaint, that is, reappears as the subject's question to himself. Lacan calls this questioning "subjectivization." What this means is that Hegel's conceptualization of the end of art and its derivatives are not only a repetition of the death drive in culture with respect to art, but also constitute a cultural subjectivization of this repetition.

Hegel's *Aesthetics*, first published posthumously in the 1830s, is the most distinct source of the idea of the end of art as we know it today. But decades earlier, Kant had already pondered the possibility of art's continued existence in the far future, wondering what form this existence might take. Kant's limited speculation is of course very far from Hegel's elaborate conception of the end of art, but even Kant's tacit articulation of the possible mortality of the fine arts indicates that the structural change which reaches its clearest form with Hegel had begun to burgeon earlier. Toward the end of the *Critique of Judgment*, Kant argues that the production of fine art in its highest degree requires a departure from familiar precepts:

> The propaedeutic to all fine art, so far as the highest degree of its perfection is what is in view, appears to lie, not in precepts, but in the culture of the mental powers produced by a sound preparatory education in what are called the *humaniora*—so called, presumably, because *humanity* signifies, on the one hand, the universal *feeling of sympathy*, and, on the other, the faculty of being able to *communicate* universally one's inmost self-properties constituting in conjunction the befitting *social spirit* of mankind, in contradiction to the narrow life of the lower animals. [32]

Art finds its origin in the human spirit arising from culture—it is uniquely human. Later on in the text, Kant hypothesizes an archaic state of humanity in which a battle raged between "man's natural propensity to sociability" and the possible enforcement of social law. According to Kant:

> And such must have been the age, and such the nation, that first discovered the art of reciprocal communication of ideas between the more cultured and ruder sections of the community, and how to bridge the difference between the amplitude and refinement of the former and the natural simplicity and originality of the latter—in this way hitting upon that mean between higher culture and the modest worth of nature, that forms for taste also, as a sense common to all mankind, that true standard which no universal rules can supply.[33]

The birth of art, more precisely the birth of the judgment of taste which determines beauty in nature or art, relies on the idea of a common sense: the possibility of reaching a consensus regarding an object of beauty. This consensus is not based on established rules but on a taste reflecting a given culture. Kant goes on to discuss the future of common taste, arguing that even in the furthest possible future, this ancient standard is unlikely to be given up, since without it the judgment of beauty would be impossible.

Kant, however, does not stop there. He later complicates matters by claiming that taste cannot be reduced to the finding of a common denominator, as he had claimed in the two previous paragraphs, but must comply with moral ideas. What will "lay the foundations of taste," Kant writes,

> is the development of moral ideas and the culture of the moral feeling. For only when sensibility is brought into harmony with moral feeling can genuine taste assume a definite, unchangeable form.[34]

Although Kant does not directly address the question of the end of art as Hegel would later articulate it, he does make a serious assumption regarding the birth of aesthetic judgment as a cultural practice with a social significance, from whence he derives, even if indirectly, the conditions for the creation of a taste that would be genuine, definite, and unchangeable. While the conditions that led to the birth of the judgment of taste may be conjectured as part of a past, Kant says, the conditions that might determine taste are not at our disposal since they are not historical but transcendent. For an absolute and stable taste to be formed, it must be compatible with moral feeling. This is because "taste is, in the ultimate analysis, a critical faculty that judges of the rendering of moral ideas in terms of sense."[35] The birth of taste, then, necessitates more than finding a common denominator for a given public. Taste may be established only if molded with moral ideas, may be made permanent and eternal only after it has been connected and adjusted to the moral domain. However, like all ideas, for Kant, the moral idea, because transcendent, is never completely given. Intended and aspired toward, it shall always remain but an aspiration. This is because in Kant's moral philosophy, even if the moral law is immanent in every subject, a thoroughly moral community will always remain an object of striving. What this means is that in Kantian terms, art and the taste that determines it as beautiful will remain mortal as long as they do not reach the haven of complete compatibility with the moral ideal. Thus, even if Kant does not directly refer to the end of art, what he argues implies that art is not immune to such an end. As long as art is not completely compatible with a moral idea, its end is possible. In other words, the possible end of art is always already on its horizon.

Hegel presents Kantian aesthetics as one of the cornerstones of his theory, alongside the positions of Friedrich Schiller, Johann Joachim Winckelmann, and Friedrich Wilhelm Joseph Schelling.[36] After briefly outlining Kant's four moments of the judgment of taste, Hegel shows how Kant's conception of the beautiful allows him to resolve the fundamental dichotomies between universal and particular, end and means, concept and object. Nevertheless, Hegel argues, in Kant's philosophy these dichotomies ultimately remain unresolved, for ultimately their reconciliation is "only subjective in respect of the judgement and the production [of art]."[37]

Hegel's analysis of Kant's aesthetics makes it possible to understand the difficulty in achieving a complete amalgamation of taste and moral idea, an amalgamation Kant leaves an unrealized suggestion for a hypothetical future. Hegel then sets out to develop an aesthetics which would be based on Kant's but surmount its flaws, one which would make it possible to at once understand beauty in art and grasp the true unity of need and freedom, particularity and universality, the senses and the intellect. Hegel's philosophy of art, that is, is offered as what would make it possible to refine Kant's view of art as a bridge between the sensual and the spiritual, form and content, while transposing it to a beyond of particular subjective experience.

To achieve this, Hegel embarks on an intricate trajectory which traces the complex relation between content and form, meaning and expression in the artistic object, as it unfolds in three historical and developmental stages. The first stage is that of symbolic art, in which content and form aspire in a variety of ways toward a unity which is never attained. The second stage is that of classical art, in which such unity is first achieved. The third and last stage is that of romantic art, in which divinity itself is embodied.

Art, Hegel says, can be used as a means for pleasurable recreation or decoration. In such cases, art is ancillary to an end and therefore not free. Art such as is the focus of his discussion, however, is free alike in its end and its means. It is therefore close to thought, for thought too can be at once ancillary to an end and elevate itself toward truth for its own ends alone.[38] Only free art is truly art, an art that fulfills its highest purpose and positions itself in the same sphere as religion and philosophy, that is, as a means for expressing the Divine that would make it possible for the truth of the spirit to emerge.[39] "The beauty of art is beauty born of the spirit and born again," Hegel states in the opening words of his *Aesthetics*.[40] T. M. Knox, the text's English translator, notes that an earlier English translation interpreted this sentence as an allusion to Jesus's words to Nicodemus: "born of water and of the spirit" (John 3:12). Knox, who does not agree with this interpretation, argues that the meaning of Hegel's sentence is that "we have beauty originated by man's mind and also what is reproduced by his mind in his natural world."[41] That is, Knox interprets the rebirth that repeats itself that Hegel speaks of as the activity of human consciousness.

Hegel's obscure sentence regarding the birth of art, however, may also be read by means of another of Hegel's famous statements on art: "art . . . is and remains for us a thing of the past."[42] Reading this statement in terms of the common conception of linear and progressive time raises the question of how to explain the artistic life that persists beyond the end of art. Read in psychoanalytic terms, however, this statement becomes clear. As Freud would later do, Hegel supposes a temporality that is not simple, that involves a reshuffling of diachrony. For Freud, every traumatic repetition is in effect the emergence of the subject's past from his future, for it will continue to revisit the subject for the duration of his life. In a similar shuffling of temporalities, for Hegel all art to be created will remain a thing of the past, just as the beauty born of the spirit will always be born again. In their different ways, both Freud and Hegel speak of a past that does not end, returning from the future in a different guise. The Hegelian concept of the end of art is thus not art's annihilation but its reappearance at a higher level.

Hegel's theorization of the end of art, we would like to suggest, has a status different from theories linking art and death discussed above, whether written before or after Hegel. Hegel's theorization is not one more of the many arguments connecting art to death. It constitutes the raising of this argument to a higher power where what becomes at stake is the death of art itself. Such raising of a signifier to a higher power or "second degree" is of the same structure as what Lacan calls "subjectivation": no longer only a description of a state of affairs but also its reflexive reading from another plane.

The category of the spirit (*Geist*) is central to Hegel's theorization of the end of art and to Hegelian thought in general. An essentially secular philosopher, Hegel does not presuppose a transcendental being whose abilities exceed those of the subject, such as divinity in its various forms. Instead, divinity as Hegel conceives it is located in the subject himself. The spirit, according to Hegel, exists by means of a self-conscious subject. Self-consciousness is a highly evolved manifestation of the spirit. Hegel lists three forms by means of which the spirit may appear: art, religion and philosophy. In each of these spheres, the spirit appears in different form: in art it appears by means of representation, in religion by means of faith, and in philosophy by means of thought. Hegel aligns each of these forms of the spirit with a stage in its evolution. While philosophy is situated as the highest stage of the evolution of the spirit, art is situated as the lowest,[43] for in it the manifestation of the spirit takes material form. However, what Hegel shows throughout his *Aesthetics* is that the status of art as a particular manifestation of the spirit in matter is precisely the source of the strength of art.

It is when he introduces classical art that Hegel sheds some light on art and its relation to the spirit. The center of art, Hegel writes, is the unification of content and a form completely compatible with this content, which coincides with the idea of beauty. The inner being of classical beauty is "free independent meaning," a meaning that is not any particular sense but meaning itself. This is spirit, which in general makes itself into an object to itself.[44] In other words, the spirit is identified with sense and meaning, yet this sense is not specific, nor is it intellectual, articulated, and conceptualized. Beyond any particular content, this sense emerges as the very essence of the act of signification, precisely from its manifestation in matter, in form, in the beauty of the work of art.

What brings the human being to create art? Hegel finds a possible answer to this question in the fact that man is a thinking consciousness, which takes itself as well as the world as an object of contemplation. As spirit, man creates himself, represents himself to himself, thinks his very existence. It is only on the strength of these actions of placing himself before himself that it is possible to think of him as spirit.[45] This bringing himself before himself is at once theoretical and practical. In theory, man must bring himself into his own consciousness, represent himself to himself, think of himself as though he were an external object in the world. Practically, man brings himself before himself by internalizing external objects and recognizing himself through them.

The creation of art, for Hegel, constitutes an evolved form of the fundamental procedure of self-reflexivity, founded in man's aspiration to do something with his being a consciousness that thinks itself. In the beginning of his discussion of symbolic art, Hegel develops the idea that art begins when the self is projected onto an external object. According to Hegel, at the early stages of human development man has no actual interest in the external environment. Man is closed off from it since he has yet to clearly differentiate himself from it. Only when he notices the outside world and wonders about it as an otherness separate from him yet given to him as an object of perception on which he might impress the seal of his inner being does man evolve to a higher stage. It is from this stage that the conception of art as the ability to observe the external environment from a position of self-consciousness for the spirit will later develop.[46]

Art, Hegel argues, is present sensually: we experience it as we experience nature. Yet art is not completely given to sensuous apprehension. Its uniqueness is in its being given also to apprehension by the spirit: "the spirit is meant to be affected by it [the work of art] and to find some satisfaction in it."[47] Art interests Hegel since, like religion and philosophy, it makes it possible for truth to emerge. But in art truth, whose essence is spiritual, emerges sensually. The senses through which the object of art is made present are sight and hearing. It is by means of these senses that art creates a shadow world of forms, sounds and sights. This shadow world of the senses exists not only for itself but aspires at higher levels of spirituality, since the forms, sounds and sights have the power to call forth from all the depths of consciousness a sound and an echo in the spirit. The sensual aspect of art becomes spiritual, for the spirit appears in art as made sensuous. Sensuality and spirituality, then, are not separate aspects of the art object but intertwined in it.[48] This intertwining is complex, for though in artistic production sensuous and spiritual aspects must be as one, art makes it possible to free man from the sensual sphere where its manifestations appear and elevate him to the spiritual sphere; hence its edifying power.[49] Art combines within itself the spiritual and the sensuous, the universal and the particular. Its ultimate aim, like that of philosophy and religion, is to effect moral improvement. This does not mean, Hegel writes, that moral improvement exhausts the purpose of art. Such erroneous thinking presupposes that the substantial purpose of art is external to it, to be measured by means of extra-artistic values. Against such thinking, Hegel argues that the purpose of art is to "unveil the truth in the sensuous artistic configuration." It is precisely thus that art bridges and reconciles the fundamental antagonism between spirit and matter.[50]

This is Hegel's way of settling the dichotomy he deems emerges from Kant's discussion. By means of his conceptualization of the beautiful, Kant is indeed able to annul the distinction between universal and particular, means and end, concept and object. But for Kant, the resolution of these contraries has to do with beauty as it appears in the eyes of the beholder. Hegel, for his part, concerned as he is with the place of art in the development of the spirit, transposes this resolution beyond the particular experience of a specific observer. It is with this conceptual move that Hegel marks the end following which art continues to appear on a higher plane.

This move, we would like to suggest, is tantamount to a subjectivization of the conception of art in Western culture, a conception that always intertwines art and finality, indexing the origin of art in a loss it embraces as its condition of possibility.

In the beginning of his discussion, Hegel claims that art has the status of what has already taken place, of something belonging to a past.[51] It is thus that he sets the stage for an idea he will develop throughout his *Aesthetics*, the idea of the end of art. If Pliny the Elder and Alberti connect the birth of the painting to death, Hegel explains the end of art inversely, by hypothesizing its beginning. Unlike those who believe that art has a purpose that lies beyond it and is alien to its nature, Hegel claims that when art is present in its supreme perfection, it contains the kind of exposition most essential to the content of truth precisely in its figurativeness. Thus, for instance, for the Greeks, art was used for the highest representation of the gods, thus providing an awareness of truth. This is why the artists and the poets were the ones to create the gods and give a definite content to religion.[52] It is not, Hegel stresses, that artists and poets first formed religious ideas and then embodied them in works of art. On the contrary, what fermented in these artists and poets could crystalize only in the form of art and poetry. This point is significant for the understanding of Hegel's concept of art, for what transpires from it is that far from embodying divine essences in matter, classical sculptors in effect created the gods. What this means is that the very act of creating in matter makes it possible for something more to emerge: the spirit, and by means of the spirit—truth. It is the very beauty of the object which endows it with divine qualities. Hegel thus in effect situates the birth of art not as a response to an event external to art itself. Art stems from the artist as what is immanent in him. Its embodiment and essence are one.

Just as it is possible to hypothesize the birth of art and the state of affairs preceding it, it is possible to hypothesize what will come after it, the state of affairs exceeding art and the possibilities of understanding and representing which are unique to it. It is against this backdrop that Hegel formulates the idea of the end of art.

Hegel believes that at an early stage of history, thought condemned art for being a kind of illustration of divinity. This is evident in Judaism's second commandment, in Islam's aversion to the image, and even in the manner in which Plato denounces the poets. As culture progresses, Hegel continues, there comes a stage in which art points to a beyond of itself. An example of this may be found in certain aspects of Christianity, such as Christ's incarnation, which open new possibilities for art. At this stage, the Church nourishes art, but when the need for knowledge and research engenders the Reformation, religious ideas retreat from the sensual to the intellectual. Hegel regards this the era "after" art, based on the aspiration of the spirit to satisfy itself by itself alone. This aspiration is awakened when art reaches a high level of sophistication. At this point, art emerges perfectly by means of its manifestations; it leaves no mysterious remainder to be yearned for. In this state of affairs, which Hegel locates in his own period, despite the perfection of the work of art, "we bow the knee no longer [before artistic portrayals]."[53]

In other words, Hegel claims that the process in which the spirit is embodied in matter, the process which is the essence of art, reaches its apex in medieval and Renaissance art, at a time when religion and art nourish one another. The paradigmatic expression of this mutually nourishing encounter between religion and art is in paintings whose subject matter is the incarnation of Christ. This state of affairs, in which art embodies religion's universal ideas in concrete and specific matter, is unique to a historical moment. Later, when the Reformation defines a spirituality distancing itself from material embodiment, this climatic moment will pass. In Hegelian terms, there will be a sublation (*Aufhebung*) of art by religion. The meaning of the German term "*Aufhebung*" is equivocal, involving at once cancellation and raising. According to Hegel, the spirit always moves forward. In a process of progressive development, the spirit rises from a lower to a higher level. This process is spiral: the higher level cancels the one preceding it at the same time that it contains it and thus does not completely negate it. This is sublation as negation that is also a raising to a higher level. Henceforth, art will be something that has taken place in the past; what will remain is art after art.

Death appears in Hegel's discussion of the end of art on both the thematic and structural registers. In both cases, the death in question is not biological extinction but a stage whose very exhaustion makes possible the sublation following which only repetition is possible. The structure Hegel describes is hence structurally close to what Freud will later conceptualize as the death drive—an end followed by a compulsion to repeat for which this end is also a condition.

As stated above, Hegel presents the development of art as consisting of three stages: symbolic art, classical art and romantic art. Symbolic art is a prerequisite for the true and developed creation of art. When he introduces symbolic art, Hegel explains the concept of the symbol by means of the relationship it maintains between content and form.[54] Unlike everyday signs such as flags or cockades, the artistic symbol displays an affinity between content and form. Symbolic art, Hegel says, may be described as an ongoing struggle between content and form, a struggle which began in ancient Persian art and reached its apex in Egyptian art. At this stage, content aspires to take over form. The symbol operates regardless of the form from which it is detached. The result is art to which beauty is irrelevant, art which often seems grotesque or tasteless. This struggle is later resolved in classical art, characterized by a spectacular unity between content and form.

Hegel lists three stages in the development of symbolic art: unconscious symbolism, fantastic symbolism and symbolism proper. Symbolism proper, Hegel claims, takes place only when "the inner becomes free and yet preserves the impulse to picture itself, in a real [form], what is in its essence, and to have this very picture before itself as also an external work."[55] It is only then that the proper impulse toward art, especially visual art, begins.

What is interesting for the purposes of the present discussion is that the transition toward symbolism proper, which is a condition for the true creation or art and for the thinking about art, must, according to Hegel, pass through the thinking of death as negation. As Hegel puts it:

> for symbolic art, as well as for fine art also, it is essential that the meaning to which it undertakes to give [form] shall not only (as happens in Indian art) emerge from the first immediate unity with its external existence. . . . but shall also become explicitly free from the *immediate* sensuous [form]. This liberation can only take place so far as the sensuous and the natural is apprehended and envisaged in itself as negative, as what is to be, and has been [sublated].[56]

It is further necessary for negation, which appears as something beyond the natural, to be accepted and understood as the universal meaning of things in general, as a component of the Divine. Negation is present in Indian art, where certain figures function as negations of the unchanging divinity. In Persian art too, negation is present, in the figure of the darkness that is Ahriman, the negation of divinity as light.

In the face of such undeveloped and undialectical conceptions, Hegel introduces a complex relation between divinity and negation which has a direct bearing on art. In this relation, negation is fixed independently by consciousness, yet regarded as only one factor in the Divine. This factor is not located outside the true divinity in the form of another god, like Ahriman. The true God, rather, appears as his own negation. Negation, that is to say, is immanent to God.[57] As death is the ultimate negation, it constitutes an inseparable part of the Divine. The death in question is not necessarily extinction. There are two faces to death, Hegel says. Death means finality; yet the death of what is natural brings forth something higher and more exalted. This is the spirit as what contains death as an inseparable part of itself.[58] What this means is that the spirit must contain within itself the possibility for its own negation. If the Persians instituted a positive god alongside a negative one, in this state of affairs there is a unity in which good and bad are held together dialectically.

The more advanced symbolic art, which makes it possible for art to ascend to a higher level, is Egyptian art. This is exemplified, Hegel suggests, by Egyptian art's constant engagement with death. In Egyptian art, life and death are intertwined: the dead, to which the Egyptians paid the highest respect, thus acquired the content of the living. The dead may be deprived of immediate existence, but they still preserve a relation to the living from which they are separated.[59]

The Egyptians were also the first to develop the idea of immortality. Life and death were for them dialectically related, each negating the other it makes possible. The Pyramid is the most consummate example of the artistic form emerging from this dialectic. Meaning is literally concealed within it. Its form, not taken from nature, envelops a hidden content. The Pyramid is, then, the creation of man as utilizing possibilities of representation exceeding nature.[60]

The next developmental stage of art as described by Hegel is classical art. While even in the most elaborate forms of symbolic art the gap between form and content remains present, the greatest achievement of classical art is a wonderful harmony of form and content. This harmony finds its expression in the beauty of the Greek sculptures. The inner being of classical art, Hegel says, is in its free independent meaning, which is "not a meaning of this or that but what means [*Bedeutende*] itself and therefore intimates [*Deutende*] itself."[61] This is the spirit, which makes itself into an object for itself. In classical art, beauty appears for itself, not at the service of any idea, yet carrying meaning. This is free and independent beauty from whence the spirit may emerge, for in the act of giving inner meaning to an art object the spirit has the possibility to grasp itself.

How does classical art manage to bridge the gap between content and form? Hegel claims that this is possible only when the artistic representation of the human body takes center stage. Only then does the spirit attain its adequate existence in sensuous and natural material. This applies also to human feelings, impulses, deeds, events and actions. The representations of these are not only natural but spiritual, instances where the inner side of man is brought into an adequate identity with the outer.[62]

Classical art achieves more than earlier forms of art also in the developed form in which it links particularity and universality.[63] *The Odyssey*, for instance, may be read as an epic which is mythical and as such universal, but what makes it persuasive and captivating is the particularity of the stories by means of which it embodies myth. For instance, to demonstrate the way in which the universal is beautifully manifested in the particular in classical art, Hegel turns to the Homeric lamentation for the death of Achilles, specifically the part describing the grief of his mother, who rises from the sea surrounded by the immortal sea-nymphs to meet with her dead son:

> But around thee stand the daughters of the Father of the Sea, lamenting and clad in ambrosial garments; the Muses too, all nine, wailed by turns in beautiful song and then indeed no Argives were seen without tears, so moved were they by the clear-toned song.[64]

Hegel emphasizes the way in which the lament presentifies a mother at once archetypal and particular. Here as at many other points throughout the *Aesthetics*, the example Hegel provides is a representation whose content is death. This repeated exemplification of art by means of representations which take death as their topic is yet another index of the structurally crucial place of death in its relation to art in Hegel's philosophy.

Hegel proceeds to show how classical art reaches its end precisely in the same manner in which it reached its grand achievements. The more elaborate classical sculpture's modes of representation become, the more serene its represented characters. Classical sculpture thus comes to presentify a harsh contradiction between loftiness and the particularity of bodily form. It is this contradiction that would eventually drag classical art itself to its ruin. What this means is that the very same gap between content and form which characterized symbolic art and which classical art managed to bridge returns to center stage, undermining the balance once struck. When form reaches perfection, sculptures increasingly become objects whose major purpose is to give pleasure to the eye. Consequently, form loses its harmony with content.[65] Here too, Hegel exemplifies the process he describes by means of representations of death, this time turning to sculptures of gods in mourning. These sculptures, where the representation of a particular character in the throes of mourning reaches a high level of sophistication, mark a retreat from embodiment toward the spirit. This retreat is an inevitable outcome of perfect embodiment itself, which necessarily points to its beyond. The particular aspect of these sculptures is no longer compatible with the universal, which now seems to subsist in a different sphere, transcending their embodiment in matter.[66] Hegel thus finds that the downfall of classical art is already implicit in its anthropomorphism.[67] It is at this point, he argues, that the road is paved toward art's next developmental stage, in which a transition takes place from the representation of divinity in classical gods to its representation in human form, the form of Christ.

The embodiment of Christ in the flesh, Hegel's paradigmatic example for the pinnacle of art, which appears in the developmental stage which he calls "romantic art," is inextricably intertwined with death. While classical art achieved a harmonious union of content and form which made it possible for the spirit to emerge, romantic art is a higher phase, in which the spirit folds into itself, no longer requiring matter as support or mediation. Romantic art dissolves the unity of form and content achieved in classical art in order to raise the spirit beyond its embodiment in matter. The unity that comes with romantic art is a unity that knows itself.

Romantic art is an art that transcends itself, rises above its embodiment in matter, referencing a spiritual being which needs no physical or material support. Hegel argues that while the eyes of the Greek sculptures of the gods are empty and sightless, the God of romantic art appears seeing, disclosing his inner being to man's inner being so that soul meets soul.[68] The mode of representing the eyes of the divinity exemplifies what Hegel considers the difference between two phases of art. The holes that appear in the place of the eyes of the gods in classical sculpture exemplify the formal limits of embodiment in matter. Romantic art, by contrast, seems to exist in a sphere beyond matter; a sphere which can only be spoken about in metaphors.

If in classical art death is conceived by way of negation, as manifest for instance in Achilles's reluctance to lead the shadows of the dead in the underworld, in romantic art death appears as the negation of negation.[69] Hegel states:

> In romantic art . . . death is only a perishing of the natural soul and finite subjectivity, a perishing (related negatively only to the inherently negative) which cancels nullity and thereby is the means of liberating the spirit from its finitude and disunion as well as spiritually reconciling the individual person with the Absolute. For the Greeks what was affirmative was only the life united with natural, external, and mundane existence, and death therefore was just a negation, the dissolution of immediate reality. But in the romantic outlook death has the significance of negativity, in the sense of the negation of the negative return to self . . . . death [as the negation of negation] is a process through which the spirit, now independent of what negates it externally, must itself go in order truly to live.[70]

We would like to suggest that this negation of negation is precisely the return of art after the end of art. Hegel's words shed new light on Holbein's *The Body of the Dead Christ in the Tomb*, analyzed by Kristeva. Kristeva reads Holbein's painting as existing "at the very place of a severance of representation."[71] This severance, according to Kristeva, is cultural and historical, a severance between a Catholic paradigm of representation and that of the Reformation.[72] The painting's existence at the very place of a severance is manifest in its expression of death by means of a mode of a representation which does not belong to either of these paradigms. Hegel's *Aesthetics* points toward the very same severance but explains it as structural rather than historical. In terms of Hegel's *Aesthetics*, what is at stake in Holbein's painting is indeed an "abyss,"[73] a twilight zone between paradigms of painting; but these paradigms differ not in historicity but in structure. Holbein's painting exists at the very place of a severance between a paradigm of representation in which the image is a religious object, so that art and religion are in complete accordance, and a paradigm of representation in which religion steps toward spiritual realms. Read in terms of Hegel's *Aesthetics*, Holbein's painting exists at the place of a severance between a paradigm of representation in which death is negation and one in which death is a negation of negation, and in which art is left behind by the spirit to contemplate its end, until beginning to manifest itself again.

The repeated manifestations of art produced after Hegel's articulation of the end of art only confirm his thesis, even though they do not necessarily stem from it. From Gustave Courbet to Marcel Duchamp, from Édouard Manet to Andy Warhol, art history has witnessed an exciting and intensive period, which began to ripen shortly after Hegel's *Aesthetics* was first published. In the mid-1980s, a series of repetitions emerged, this time not of artworks but of the Hegelian move of theorizing the end of art itself.

One of the clearest examples of this repetition can be found in the work of Arthur Danto, rife with repeated attempts to confront the idea of the end of art. Danto's recurrent engagement with the topic of the end of art refuses to come to an end with almost the same persistence in which art refuses to stop dying. The difficulty emerging from Danto's work, which is also the challenge driving it, is his wish to qualify Hegel's conception of the end of art while linking it to concrete and historically specific artistic work and at the same time providing an exhaustive explanation of the way in which art continues to vigorously create itself.

Thus, in a book published in the mid-1980s, Danto devotes an entire chapter to the idea of the end of art.[74] In a complex move in which he examines the history of art against the backdrop of two major paradigms, Danto asks what the prospects of art might be, where it is headed, and whether its future may be predicted. In light of *The Phenomenology of Spirit* and Hegel's aesthetic philosophy, Danto concludes that art, at least from the twentieth century, is engaged with the question of its own identity.[75] Answers suggested to this question seem insufficient to Danto, who offers an answer of his own. Alluding to Kant's third moment of the judgment of taste, "finality without an end," Danto defines art as "conceptuable without satisfying any specific concept."[76] Like the heroine of the female *Bildungsroman*, who simultaneously asks herself two questions, who she is and what it means to be a woman, art, Danto suggests, turns to philosophy so that it might define it and explain its essence.[77] Danto finds the source of this structure in Hegel's claim, in the *Phenomenology of Spirit*, that the spirit moves in the direction of "self-knowledge and self-realization through self-knowledge."[78] Art is one of the excruciating paths toward redemptive and final self-consciousness. For Hegel, philosophy is the most elevated form of the spirit by virtue of its reflexivity, the way in which self-exploration is part of its essence. Danto believes that the history of art can be understood as a history that produces the philosophy of art. But from a certain point, which Danto locates in twentieth-century art, art and philosophy become intertwined and self-reflexivity becomes an essential part of the art object itself. Thus, according to Danto who reads Hegel, the history of philosophy reaches its end in a final moment of self-enlightenment, as does the history of art.

Contemporary art does seem to bear out Danto's argument, increasingly dependent as it is on theory for its existence as art. Theory, for its part, becomes an element intrinsic to the work of art, and so to understand its object it must also understand itself. But the more self-reflexivity, that is to say, theory, art involves, Danto argues, the more its object begins to vanish. Thus, art evaporates in the blinding light of pure thought about itself.[79] In other words, for Danto the reshuffling of the relationship between the art object and its interpretation is one of the manifestations of the end of art.

The greater the part theory plays in the art object, the more important interpretation becomes, for theory can be extrapolated from the art object only by means of interpretation. As Danto puts it, "interpretation is not something outside the work: work and interpretation arise together in aesthetic consciousness."[80] Combined, the increasingly larger role played by theory in the art object and the increasing importance of interpretation eclipse the materiality of the object. The more the observer focuses on theory and interpretation, the less attention he pays to the object's material attributes. Thus, one of the outcomes of modernism is expediting the end of art, whose materiality might evaporate into philosophical discourse. In a later book, *After the End of Art: Contemporary Art and the Pale of Modernism*, Danto accentuates this conclusion by quoting Joseph Kosuth's claim that the only role of the artist is to explore the nature of art. This statement follows the same logic as Hegel's claim that "art invites us to intellectual consideration, and that not for the purpose of creating art again, but for knowing philosophically what art is."[81]

In his later writings, Danto's position becomes somewhat more moderate, even though he continues to return to the category of the end of art in his attempt to respond to the interpretive challenge posed by Hegel with a solution that would reconcile the Hegelian position with contemporary artistic production. Danto argues that the Hegelian notion of the end of art implies neither the actual cessation of artistic endeavor nor the exhaustion of any particular artistic genre. He insists on a careful distinction between the "end of art" and the "death of art," a category he does not underwrite.[82]

In the course of his argument, Danto engages Hans Belting's discussion of the end of art history, published shortly before, in which Belting claims that the history of art can no longer be grasped as a coherent and universal narrative.[83] In his book about images which preceded any concept of art, Belting argues that the status of art as a cultural phenomenon is not necessarily congruent with the actual production of different forms of art. Art, Belting claims, begins when a conception of art appears, as happened in the Renaissance.[84] Phenomena such as Veronica's veil in the Christian myth which allegedly bears the imprint of the face of Christ on the Via Dolorosa cannot be considered products of artistic work nor part of a conception of art, since in them the work of painting is believed to be a "true image" (*vera icon*)—a miracle or a concrete object—not the work of an artist operating within an artistic context.[85] Quoting Vasari's claim that when Raphael died, "the art of painting might well have died with him," leads Belting to conclude that this was the historical moment in which "the image was now the work of the artist and a manifestation of art," since as Vasari continues, Raphael's last picture, *Transfiguration of Christ*, was posited behind the bier and "the image seemed alive, although its creator was dead."[86] Like Belting, Danto refers to the "end of art" as a certain moment after modernism, a moment after which art, although it may not cease to exist, will exist differently. The end of art has the status of a finish line, of having reached a haven. "Art came to an end," Danto writes, "when it achieved a philosophical sense of its own identity."[87]

According to Danto, it is only from the moment of an end that art can be an object of philosophical contemplation. But what might be the nature of this art after art?[88] The art preoccupied with itself, created during periods when each artistic practice or movement had a manifesto clearly articulating the nature of art and its frame of reference, ultimately exhausted itself, transferring its conceptual freight to philosophers. At this point, tacitly alluding to Marx and Engels's claim that in the post-historical era, man will no longer be committed to one activity alone but could move among occupations, Danto claims it is possible to move among artistic movements and styles, to be a different kind of artist every week. In its late formulation by Danto, then, the "end of art" is the end of a certain narrative that had dictated the history of art. This narrative reached closure when art ceased to obey manifestos, opening the way to infinite artistic possibilities.[89] Like Hegel before him, then, Danto identifies the end of art with its philosophization. It is this very philosophization that functions as the condition for art's return and repetition, articulated, in this case, as the opening up of an infinity of artistic possibilities.

Another voice in the debate surrounding the category of the "end of art" during the 1980s is that of Gianni Vattimo, who links the Hegelian notion with the Frankfurt School's work on mass culture, eventually proposing a solution grounded in Martin Heidegger's thinking on art.[90] Vattimo claims that the category of "the death of art" is an event dictating culture, a prophecy about a society in which art no longer constitutes a distinct phenomenon because existence itself is aestheticized. The avant-garde of the 1920s created art forms which transgressed at once the limits of artistic institutions and the limits of neo-Kantian philosophy. Refusing to be labeled simply "other," the avant-garde demanded the privileged status of a knowledge in the form of recognition as a true instrument for social action. This is why it did not limit itself to exhibiting art in conventional spaces such as the museum, the gallery, or the concert hall. No longer seeking admission into the institution, art attempted to challenge the institution no less than its own existence.[91] No mere self-reflexivity such as inherent in any art as such, the challenge of the avant-garde was an instance of self-directed irony. It is this self-directed irony that Vattimo finds relevant to the discussion of the end of art. While grounded in Hegel's argument, Vattimo's conception of the end of art emerges specifically from the consideration of avant-garde art, which brings self-reflexivity to new heights of self-negation through irony.

Vattimo claims that technology in the sense of mechanical reproduction as articulated by Walter Benjamin plays a significant role in the end of art, as it makes a general and aura-free aestheticization possible. The responses of various artists to mass culture too, Vattimo claims, are another aspect of the death of art, in this case, death by suicide. In the face of the flatness and shallowness of mass culture, art, which seeks to distinguish itself, makes itself expressly uncommunicative, as evident in the case of Samuel Beckett. Such a suicidal, self-destructive response to mass culture is what is at stake in the avant-garde's opposition to traditional artistic canons exalting the pleasurable or beautiful.[92]

Vattimo, then, links the death of art with the avant-garde movement of the turn of the twentieth century upon its aspiration to break the traditional boundaries of aesthetics by negating the very site in which the aesthetic had traditionally resided. One result of the avant-garde's move is the plurivalent status of contemporary art. No longer measured by a given set of values, art defines its success precisely by problematizing this set, whose boundaries it challenges. The ability of art to put its own status into question hence emerges as a new criterion for artistic value, stemming from art's aspiration to distinguish itself from mass culture and kitsch:[93]

> In a world where consensus is produced by manipulation, authentic art speaks only by lapsing into silence, and aesthetic experience arises only as the negation of all its traditional and canonical characteristics, starting with the pleasure of the beautiful itself. Even in Adorno's negative aesthetics, as in the case of the utopia of a general aestheticization of experience, the chief criterion for evaluating the work of art is its greater or lesser capacity for self-negation. . . . In a sense that needs to be more closely examined, the work of art, in present conditions, displays characteristics analogous to Heidegger's notion of Being: it arises only as that which at the same time withdraws from us.[94]

The end of art, according to Vattimo, is manifest in three ways: the thinking of art as a utopia of reintegration, the aestheticization of the masses, and the silencing and suicide of artistic action. Yet this tripartite classification of the manifestations of the death of art does not seem to Vattimo to adequately respond either to the repeated occurrences of art nor to differentiations of artistic value which continue to elude it.[95]

Nevertheless, Vattimo claims that contemporary art does engage these three manifestations of the death of art. In effect, in contemporary art it is no longer self-irony but the interplay among these three manifestations of the death of art that becomes the central element in the persistent life of art and its products. It is with this situation in which interrelations between different manifestations of the end of art become the very life of art that the contemporary philosophy of art must contend. Since it involves the repeated announcement and deferral of the death of art, this situation, Vattimo says, may also be called the decline of art.[96]

Traditional aesthetic philosophy with its categories of the beautiful, the genius, or the ideal finds it difficult to contend with this situation, characteristic of contemporary art. Thus, what the death of art mirrors is the death of aesthetics.[97] It is in Heidegger's "The Origin of the Work of Art" that Vattimo finds a way to philosophically articulate the death of art. At the end of a complex argument saturated in Heideggerian conceptualizations, Vattimo reaches the conclusion that aesthetics can fulfill its purpose as philosophical aesthetics if it is able to recognize in the various elements which are assumed to signal the death of art the announcement of an epoch of Being in which "thought may open itself up to the only partially negative . . . meaning which the experience of aestheticity has acquired in the era of mechanical reproduction and mass culture."[98]

Vattimo's repetition of the structure of Hegel's argument regarding the end of art involves various definitions of the "end" (the thinking of art as a utopia of reintegration, the aestheticization of the masses, and the silencing and suicide of artistic action). What is beyond the end is conceptualized as the opening up of consciousness to a meaning founded upon aesthetic experience. What is new in Vattimo's argument is his introduction of Heideggerian and Frankfurt School conceptualizations to the philosophical debate concerning the end of art. Other than this innovation, Vattimo's argument is a variation on the structure that repeats itself from the inception of the discourse on art in Western culture: art as conditioned by loss and persisting beyond it, a structure raised to a higher power in the Hegelian discussion of the end of art and its derivatives.

Jacques Derrida's discussion of Hegel's *Aesthetics* in *The Truth in Painting* constitutes yet another sublation, and subjectivation, of this structure. Revisiting the Hegelian thesis of the end of art, Derrida writes:

> The fact remains that here art is studied from the point of view of its end. Its pastness is its truth. The philosophy of art is thus a circle in a circle of circles: "a ring" says Hegel, in the totality of philosophy. It turns upon itself and in annulling itself it links onto other rings. This annular concatenation forms the circle of circles of the philosophical encyclopedia. Art cuts out a circumscription or takes away a circumvolution from it. It encircles itself.[99]

What Derrida adds to the Hegelian thesis on the end of art is its clarification as bound up with the figure of the circle that he finds forms and informs discourses on art.[100] More than a stage in the development of the spirit, art is what encircles itself within it so as to cut itself out from it. It is, then, what is defined by a limit, a circumference such as subtends phenomena in the visual arts such as the painting's *passe-partout*, the *cartouche* or elliptical ring delimiting inscriptions on ancient caves, or the parergonal ornaments on painting frames. Given Derrida's choice of Hegel's thesis on the death of art as the point of departure for the series of circles "around painting"[101] which constitutes his book, it is perhaps not incidental that one of these circles should be a discussion of works exploring a form in which death is literally delimited in human culture: Gérard Titus-Carmel's exhibition *The Pocket Size Tlingit Coffin and the 61 Ensuing Drawings* of 1978.[102] But for Derrida, art is not only what in annulling itself makes itself a link in an annular concatenation, that is to say, not only what in dying makes drawing and other arts ensue in their circumvolutions. Raised to a higher power, the act of encircling defining art comes to subtend the discourse on art as well. "Discourses on painting," Derrida writes, "are perhaps destined to reproduce the limit that constitutes them."[103] If since Hegel art is studied from the point of view of its end, to Derrida it reveals itself not only as what is reproduced beyond this end or limit but as reproducing this limit whenever it is taken as an object of a theoretical discourse, what in Lacanian terms amounts to a cultural subjectivation. What persist in an endless "com[ing] around" beyond the having "gone" of the death of art as theorized by Hegel is not only art but the discourse on art which carries this death within itself as a structuring limit.

There are, of course, fundamental differences—thematic, conceptual and historical—between the arguments of philosophers such as Hegel, Danto, Vattimo and Derrida and earlier writers on art such as Pliny the Elder and Alberti. Nonetheless, a similar structure recurs in the writing on art of all of these authors. Psychoanalytically speaking, this recurrence may be viewed as symptomatic repetition. The manifestations of this repetition are not identical, for each of its instances takes on a different content or form. Each instance, however, is a masked reconstruction of a primal trauma (of loss) whose purpose is none other than to treat this trauma.

"The real is that which always comes back to the same place—to where the subject in so far as he thinks . . . does not meet it," Lacan writes in his eleventh seminar in relation to repetition in psychoanalysis.[104] He adds that repetition, as Freud defines it (*Wiederholen*), is not reproduction (*Reproduzieren*) such as occurs in reproductions of canonical paintings. It is repetition under a symbolic veil.[105] Lacan's conceptualization of repetition makes it possible to show how different phenomena in the history of thinking about art, seemingly disparate in terms of content, historical context and discipline, are nothing but repetitions of something of a real which is forever traumatic in culture. These repetitions appear in different symbolic guises precisely because they involve a structural recurrence of what always comes back to the same place. And indeed, as we will show in the chapters that follow, these repetitions appear not only on the level of the discourse about art but in artistic practice's own treatment of death. This treatment is not the ubiquitously discussed theme of death in art, for death, as Freud shows, is precisely what cannot be represented in the unconscious. It is what appears in art as an end that generates an invigorated repetition, beyond the pleasure principle.

Notes

1 Pliny the Elder, *Natural History*, trans. H. Rackham (Cambridge, MA: Harvard University Press, 1995), p. 336.
2 Ibid., p. 325.
3 Jacques Derrida, *Memoirs of the Blind*, trans. Pascale-Anne Brault and Michael Naas (Chicago: Chicago University Press, 1993 [1990]), p. 49; Hagi Kenaan, "Tracing Shadows: Reflections on the Origins of Painting," in *Pictorial Languages and Their Meaning*, ed. G. Fishof and C. Versar (Tel Aviv: Tel Aviv University Publishing, 2006), pp. 17–28.
4 Leon Battista Alberti, *On Painting*, trans. John R. Spencer. (New Haven, CT: Yale University Press, 1970 [1435–1436]), p. 18.
5 Ibid, p. 63.
6 Ibid.
7 Norman Bryson, *Vision and Painting: The Logic of the Gaze* (New Haven, CT: Yale University Press, 1983), pp. 104–6.
8 Ibid., p. 106.
9 Ibid., p. 106.
10 Ibid., p. 107.
11 See also Efrat Biberman, "Of the Gaze as Topological Locus: Alberti and Lacan," *(Re)-Turn: A Journal of Lacanian Studies* 3 & 4 (Spring 2008): 135–49.
12 Julia Kristeva, *Black Sun: Depression and Melancholia*, trans. Leon S. Roudiez (New York: Columbia University Press, 1989 [1987]), p. 103.
13 Ibid., 137.
14 George Bataille, *The Tears of Eros*, trans. Peter Connor (San Francisco: City Lights Books, 1989 [1961]), p. 32.
15 Ibid., p. 33.
16 Ibid., p. 34.
17 Ibid., p. 42.
18 Ibid., p. 45.
19 Jacques Lacan, *The Seminar of Jacques Lacan, Book XIX: . . . Ou Pire [. . . Or Worse]* (1971–1972), trans. Cormac Gallagher (unpublished manuscript), lesson of 17 May 1972, p. 10.
20 Jacques Lacan, *The Seminar of Jacques Lacan, Book XIXa: The Knowledge of the Psychoanalyst* (1971–1972), trans. Cormac Gallagher, lesson of 1 June 1972.
21 Jacques Lacan, *The Seminar of Jacques Lacan, Book XIII: The Object of Psychoanalysis* (1965–1966), trans. Cormac Gallagher (unpublished manuscript), lesson of 4 May 1966.
22 Philippe Dubois, *L'acte photographique* (Paris, Bruxelles: Nathan Labor, 1983), pp. 117–19.
23 Walter Benjamin, "A Short History of Photography," trans. Stanley Mitchell, *Screen* 13, no. 1 (1972 [1931]): 5–26.
24 Roland Barthes, *Camera Lucida: Reflections on Photography*, trans. Richard Howard (New York: Hill & Wang, 1982 [1980]).
25 Walter Benjamin, "The Work of Art in the Age of Mechanical Reproduction," in *Illuminations: Essays and Reflections*, trans. Harry Zohn (New York: Schocken Books, 1968 [1936]), p. 226.
26 Thierry de Duve, "Time Exposure and Snapshot: The Photograph as Paradox," *October* 5 (1978): 113–25.
27 Dubois, *L'acte photographique*, p. 160.
28 Bryson, *Vision and Painting*, p. 106.
29 The Hebrew word סוף */soph/* means "end."
30 Jacques Lacan, *The Seminar of Jacques Lacan, Book II: The Ego in Freud's Theory and in the Technique of Psychoanalysis* (1954–1955), trans. Sylvana Tomaselli (New York: W.W. Norton, 1988), p. 42.
31 Ibid.

32 Immanuel Kant, *The Critique of Judgment*, trans. James Creed Meredith (Oxford: Clarendon Press, 1952 [1790]), § 60, p. 226.
33 Ibid., p. 227.
34 Ibid.
35 Ibid.
36 G.W. F. Hegel, *Aesthetics: Lectures on Fine Art*, trans. T. M. Knox (Oxford: Clarendon Press, 1988 [1835]), pp. 56–61.
37 Ibid., pp. 60–61.
38 Ibid., p. 7.
39 Ibid.
40 Ibid., p. 2.
41 Ibid.
42 Ibid., p. 11.
43 We would like to express our deep gratitude to Prof. Zvi Tauber for his illuminating comments on this topic.
44 Hegel, *Aesthetics*, p. 427.
45 Ibid., p. 31.
46 Ibid., pp. 315–16.
47 Ibid., p. 35.
48 Ibid., p. 39.
49 Ibid., p. 49.
50 Ibid., p. 55.
51 Ibid., p. 11.
52 Ibid., p. 102.
53 Ibid., p. 10.
54 Ibid., p. 304.
55 Ibid., p. 351.
56 Ibid., p. 347.
57 Ibid., p. 348.
58 Ibid., p. 349.
59 Ibid., p. 355.
60 Ibid., p. 356.
61 Ibid., p. 427.
62 Ibid., pp. 434–35.
63 Ibid., pp. 476–77.
64 Ibid., p. 481.
65 Ibid., p. 485.
66 Ibid., p. 503.
67 Ibid., p. 504.
68 Ibid., p. 521.
69 Ibid., p. 523.
70 Ibid., pp. 523–24.
71 Kristeva, *Black Sun*, p. 136.
72 Ibid.
73 Ibid.
74 Arthur C. Danto, "The End of Art," in *The Philosophical Disenfranchisement of Art* (New York: Columbia University Press, 1986), pp. 81–115.
75 Ibid., p. 110.
76 Ibid.
77 Alain Badiou offers a similar idea when he refers to Lacan's formulation of the discourse of the hysteric. See Alain Badiou, *Handbook of Inaesthetics*, trans. Alberto Toscano (Stanford, CA: Stanford University Press, 2005), p. 1.
78 Danto, "The End of Art," p. 110.
79 Ibid., p. 111.

80 Ibid., p. 45.
81 Hegel, *Aesthetics*, p. 11; quoted in Arthur C. Danto, *After the End of Art: Contemporary Art and the Pale of Modernism* (Princeton, NJ: Princeton University Press, 1997), pp. 13–14.
82 Ibid., p. 3.
83 Hans Belting, *The End of the History of Art?*, trans. Christopher S. Wood (Chicago: University of Chicago Press, 1984), p. IX.
84 Hans Belting, *Likeness and Presence: A History of the Image before the Era of Art*, trans. Edmund Jephcott (Chicago: University of Chicago Press, 1994), p. 471. By excluding the paintings of Veronica from the sphere of art, Belting follows the logic of Hegel's conceptualization of art, since for Hegel art, in its early stages, or art before art, is characterized by a fetishistic conception of itself and is hence not art at all. Hegel, *Aesthetics*, pp. 315–16.
85 Belting, *Likeness and Presence*, p. 49.
86 Ibid., p. 471.
87 Arthur Danto, *The Wake of Art: Criticism, Philosophy, and the Ends of Taste* (Amsterdam: B+G Arts International, 1998), p. 119.
88 Danto, *After the End of Art*, p. 47.
89 Ibid., p. 37.
90 Gianni Vattimo, "The Death or Decline of Art," in *The End of Modernity: Nihilism and Hermeneutics in Postmodern Culture*, trans. Jon R. Snyder (Cambridge: Polity Press, 1988), pp. 51–64.
91 Ibid., pp. 53–54.
92 Ibid., p. 56.
93 Ibid., p. 52.
94 Ibid., pp. 56–57.
95 Ibid., p. 58.
96 Ibid., p. 59.
97 Ibid., p. 59.
98 Ibid., p. 64.
99 Jacques Derrida, *The Truth in Painting*, trans. Geoff Bennington and Ian McLoed (Chicago: University of Chicago Press), p. 26.
100 Ibid., p. 23.
101 Ibid., p. 9.
102 Ibid., pp. 185–247.
103 Ibid., p. 11.
104 Jacques Lacan, *The Seminar of Jacques Lacan, Book XI: The Four Fundamental Concepts of Psychoanalysis*, trans. Alan Sheridan (New York: W.W. Norton, 1981 [1964–1965]), p. 49.
105 Ibid., p. 50.

3

ON THE ARTWORK AS CEDABLE OBJECT

> The objet petit a is qualified
> as what is most myself in myself
>
> —*Jacques-Alain Miller, 2005*

At the end of his essay on "Negation," Freud writes that the condition for the creation of psychic reality as a reality of representation is the loss of objects that once brought real satisfaction.[1] What follows is not the retrieving of this real satisfaction, nor the retrieving of the satisfaction involved in loss, but, as Freud explains in the same article, a return in the symbolic register: a return to representation as a site where something of primordial satisfaction may be regained.[2] As Freud's earlier *Three Essays on Sexuality* (1905) indicates, such return takes place by means of objects of the drive (oral, anal, scopic, invocatory), themselves already representations of or concrete veils for the primordial satisfaction that has been lost, that in Lacanian notation is the object a.[3] It is thus hardly surprising that in the field of visual arts, the repetition whose trajectory we follow—a repetition whose condition is loss and that persists beyond this loss—is manifest in works of art by means of a concrete object. This chapter focuses on visual artworks foregrounding the object a as cedable object one moment before its ostensible loss. From the many examples of such artworks, we have chosen the cases detailed below.

"Perhaps it is an attempt to renounce the splendor of beauty and in exchange gain the splendor of death—or what in Western culture is called 'eternity.'"[4] With these words, Israeli artist Shosh Kormosh describes her photographic collage/montage works. Like the artworks discussed in the sixth chapter of this book, Kormosh's works occupy a space between photography and painting, as in the relatively few years of her work, Kormosh treated the photographic medium in a unique fashion. Collecting photographed objects from various sources and placing them alongside objects she herself photographed, Kormosh created new combinations in which the image is rent, cut, divested of its background, conjoined with other images and pasted onto an alien environment, on a black or white background without shadows and reflections. The photographed objects float on a clean, pristine background, and despite the alienation between them and the new background they have been given, they appear to be immaculately positioned in their proper place, in accordance with the title of Kormosh's series of works from 1994 to 1995: "Order and Cleanliness: A–."

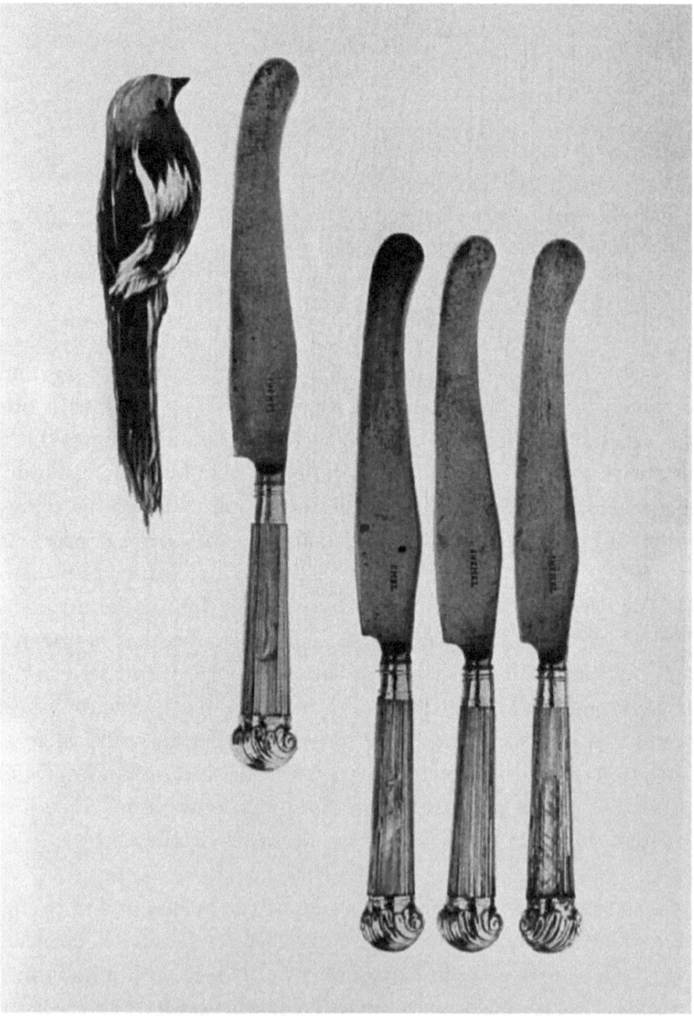

FIGURE 3.1 Shosh Kormosh, *Untitled (M19)*, 1991–1993. Image reproduced with the kind permission of the artist's family.

The materiality of the different mediums of photography and painting is present in these works. Photography is present in its black-white contrasts, in the printed photographic paper, in the qualities of the image. Painting is present in the traces of the brush strokes that color the background, in the thickness of the white paint which divests the image of its original surroundings. Yet despite the almost blatant allusion of Kormosh's works to photographic montage and to surrealism, any mention of those seems redundant, for the most salient feature of these series of photographs is that in them, the image is cut from its background. The photographed objects are wrenched from their original habitat and meticulously placed and rearranged in the photographic framework. The object's status as cut off eclipses the connection between artistic mediums in Kormosh's work. The object appears as cut off on several levels. First, the image is taken from a source external

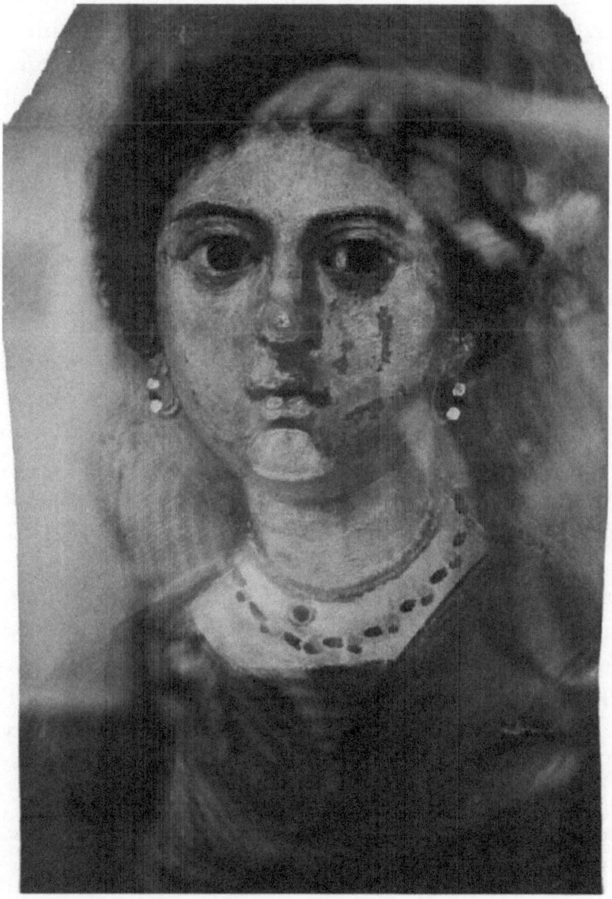

FIGURE 3.2 Shosh Kormosh, *Untitled (E3)*, 1987–1990. Image reproduced with the kind permission of the artist's family.

to the world of art, an auction-house catalogue. Second, the object is divested of its background and from the shadow it once cast and placed on a monochromatic background. Third, not only is the image divested of its previous background; it is not integrated into the new background it was given but glides within it. Whether the work features a single object connected with other objects or a single object duplicated into a group, the image as a whole seems cohesive, a unified combination against a backdrop which is foreign to it.

One of Kormosh's early works features the portrait of a female figure, taken from an Egyptian burial painting. While at first glance the viewer is captivated by the photographed portrait, a second glance encounters, above the head of the figure, the blurred shape of a human hand, lightly resting on the head of the drawn figure. As curator Tali Tamir discloses, this is a reflection of the artist's own hand during the photographic act.[5] This hand, which emerges as an absent-present ghost, points toward Kormosh's later works, in which the image of the human body is present only as a body part, as a garment from which this body has been removed, or as a utensil such as a comb or a mirror which fashions the body's appearance and makes it possible for its reflection to emerge. This is suggested, for instance, by a work that shows two rows of starched collars of men's shirts with dotted textures resembling butterfly wings planted into their inner side, or by series of works featuring ironed aprons, combs, braids tied with ribbons, or decorated chairs.

Although these works clearly deal with a photographed object that has been displaced, cut out and pasted, and although the human body is present in them in various ways, they also function on the linguistic register. This is indicated by the equivoque in the Hebrew title of the series of works from 1991 to 1993: "*Munakhim.*" This signifier is both a noun and a verb. As a noun, it designates a linguistic category, "term"; as a verb, it designates the objects cast before the spectators' eyes. The English signifier "term" evoked by the title is a noun whose denotations include a specialized word or expression and an end. The latter echoes the Hebrew sense of the cast object as well as the relation to still nature and finality. Kormosh described her series in these words:

> I have tried to endow my photographs with the status of facts, or in other words, to create an encyclopedia of terms. I made a kind of fusion of encyclopedic terms [*munakhim*] and objects laid out [*munakhim*] on a table, with the intention of turning a still object into a still term [*munach*]. The result is a photograph without any occurrence, transience, or anecdotality. The genre of still-life allows me to relate to an artistic genre whose life has ended and which now belongs to the remote past. Simultaneously, I deal with domestic dreams that subsist secretly, by penetrating an interior space relegated to catalogues by bourgeois good taste.[6]

Kormosh's works, we claim, invite a reading that combines their two salient features: their giving the art object the status of cast object [*munakh*], and their relating this object to a human body part which at a certain moment is amputated from the body yet continues to exist beyond it. In what follows, we will explore the relation between these two features and interrogate its significance as a manifestation of the compulsion to repeat. This chapter will, then, examine another aspect of the artwork in its relation to the death drive. This aspect has to do with the artwork as cedable object, as a body part that falls yet persists despite its seeming ruin. In the field of visual art, this aspect appears most prominently in the genre of the self-portrait.

Autobiography or automortography

A number of art theorists and historians have treated the self-portrait in its relation to finality, among them Victor Stoichita, in a chapter of his book on theories of painting at the threshold of modernity.[7] According to Stoichita, the rise of the Reformation brought with it not, as one would expect, the end of the visual image, but a crisis in art's conception of itself. Stoichita identifies the product of this crisis in the publication, in 1550, of Giorgio Vasari's *Lives of the Artists*, which, he claims, may be read as the birth of art history.[8] Stoichita, whose discussion bears the traces of Hegel's discussions of aesthetics, argues that Vasari's book, which could only have emerged from the very heart of Catholicism, "was both a symptom and a premonition: a 'history of art' cannot be made until it is in decline. Art—from Cimabue to Michelangelo—has a *story*: To tell it (or retell it) marks its end."[9] According to Stoichita, then, the history of art is a paradoxical phenomenon, including at once the birth of the art history and its demise, as the story of art, the notation of its history, could only have taken place retroactively, once this story had already reached its terminus.

Stoichita writes that the rise of Protestantism alongside Catholicism generated two conceptions of the image: that of the "white wall," identified with one of the currents of the Reformation, and that of the mirror, identified with the immanent visuality characteristic of Catholicism. Evidently, however, even the "white wall" conception does not completely invalidate the visual image; it generates a new understanding of the image and a significant change in its status. In a certain sense, Stoichita claims, the Protestants, who grasped art in terms of function, reception, and context,[10] were those who dialectically created the modern view of art. And indeed, the image of the white wall cannot but remind us of the white cube, that quintessentially modern conceptualization of the museum space. One of the expressions of the conceptual shift at stake, Stoichita later shows, is amply demonstrated by complex practices of self-representation.

The trajectory Stoichita traces is as follows: the Reformation causes a crisis in the view of art. One of the products of this crisis is the beginning of the notation of the history and theory of art—a notation made possible only once art reaches its end. The new views of art, the result of the displacement of visuality from the domain of the Church, also bring about a shift in artists' conception of themselves and in their awareness of their craft. This trajectory is manifest, *inter alia*, in paintings that place the self-portrait at their forefront. Unlike before, the image of the artist is not only integrated into the visual narrative, nor does it appear as self-representation pure and simple. What now emerge are complex conceptualizations of self-portraiture involving the presentification of the painting self. In other words, the artist's self-portrayal as the picture's painter rather than as a figure participating in the narrative the picture presents is one of the manifestations of a new view of art. What, then, is the status of the act of self-portrayal, and is the self-portrayal of the artist distinct from art's portrayal of itself, art history? If art may note its own history only in the aftermath of its end, is the artist's self-portrayal subject to a similar logic? Does the act of self-portraiture involve the inscription of life, the presentification of the painting self on the canvas, or does this inscription spell the artist's removal from the field of life, just as the notation of the history of art heralds its end as having already taken place?

The answer Stoichita offers to these questions is complex. Self-representation, he argues, necessarily involves a paradox. This paradox may be observed in several examples in which the function of the self-portraying artist is double: that of the painting's creator, and that of its subject matter. At times, artists point toward this twofold function by painting the artist as someone about to break out of the frame of the painting. The question more essential to this discussion relates to the actual act of self-portraiture: does this act preserve life and presentify the painter, or is it, inversely, an inscription whose nature is the tracing of what has already passed away? Does an artist who paints self-portraits throughout his life give expression to life, or to life's approaching end?[11]

The first part of this chapter presents answers to these questions from two contrasting theoretical perspectives. According to the first, which stems from Hegel's aesthetics, the act of self-portraiture partakes of the essence of art as a manifestation of the spirit, and hence imbues the art object with life. This is the approach taken by a number of art theorists who have written about the self-portrait. The second perspective appears approximately one hundred and fifty years after Hegel, in Paul de Man's work on autobiography in literature. De Man conceives of autobiography as an erasure, an act of mortification.

The second part of the chapter offers a psychoanalytical position different from these two contrasting perspectives on the nature of self-portraiture. Analyzing a number of self-portraits from various periods in which the painter inscribes himself as a leftover, as a body part ceded from the artist's living organism in the form of lifeless matter, while bringing to bear Lacan's notion of the object a as cedable object, will enable us to provide a better answer to the question of the relation between self-portraiture and the death drive. As we shall show, portraying the self as a fallen body part means grasping the object of art as a cedable object. The moment of the object's being cut from the living body can no more be represented or articulated than the death and destruction of this body. Yet the self-portrait as a cedable object offers a way of manifesting this impossible moment in art. This manifestation, we shall claim, is situated beyond the pleasure principle, that is to say, as repetition compulsion. Such situating of representation beyond the pleasure principle which the self-portrait genre points to has implications exceeding the genre itself. It is at the heart of any artistic work, whose products are, constitutively, cedable objects.

Inscribing the body/inscribing life?

How might we, from a psychoanalytical perspective, conceive of the self-portrait as a manifestation of a cedable object? How is this perspective on self-portraiture different from those of philosophy and art theory? At this point we might reconsider Stoichita's argument as reverberating Hegel's aesthetic theory of self-representation. As we have shown in the previous chapter, in the introductory chapters of his *Aesthetics*, when attempting to answer the question of why man creates art, Hegel claims that one of the reasons for the creation of art is man's identification of himself in what is external to him.[12]

Man's self-conception emerges in part through external objects by means of which he identifies himself. Man attains such self-identification also by leaving his mark on external objects and thereby changing them.[13] Man, who does this as a free subject, wishes to strip the external world of its alienating qualities so that he might identify himself within it.[14]

Hegel's example for this procedure is a child standing on a riverbank and throwing pebbles into the river to observe the ripples they leave in the water. What the child obtains by means of his observation, Hegel claims, is an intuition which is the product of his actions.[15] Hegel suggests that by observing the ripples on the water, the child leaves his mark on the environment, which thus becomes a part of him. A similar procedure appears in art in various ways, and involves not only objects external to man but also his body and his appearance. The procedure of projecting the self onto objects also subtends forms of self-fashioning. This is how Hegel explains phenomena such as dress and makeup, so typical of civilized individuals and originating in their spiritual development.[16] In order to validate himself and attain recognition, man transforms his appearance just as he transforms his environment. This procedure involves a complex relationship between outside and inside, a relationship in which man and his environment are intermingled and assimilated into one another.

It is against this backdrop that Hegel understands the human need to produce art. Art is man's act of raising his internal and external worlds to spiritual consciousness in order to find himself through these worlds. In externalizing his inner world, man satisfies his need for spiritual freedom. By doubling his inner self, man attains perception and understanding of himself and of those around him.[17]

Hegel, then, supposes that artwork, which to him is nothing but the manifestation of the spirit, must be understood as a means of realizing self-consciousness as at once an externalization of the subject's inner world and an internalization and understanding of the external world. The self-portrait is a paradigmatic case of the process described by Hegel. The subject who paints himself, whether portraying his face, inserting himself into a fictional pictorial scene as one of its protagonists, or using any other form of artistic self-representation, gives positive expression to his being.

This aspect of Hegelian aesthetics becomes more complex in view of what Hegel writes in the introductory chapters of the *Aesthetics*, before the discussion of self-realization. Hegel discusses the common perception regarding the hierarchical relations between nature and art.[18] It is customary to think, Hegel claims, that the products of nature are superior to the products of art, since nature is alive while the object of art, whether it is a marble statue or a painted canvas, is lifeless. The object of art "attains the appearance of life only on its surface,"[19] but the object itself lacks life. Since the inclination is to prefer the living over the dead, the product of nature is preferred over the artwork. However, Hegel argues, such is not actually the case, since the object of art is not measured by its external existence. The object of art becomes what it is because the source of its existence is the spirit, which endows it with life. The object of art is an object baptized by the spirit, and its form is created in harmony with it. In other words, the spirit as a source of art breathes life into the object of art. In contrast to natural life, this life given by the spirit is not finite.

Self-consciousness is thus at the origin of every work of art, and the internalization of the external environment is part of this self-consciousness. The product of artistic activity is not an object that is inert like the materials from which it is made, but an object brought to life by the spirit. Artwork portraying the human body is one of the most pervasive formations of such an object. And indeed, when defining sculpture, Hegel states that the human body is its most prominent and worthy subject matter.[20]

According to Hegel, then, the subject's self-consciousness, his projecting himself onto the environment and internalizing it, is at the source of all artistic activity. This conception tacitly connects the production of art and the human body. In Hegelian terms, the self-portrait is an inscription of life which is not organic but emerges from the spirit. Of course, for Hegel, not every self-portrait would necessarily be a work of art, since in order to be such, a portrait would have to meet the strict conditions Hegel posits throughout his work, such as a proper ratio between universality and particularity. However, it is ultimately possible to say that in Hegelian terms, self-portraiture is an inscription of life.

Indeed, although art theorists treat the phenomenon of self-portraiture in various ways, most of them share the basic assumption that the self-portrait has to do with an inscription of life, whether this be the diligent tracing of the painter's mirror image suggested in Michael Fried's analysis of Courbet's early self-portraits[21] or the painter's paradoxical attempt to capture his image via various costumes and roles outlined by Svetlana Alpers in what she calls "The Theatrical Model."[22] Alpers claims that Rembrandt, who worked mostly from his atelier, would, much like a skilled theatre director, plan richly detailed scenes for his paintings. Rembrandt's self-portraits, Alpers argues, should be understood along these lines. Rembrandt not only traces his own image but also directs himself in a variety of roles and characters. Thus, for instance, in *Self Portrait from Kenwood House*, Rembrandt paints himself as the painter, and his brushes seem an inseparable part of his hand or a prosthetic hand of sorts.[23] In *Self Portrait with a Dead Bittern*, Rembrandt paints himself as a butcher. According to Alpers, in this painting, Rembrandt identifies himself as painter in the figures of both the executioner and the sacrifice.[24] Rembrandt's painting himself in a double role of butcher and butchered animal is analogous to Rembrandt's position as painter and painted object.

Alpers points out the relation between the subject's identity and its representation as other and demonstrates this relation by means of Rembrandt's changing appearances in his self-portraits. But beyond the variety of Rembrandt's donned appearances, the passage from one of Rembrandt's self-portraits to another points to something else, something which emerges when these self-portraits are examined as a series he created in the course of his life. This form of examination naturally involves an attempt to locate details preserved throughout Rembrandt's self-portraits, details that insist in the transition from one stage to another and from one medium to another, unlike other details that are relinquished and lost, or those which appear only in one portrait and for an instant, leaving no trace behind in the portrait that follows. A linear transition is thus formed between one image and the next, like in a relay race or in the game of Chinese whispers: the information present in the first image slowly disappears and only a trace of it, if anything, is preserved up to the last image in the series of self-representations, which stops only with Rembrandt's death but in fact continues to exist in the discourse of art. It seems, then, that the structure whose repetition on the theoretical register we traced in the previous chapter appears also in the praxis of art.

In what sense is what is at stake in these portraits an auto-bio-graphy, that is, a self-inscription of life? After all, the very inscription of life manifests the perishable aspect of life emerging from the series of images: the texture of changes which transpires in its course alongside the characteristics that remain permanent. What, then, is actually registered in this series—life, or its slow decay, its progression toward its terminal point? Or perhaps the dialectical relation between life and its inevitable ending, death, as it is manifest in the death drive qua repetition? And if indeed self-portraiture involves not only the inscription of life but also the inscription of death, how *is* death registered—as the inverse of life, as what is divested of life or opposed to it, or by means of an utterly different form of inscription, one that unlike the inscription of life, does not proceed by means of the coherent image? Furthermore, in what way does painting, upon its singular abilities, make possible the inscription of the death drive, and what is the significance of this inscription for our understanding of the act of painting as such? What is the particularity of the manifestations of repetition in the pictorial medium, and might this particularity teach us something more about the structure of repetition?

Stoichita's position on some of these questions is a complex one. The complexity of his treatment of self-portraiture may be demonstrated by means of two antithetical examples. The first is Bartolome Esteban Murillo's self-portrait from 1670, in which the painter's hand holds the painting's painted frame, seemingly trying to break through its boundaries, to be in the portrait as an ostensibly concrete presence beyond appearing in it as representation. Beneath the painted frame is an inscription stating that Murillo is the picture's painter. Stoichita uses this painting as an example of a self-portrait that aspires to push the boundaries of

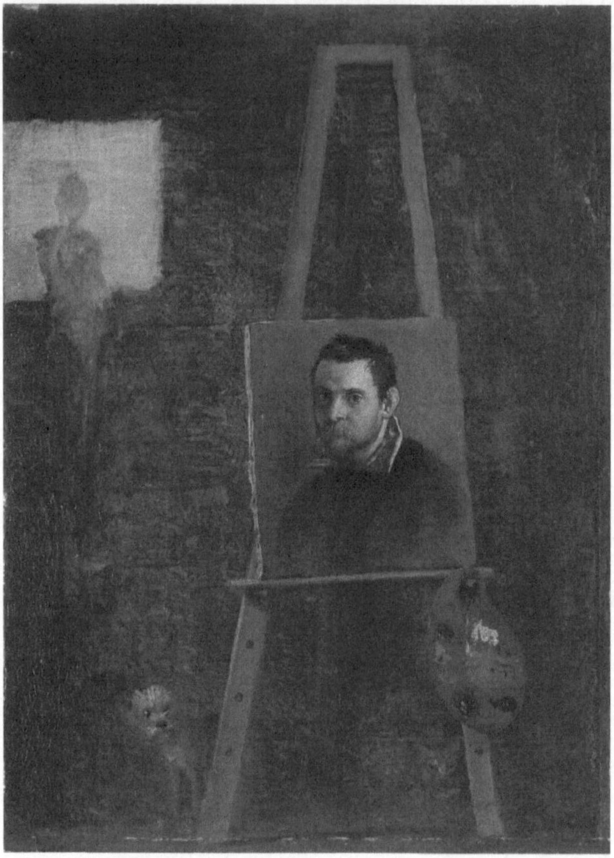

FIGURE 3.3 Annibale Carracci, *Self-Portrait at the Easel*, 1604. © The State Hermitage Museum, St. Petersburg. Image reproduced with the kind permission of the State Hermitage Museum.

representation to a point in which the act of representation would bring about the presentification of the artist himself.[25] As a contrast to this painting, Stoichita positions Annibale Carracci's self-portrait of 1604. In Carracci's painting the artist's portrait appears on an easel in the studio, his color palette hanging on its right.

While Murillo's self-portrait (much like Nicolas Poussin's self-portrait of 1605, which will be discussed below) serves Stoichita as an example of the expansion of the boundaries of representation to the point of the seeming eruption of the artist's presence toward the spectator's reality, Carracci's portrait demonstrates an opposite state of affairs, in which the portrait's painter does not appear in it, his presence reduced to the mere indexicality of the portrait and palette. Stoichita, that is, presents two inverse models for understanding self-representation. In the first, pictorial and conceptual effort is invested in making the painter maximally present, in reinforcing his living presence in the painting. In the second, what is attained is the opposite result: self-representation is shown as what to an extent drains the painter of life or at least foregrounds his absence, leaving a representation (the painted portrait, the palette) as the mere index of his absent presence. This case is a pictorial embodiment of Lacan's claim, outlined in the first chapter, that "the word kills the thing," that is, that the very act of representation necessarily involves something of death.

What is, then, the status of self-portraiture, and does the spirit indeed breathe life into it, as Hegel believed, or is self-portraiture, as Stoichita shows by means of Carracci's portrait, precisely what generates the absence of the artist painted in it, just as the art that registers its own history thereby heralds at once its end and its existence beyond this end?

Inscribing the body/inscribing death

In his mid-1980s article "Autobiography as De-Facement," Paul de Man, a literary theorist identified with post-structuralism, examines the properties of autobiography and analyzes the rhetorical devices it employs.[26] While many literary critics regard autobiography as a genre emphasizing its relation to a referent in the world, a genre that is a product of the historical reality of the writer's life, de Man claims that life itself is just as much an effect of autobiography. The documentary semblance characterizing this form of writing is a poetic device like any other. It does not have a privileged relation to the truth; in effect, it too constitutes a form of fiction.

According to de Man, "autobiographies, by their thematic insistence on the subject, on the proper name, on memory, on birth, eros, and death, and on the doubleness of specularity, openly declare their cognitive and tropological constitution."[27] At the same time, de Man states, autobiographies "are equally eager to escape from the coercions of this [cognitive and tropological] system."[28] In other words, autobiography necessarily operates in two contradictory trajectories. On the one hand, it makes extensive use of literary devices to preserve its fundamental properties, such as first-person narration and the use of personal memories. On the other hand, to reinforce the illusion of concrete self-representation, autobiography is obliged to disown the use of rhetorical devices. It wishes to persuade its reader that it is the thing itself and not the semblance of the thing, not a fictional literary construct. This argument leads de Man to claim that autobiography's extensive use of figurative language, for instance the use of allusion, personification (prosopopeia)[29] and metaphor, serves it as a cover, similar to a garment that covers the body. However, such language is no innocent cover; it is a garment that can, on occasion, be fatal to the one who wears it.[30] Figurative language, de Man believes, is not the thing in itself but a representation of the thing, its picture. "As soon as we understand the rhetorical function of prosopopeia as positing voice or face by means of language, we also understand that what we are deprived of is not life but the shape and the sense of a world accessible only in the private way of understanding. . . . Autobiography veils a defacement of the mind of which it is itself the cause."[31] De Man claims that autobiography, which supposedly represents a particular life and as such endows this life with a particular voice, is itself, because of its rhetoricity, a defacement of this life. This rhetoricity, which in fact characterizes any form of writing, and which comprises universal forms, always negates the private voice it supposedly presentifies through prosopopeia. "Death," de Man writes, "is a displaced name for a linguistic predicament"[32] that is the predicament of every writer.

De Man's claim is structurally similar to Stoichita's claim regarding Carracci's self-portrait as foregrounding the limits of representation. Unlike self-portraits such as Murillo's that stretch the limits of representation by including the painter within the self-portrait, a self-portrait like Carracci's presentifies its maker only as an absence, as what can be manifest only by means of re-presentation. In effect, the absence of the painter itself is an effect of the act of representation. Similarly, de Man shows that the presence of the author of an autobiography, to whom the text ostensibly gives voice, is taken away from him by his very use of figurative language. However, according to de Man, autobiography not only presentifies the author as absent. After having shown how autobiography makes use of rhetorical devices to attain seeming authenticity, de Man claims these rhetorical devices embalm the particular voice they are supposed to engender. Furthermore, they infuse this particular voice with a lethal poison that fossilizes and deadens it.

How might one bring de Man's observations to bear on self-portraits? In what sense does the self-portrait qua autobiography simultaneously preserve and fossilize, restore and deaden life? Alpers pointed to the characteristics Rembrandt uses in his self-portraits so as to generate his self-representations as something external to him. Despite the immense theoretical divide between Alpers and de Man, Alpers's argument concerning Rembrandt evinces the same paradoxical logic posed by de Man concerning the writer of an autobiography: in both cases an attempt is made to represent the self through the use of artistic devices which make the portrayed object distinct from the procedure of its portrayal; and in both cases the procedure of self-portrayal cancels itself out so as to attain its goal. Rembrandt paints himself as other so as to create a difference and a distance between himself and the object he represents. The ultimate role of this difference is the attainment of maximum objectification, that is, the emergence of the self-portrait as such, detached from the actual presence of its creator. Rembrandt does not paint himself in various roles to say something about the diverse aspects of his personality. Rather, to make himself present, he ostensibly divests himself of the immanent core which necessarily appears in every one of his self-portraits and paints himself as someone completely foreign to himself. Like Alpers, de Man describes autobiography as a practice that makes use of artistic devices while also disavowing them. The object is distinguished from the describing self in the interest of reliability and exactitude, but in the same interest the object must disown the characteristics of the artistic praxis that engendered it.

De Man, however, takes a step further when he links self-representation to effacement and death. Ostensibly, every representation manifesting the body's gradual decay necessarily presentifies death and the inevitable march toward it. However, de Man's argument puts the matter in a different light: the link between self-representation and death is not in correspondence with the fact of mortality. Every autobiographical procedure necessitates the negation of life as an effect of the very attempt to preserve it. The death emerging from autobiographical representation is not caused simply by the term toward which life progresses. Instead, death is immanent to the very attempt at self-representation, an attempt whose very nature involves a mortifying presence: the presence of the language of art. A similar, albeit less radical logic is implicit in Stoichita's analysis of Carracci's self-portrait, in which the represented self-portrait is shown to substitute for the artist's presence. De Man explains the mortification involved in such cases as the result of the very use of existing forms of representation. The argument we will suggest, from a psychoanalytic perspective, will explain the mortification involved in self-representational art, as exemplified in visual self-portraits, differently, and in a way that might shed new light on art in general.

The self-portrait as cedable object

Stoichita teaches that what we know today as the pictorial genre of the self-portrait, the self-portrayal of the artist's torso, is a product of the rise of modernity. The self-portraits we know were preceded by what Stoichita calls "contextual self-projection" portraits. Carracci's and Murillo's portraits discussed above are of this kind. While the topic of these paintings may be the painter who created them, the relationship between painter and painting they evince is complex. To further delineate this relationship Stoichita turns to another example, a self-portrait painted by Nicolas Poussin. This painting was made following the request of an art collector who was a friend of the painter. The collector requested a portrait of Poussin painted by someone other than himself. Poussin consented to his friend's request and ordered a portrait of himself to be made, but disappointed with the result, he decided to take the mission into his own hands. The result is a painting of Poussin without the typical attributes of a painter such as a palette or brushes. Poussin is painted standing before several paintings, only one of which can be seen. According to Stoichita, who quotes Rosalie Colie, the paradox this self-portrait invokes may be formulated thus: "This is not a self-portrait. What you see is Poussin waiting for someone to come along who is capable of recording it next to his name."[33] Poussin, that is, paints himself neither as himself nor as a stranger nor as himself in a costume, neither as his imaginary reflection nor as a hero from a fictional scene. But nor does Poussin inscribe himself in the painting as an empty place that can be occupied by various entities. He seems to try and have it both ways: to represent himself as someone who is not included within the representation. By painting his external appearance, he indicates his presence in the painting as someone else might have painted him. This is no longer the self-portrait of a Cartesian *Cogito*, a consciousness congruent with the human body that contains it. Instead, Poussin relates to his body as something external to him, as an object separated from him. This constellation can be found in more extreme forms in other self-portraits such as painted throughout history and such as continue to be made to this day, in which the artist represents himself as a cut-off body part, as an object separated from the body.[34]

In the famous fresco from the Sistine Chapel, *The Last Judgment* of 1536–1541, Michelangelo paints Saint Bartholomew, who was flayed and tortured to death.

What is striking about this fresco is that Michelangelo chooses to give the slough of the saint's face the form of his own face. In a painting from 1609–1610, Caravaggio paints himself as Goliath's severed head which David holds by the tuft of his hair. In a similar painting from 1623, Hendrick Ter Brugghen too chooses to represent himself as Goliath's severed head. Around 1610, Cristofano Allori paints himself as Holofernes's severed head moments after his beheading by Judith.

It is possible to read these cases in terms of Alpers's analysis of Rembrandt's portrait with a dead bittern, in which Rembrandt appears as both slayer and slain.

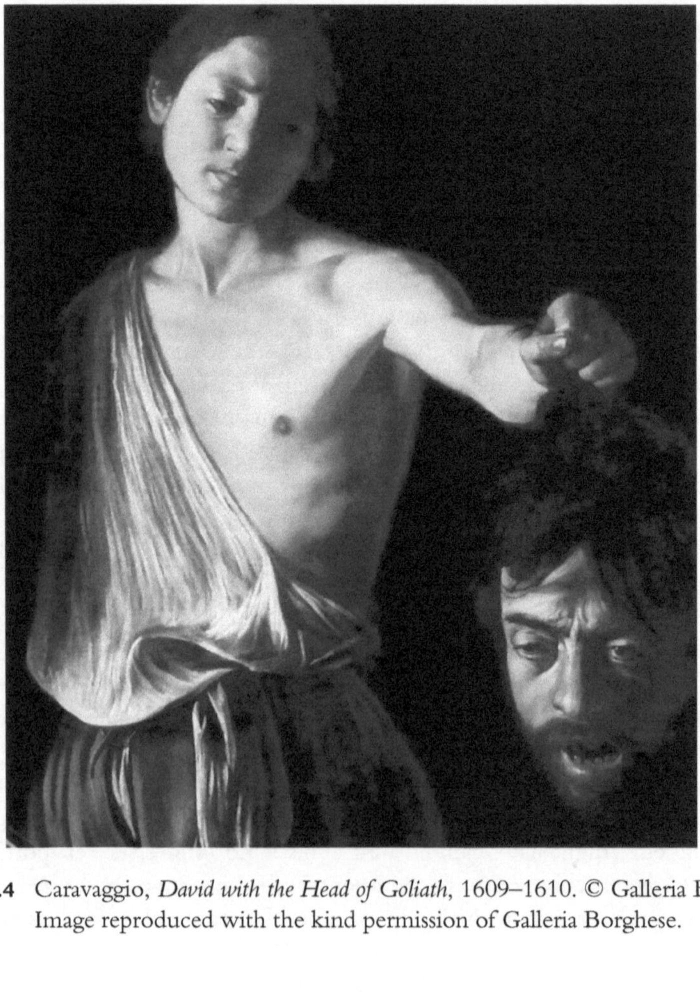

FIGURE 3.4 Caravaggio, *David with the Head of Goliath*, 1609–1610. © Galleria Borghese. Image reproduced with the kind permission of Galleria Borghese.

But these cases exceed the logic of the artist's self-portrayal as a dead body. They involve self-portrayal as a body part that has been severed and cut off, which has been not only removed from the sphere of life but ripped away from it.

The self-portraits mentioned seem to characterize a specific cultural moment which took place between the fifteenth and sixteenth centuries. Yet twentieth-century art conjures anew quite a few self-portraits as a ceded object, or self-portraits involving matter ejected from the body, some of them by leading artists. Thus, for example, in Bruce Nauman's *Self-Portrait as a Fountain* of 1966, the artist is photographed as a jet of water squirts out of his mouth. In *From Hand to Mouth* of the following year, Nauman creates a latex cast of part of his body as a slough. Other examples are Mark Quinn's self-portrait of 1991, a statue in which the artist's own head is cast from his frozen blood, and Maurizio Cattelan's 1997 *Spermini*, a self-portrait consisting of multiple casts of his head hanging on a wall.

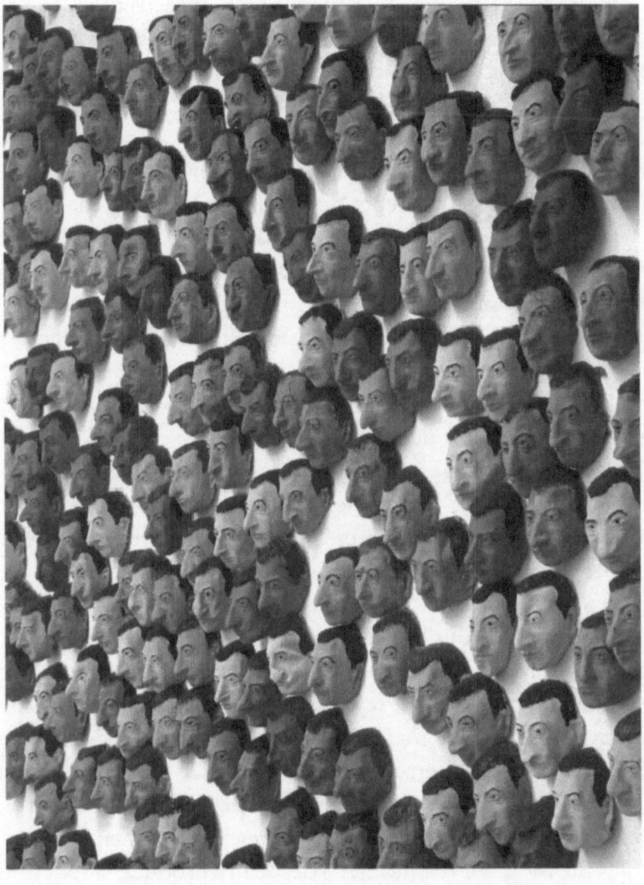

FIGURE 3.5 Maurizio Cattelan, *Spermini*, 1997. Painted latex masks, 17.5 × 9 × 10 cm each. Photo Attilio Maranzano. Image reproduced with the kind permission of Maurizio Cattelan's archive.

These contemporary manifestations of the self-portrait as ceded object may seem less narrative than their historical precedents, but they retain the fundamental logic of the portrayal of the self as leftover, as something emitted or cut off from the body.

The cases detailed above of self-portraiture as ejected body part are a manifestation of repetition in the history of art. How might we read this manifestation of repetition, in which the self-portrait appears as a cedable object, and what might we learn from it from the point of view of psychoanalysis? Hegel, it will be recalled, claims that the point of departure for artistic endeavor is the subject's need to do something with his environment. Hegel's example is the boy who throws pebbles into the river and observes the ripples their fall generates.[35] It is instructive at this point to recall another boy who throws objects for his own pleasure and watches them fall—Freud's infant grandson playing with a reel of string.[36] As we explained in the first chapter, the infant's game with the reel of string does not involve mere pleasurable imitation; it manifests something which exceeds the pleasure principle: the pleasure derived from repetition in and of itself.[37] As we may recall, Freud links this repetition to the compulsion to repeat, wherein nightmares, for instance those of shell-shocked soldiers, constantly return. But beyond the pleasure in repetition, Freud's famous example points to something more, which goes to the heart of the relation between the reel of string and the playing child.

When Lacan rereads Freud on repetition in his seminar on the four fundamental concepts of psychoanalysis, he argues that the status of the reel of string with which the child plays must be understood in a different light. According to Lacan, the reel of string is not a simple representation of the mother who left the house. For the infant, the reel constitutes a small part of himself as subject, a part which disconnects from him while continuing to function as a part of him. This activity in its entirety, Lacan states, symbolizes a repetition or return, but not the need for the mother's return, since this need could have been expressed by the simple act of crying. What returns, is repeated, is the mother's departure as the reason for a split in the subject, which the infant then treats by means of the game of throwing the reel of string. The game is directed at what is not there, at what is in itself already a representation. The game itself is, thus, a "representative of representation" (*Vorstellungsrepräsentanz*).[38]

The Freudian term Lacan utilizes designates a representative of an unconscious representation. Like Freud, Lacan assumes that repressed unconscious events cannot be accessed directly, and can be represented only by means of a representative. The representative itself does not lead to what had been repressed; it presents itself alone. What is represented, then, is not the repressed but a representative of a representation that remains unconscious and unknown.[39] The reel of string is not a simple representation of the mother, but a representative of an unconscious signifier that emerges the moment the mother's departure produces a split in the subject. Lacan states that "it is with this object that the child leaps beyond the frontiers of his domain . . . . If it is true that the signifier is the first mark of the subject, how can we fail to recognize here—that it is in the object to which the opposition is applied in act, the real, that we must designate the subject. To this object we will later give the name it bears in the Lacanian algebra—the *petit a*."[40] In other words, the mother's departure, which is represented by the reel of string, does not function as the reason for the game. Rather, the reel of string is a representative of the mother's departure, and the mother's departure itself is a representative of an unconscious event that has been repressed, such as the infant's earlier separation from the breast, or even the infant's separation from the placenta at the time of his birth.

The idea is not to attempt to ascertain the nature of the repressed event (which is impossible), but to grasp that the reel of string functions as a representative of a representation (the mother's departure), which is itself a representative of an earlier repressed event that is structurally constitutive for the subject. This repressed event is linked to separation, and therefore, according to Lacan, the reel of string should be understood as an inseparable part of the subject, as a detached piece which appears only at the moment of its loss. This is the object Lacan designates as an object a: an object which does not lend itself to articulation, which slips away between stages of representation. Lacan denominates this object the object cause of desire [*objet cause du desir*]. That is, this object is not the aim of desire, and by virtue of its very definition as an object of lack, it cannot fulfill desire. Instead, it is desire's very cause.

It should be noted that this object of lack is also the object around which the drive circulates. However, while desire is propelled by lack, the drive is propelled by its very structure as a blind drive, whose primordial origins are instinctual. While desire by its very nature can never be fulfilled, the drive is always satisfied by its very orbiting around the object, which is nothing but an inseparable part of the subject himself, a part embodied in the flesh.

Lacan, then, proposes to understand the status of the reel of string as an inherent part of the subject which is nonetheless external to him, something that has been separated from his body. To understand this strange status, we ought to return to Lacan's definitive article on the mirror stage. In this article, Lacan states that at a certain moment before the acquisition of language and complete motor control, the infant encounters his specular reflection and identifies himself in it. Discovering his reflection fills him with jubilation yet at the same time institutes a fundamental gap between his fragmented perception of himself and the coherent and symmetrical reflection he receives from the outside. It is this gap that from that moment on founds his status as a subject split between the ego and the unconscious, between imaginary completeness and a sense of fragmentation.[41]

Years later, in his tenth seminar whose topic is anxiety, Lacan returns to his article on the mirror stage. While in the article Lacan describes the specular reflection as the coherent image the child yearns for, he now claims that this semblance of completion contains something more, which can never be represented in it: the lost object, that same object a. Lacan calls the phenomenal manifestations of the object a, for instance, the objects of the drive, cedable objects—body parts which are external-internal to the subject. In contravention of the commonplace assumption that at the moment of his birth the infant is completely separated from his mother's body and hereafter exists as an independent creature, Lacan shows that the mother–infant relation is much more complex. While infant and mother are always already separated by the umbilical cord and placenta, the separation between mother and infant is not definitive, and it does not necessarily take place at the moment of birth. Lacan's argument points to a possible link between the mother's departures, such as experienced in the case of Freud's grandson, and the infant's separation from the placenta or the breast.[42] Beyond the implication that the boundaries of the human body do not correspond with the anatomy described by medicine, what this means is that the human creature has a complex relation with an object that is external–internal to him. Years later, Jacques Alain-Miller would, after Lacan, describe this relation by means of the term "extimacy," which means a radical intimacy that is nevertheless experienced as something foreign to the subject.[43]

In the tenth seminar, Lacan clarifies the subject's relation to this object, at once part of the subject and separate from him, by means of the Hebrew adjective "*arel*" (uncircumcised) in its biblical significance. Lacan quotes the following verse from the book of Jeremiah: "I will smite all them which are circumcised in their prepuce" (9:25). In fact, Lacan states, this sentence is paradoxical, for how can someone who was circumcised be punished in his missing prepuce? While biblical commentators and translators tried to resolve the paradox inherent in this verse in a variety of creative ways, Lacan makes use of the paradox itself to explain the complex relation between the subject and the cedable object. What is at stake in the word "*arel*," Lacan says, is not the removed piece of skin, but the separation from a certain body part, an appendix of sorts, which is alien to the body and essential to the subject.[44] Lacan states that "lack is radical, radical in the very constitution of subjectivity. . . . I should like to set it out in the following formula—as soon as it becomes known, as soon as something comes to knowledge, something is lost and the surest way of approaching this lost something is to conceive of it as a bodily fragment."[45] This passage can be explicated as follows. The real for Lacan is what cannot be represented, reflected in the mirror image, known or symbolized. When something of the order of the real does become known, this knowledge is manifested as a loss of a body part or fragment. The separation from a body part such as a prepuce or breast, that has become disconnected from the body, functions as a condition of possibility for unconscious representation, that is, for the constitution of subjectivity, or in other words, for the constitution of the symbolic order.

Yet what is the relation between the cedable object, whose separation from the body is a condition for the emergence of the symbolic order, and the creation of an artwork? When Lacan revisits the Freudian fable of the infant and the reel of string in his eleventh seminar, he concludes his reading with the following sentence: "what will become of the *Vorstellung* when, once again, this *Repräsentant* of the mother—in her outline made up of the brush-strokes and gouaches of desire—will be lacking"?[46] These words are surprising, as nowhere in these pages does Lacan seem to engage in any way with the making of art. This sentence does, however, point to a relation between painting or artwork in general and the category of desire.

Desire is a component of the demand the subject directs at the Other. The very articulation of the demand (for instance, the demand for food) necessarily includes a component which is not satisfied by the response to the need that generated the demand. In other words, the infant's crying as a result of his need for food engenders an articulation of his demand from the side of the primordial Other, the mother. However, the milk he receives in response to the demand satisfies the need but not the demand; it makes desire emerge as the unbridgeable gap between the demand and the fulfillment of need. As emphasized above, what propels desire is not need but the object a, the object cause of desire, which is present only as an absence. It is this object that is at the basis of the relation between infant and mother, a relation of which the work of art is a later version. Yet the object a is not a concrete object but a logical consistency. How, then, we might ask, can the artwork manifest it? Lacan's examples are two paintings by the seventeenth-century Spanish painter Francisco de Zurbaran, the first depicting Saint Lucia carrying a platter of her gauged-out eyes, the second depicting Saint Agatha holding a platter with her two torn-off breasts.[47] In these paintings what evades any specular manifestation is nevertheless manifest not only in the phenomenal guise of an object of the drive (gaze or breast) but as painted. What is the painted form, then, that this object can take in examples such as those discussed above, which are concerned with self-portrayal? And in what way can painted depictions of the object a be related to desire?

In most cases, self-portraits place the imaginary semblance, the specular image, at their forefront. What is not reflected in the mirror is not directly represented in them, though it does at times appear otherwise, for instance, as something that is present in its absence. In self portraits such as those of Michelangelo and Caravaggio, something else takes place, since the artist's image, his imaginary semblance, is congruent with a fallen body part. In a sense, these self-portraits represent what is necessarily unrepresentable. How might one theoretically account for this phenomenon of the artist's representing as specular image precisely the object whose evasion of specularity makes it possible to constitute the specular image as coherent and whole in the first place?

Language, or the chain of signifiers, Lacan says, functions in accordance with the pleasure principle. "The function of the pleasure principle is, in effect, to lead the subject from signifier to signifier, by generating as many signifiers as are required to maintain at as low a level as possible the tension that regulates the whole function of the psychic apparatus."[48] That is, language makes it possible for the subject to keep a safe distance from the real that is located beyond the possibilities of representation and articulation. When this safe distance is not in place, Lacan teaches in his tenth seminar, its absence manifests itself as a bodily loss.

If we now return to self-portraits in which artists portray themselves as ceded objects, we may better grasp the complexity at work in them: instead of the complete specular image, they present an object that has been cast off from the body. However, the moment this object is symbolized and becomes part of language's treasury of signifiers, it ostensibly represents what it can never be.

This complex image is not a veil for a horrific sight which is unbearable. Rather, the way in which the terrifying sight is represented in it points to the possibility of its being situated beyond the chain of signifiers, beyond the possibilities of representation, beyond the pleasure principle. The manner in which a terrifying representation domesticates what is seemingly beyond the possibilities of representation exemplifies what is truly beyond representation—what representation itself generates as what exceeds it, such as the moment the object is cut off from the body, a moment that is present in life not as representation but in the repetitions constituting the death drive.

Lacan's argument that Zurbaran's paintings of the two martyrs carrying cedable objects are unexpectedly serene and beautiful despite their horrific contents thus becomes clear.[49] Although one of Lacan's major claims in the *Anxiety* seminar is that "anxiety is not without an object,"[50] that is, that anxiety is an affect aroused on the occasion of the subject's confrontation with the object a as real, this does not, he says, occur in the encounter with Zurbaran's paintings. Nor are Zurbaran's paintings of the two martyrs saturated with the jouissance characterizing their other pictorial depictions. Instead, Lacan argues, Zurbaran's paintings evoke desire.[51] It is the painter's unique style, his own invention of a mode of manifesting in painting what is situated beyond the pleasure principle, that enables the paintings of the two martyrs carrying cedable objects as themselves objects ceded by the painter to function as objects cause of the viewer's desire.

In the visual field, it seems, the morbid dimension of autobiographic representation which de Man points out emerges in those places where the signifier presentifies what exceeds the possibilities of representation. It is important to note that moving beyond the possibility of representation does not mean adopting an extreme form of representation; it means being situated in the field of unrepresentability, a field in which the encounter with the object is an encounter with radical alterity. The self-portrait, in which the subject is engaged with his own representation, is a convenient site for such an encounter, since it is a topological structure that disturbs the neat distinction between inside and outside. This topological structure is endemic to the self-portrait as such, but self-portraits in which the painter appears as an object remainder are its most patent exemplification, distinct cases of this structure which also foreground it.

In other words, when the treasury of signifiers located in the Other is used by a subject for the purpose of self-representation, the subject is present in that self-representation also in a way that is not symbolic. The attempt to transpose this presence and endow it with symbolic value constitutes a move beyond the treasury of signifiers, beyond the pleasure principle. As long as the painting is situated within the bounds of the treasury of signifiers, it ostensibly keeps a safe distance from the Thing situated outside the possibilities of representation. However, precisely because painting is an expression of a particular subject which utilizes common signifying mechanisms, it contains what is not possible to represent, what exceeds the treasury of signifiers but makes signification and representation possible. This is the singularity that, while not included in the common language of art, nonetheless emerges thanks to its deployment, a singularity that psychoanalysis situates as lost satisfaction. It is thus that painting steps beyond the pleasure principle and manifests the drive in its purest form, the death drive. Unlike the pleasure principle for which there is a beyond (the death drive, the compulsion to repeat), what we call the painting principle is inclusive of its beyond. It is, in effect, nothing but the movement of painting beyond its own boundaries.

The inscription of death that emerges from the self-portrait as a paradigmatic case of a cedable object in the field of visual art, or of autobiography in the visual field, is thus related to the attempt to make use of a signifier *en plus*, a signifier of another order, to make present on canvas something which is nonsymbolic in its essence, not part of the treasury of signifiers. To move beyond the treasury of signifiers is to move beyond the pleasure principle into the realm of the death drive. As Freud showed, such movement is not necessarily anti-life, since the death drive, which emerges in everyday life in the form of the repetition compulsion, is woven into the normal course of human existence. While Freud's early thinking was that repetition originates in the duplication of pleasurable activity and hence operates in accordance with the pleasure principle, Freud later discovers that the compulsion to repeat is usually accompanied by unpleasure. This discovery eventually led Freud to suppose that the origin of the compulsion to repeat lies in the death drive, a type of primordial push to return to an archaic state of nonbeing, of pre-animation. According to de Man, the rhetorical form of personification (prosopopeia) makes death present in the autobiographical art object. What de Man shows thus corresponds to the Freudian principle according to which every representation comes at a price of loss. Yet a Freudian reading of self-representation makes it possible to show something else: the very attempt to personify necessarily involves a repetition compulsion originating in an impulse to flee a state of vitality toward a primordial state of inert matter. What this means, however, is not, as de Man supposes, a mortification that is the inverse of vitalization; it means that the tenacious attempt to return to a pre-animate state is one of the characteristics of life itself.

The death drive does not posit an opposition between life and death; it is precisely what makes painting as inscription of life possible. Furthermore, painting itself has the complex status of a cedable object, an object situated in the liminal zone between life and death, for which the clear-cut distinction between life and death does not hold. In this context, the self-portrait as cedable object is a cedable object that flaunts its cedability. The status of the remainder which this variety of self-portraiture flaunts, but which typifies art in general, belies simple oppositions between life and death. Self-portraits as cedable objects, and works of art which such self-portraits structurally epitomize, continue to live after the physical death of the artist—and not as vestiges of immortality but as manifestations of the death drive.

Notes

1 Sigmund Freud, "Negation," in *The Standard Edition of the Complete Psychological Works of Sigmund Freud, Vol. XIX*, trans. and ed. James Strachey (London: Hogarth Press, 1961 [1925]), p. 238.
2 Ibid.
3 According to Freud, the object is one of the four components of the drive, in addition to pressure, aim and source. The object of the drive is in effect a material manifestation of the lost object, and it appears as what is cut off from the source of the drive, which is an erogenous zone in the body. The oral object is the object whose source is the mouth as erogenous zone; the scopic object is an object whose source is the eye and vision upon all its libidinal aspects. Lacan gives the name of "*objet petit a*" to that leftover of satisfaction which is not represented, or to use his terms, does not constitute part of the chain of signifiers. This term is in effect equivalent to Freud's lost object.
4 Tali Tamir, "Beyond the Threshold of Beauty: Tali Tamir in Conversation with Shosh Kormosh, 2001," in *Shosh Kormosh: Terms of Stillness, Works 1987–2001* (Tel-Hai Open Museum, 2008 [2001]), p. 246. English translation in the original.
5 Ibid., p. 264.
6 Ibid., p. 247.
7 Victor I. Stoichita, *The Self-Aware Image: An Insight into Early Modern Meta-Painting*, trans. Ann-Marie Glasheen (Cambridge: Cambridge University Press, 1997).
8 Giorgio Vasari, *The Lives of the Most Excellent Painters, Sculptures, and Architects*, trans. Gaston du C. de Vere (New York: Random House, 1996 [1550]).
9 Stoichita, *The Self-Aware Image*, p. 95.
10 Ibid., p. 89.
11 See Efrat Biberman, "Beyond the Painting Principle," *Machbar-Ot: Journal of the Lacanian Network* 3 (2008): 69–73. In Hebrew.
12 Hegel, G. W. F. 1988 [1835]. *Aesthetics: Lectures on Fine Art*, trans. T. M. Knox. Oxford: Clarendon Press, 30–31.
13 Ibid., p. 31.
14 Ibid., p. 31.
15 Ibid., p. 31.
16 Ibid., p. 31.
17 Ibid., p. 32.
18 Ibid., p. 29.
19 Ibid., p. 29.
20 Ibid., p. 713.
21 Fried Michael, *Courbet's Realism* (Chicago: University of Chicago Press, 1992).
22 Svetlana Alpers, *Rembrandt's Enterprise: The Studio and the Market* (Chicago: University of Chicago Press, 1998). On Alpers and Fried's discussion of self-portraits, see Efrat Biberman, *Visual Text(a)iles: Narrative and Gaze in Painting* (Ramat Gan: Bar Ilan University Press, 2009). In Hebrew.
23 Alpers, *Rembrandt's Enterprise*, p. 28.
24 Ibid., p. 81.
25 Stoichita, *The Self-Aware Image*, p. 215.
26 Paul de Man, "Autobiography as De-Facement," in *The Rhetoric of Romanticism* (New York: Columbia University Press, 1984).
27 Tropology is a theory of the use of the poetic forms that involve a semantic change in the literary text. Rhetoric distinguishes between tropology, in which one word is used to explain or modify another, and other figurative forms ("figures" or "schemes" such as analogy, repetition, or onomatopoeia) that do effect semantic alteration but function as linguistic ornaments.
28 de Man, "Autobiography as De-Facement," p. 71.

29 Classical rhetoric distinguishes between prosopopoeia and prosopography. Prosopography relates to a description of a living man who is not present, while prosopopoeia is the attribution of human qualities to what is not alive, the attempt to breathe life into what is dead.
30 de Man, "Autobiography as De-Facement," p. 80.
31 Ibid., p. 81.
32 Ibid., p. 81.
33 Stoichita, *The Self-Aware Image*, p. 211.
34 For a complete overview of artworks featuring the fragmented body or a body part separated from its context, see Linda Nochlin, *The Body in Pieces: The Fragment as a Metaphor of Modernity* (New York: Thames and Hudson, 1994).
35 Hegel, *Aesthetics*, p. 31.
36 Sigmund Freud, "Beyond the Pleasure Principle," in *The Standard Edition of the Complete Psychological Works of Sigmund Freud, Vol. XVIII*, trans. and ed. James Strachey (London: Hogarth Press, 1955 [1920]), pp. 7–63.
37 Ibid., p. 16.
38 Jacques Lacan, *The Seminar of Jacques Lacan, Book XI: The Four Fundamental Concepts of Psychoanalysis*, trans. Alan Sheridan (New York: W. W. Norton, 1998), pp. 62–63.
39 Ibid., p. 217.
40 Ibid., p. 62.
41 Jacques Lacan, "The Mirror Stage as Formative of the Function of the I as Revealed in Psychoanalytic Experience," in *Écrits: A Selection*, trans. A. Sheridan (New York: W. W. Norton, 1977 [1949]), pp. 1–7.
42 Jacques Lacan, *The Seminar of Jacques Lacan, Book X: Anxiety*, trans. A. R. Price (Cambridge: Polity Press, 2014 [1962–1963]), p. 233.
43 Jacques-Alain Miller, "Extimité," in *Lacanian Theory of Discourse: Subject, Structure and Society*, ed. Mark Bracher et al. (New York: New York University Press, 1997), pp. 74–87.
44 Lacan, *Seminar X*, p. 213.
45 Ibid., p. 134.
46 Ibid., p. 63.
47 Ibid., pp. 162–63.
48 Jacques Lacan, *The Seminar of Jacques Lacan, Book VII: The Ethics of Psychoanalysis*, trans. Dennis Porter (New York: W. W. Norton, 1986 [1959–1960]), p. 119.
49 Lacan, *Seminar X*, p. 163.
50 Ibid., p. 89.
51 Ibid., p. 163.

4

WRITING THEIR DEATHS

James Joyce and Virginia Woolf

> A thing there was that mattered; a thing, wreathed
> about with chatter, defaced, obscured in her own life,
> let drop every day in corruption, lies, chatter. This
> he had preserved. Death was defiance. Death was
> an attempt to communicate; people feeling the impossibility
> of reaching the center which, mystically, evaded them;
> closeness drew apart; rapture faded, one was alone.
> There was an embrace in death.
>
> —*Virginia Woolf, 1989 [1925], p. 163*

A genre of self-portraiture as art object in which repetition which is of the order of the drive persists beyond the subject's demise is known in the literary domain, the art of the spoken word. This genre of literary self-portraiture, or as it is commonly known, auto-bio-graphy, that is, the author's inscription of her own life, is at the same time a paradigmatic case of the inscription of death. Autobiography thus exemplifies what psychoanalysis teaches about the drive: a force "whose name is life, but whose work is death."[1] The drive, which makes the motion of life possible, Lacan teaches after Freud's "Beyond the Pleasure Principle," is in its foundation nothing other than the death drive. The features specific to literary art, of which the genre of autobiography partakes, make it possible to turn to it so as to learn something more about the way in which the death drive operates in the artistic object. The specificity at stake has to do with the materiality of the literary object, its being a combinatory of letters.

In "Lituraterre," Lacan makes use of James Joyce's well-known homophony of "letter" and "litter" to comment upon the nature of the literary.[2] Literature, Lacan says, invoking the Joycean homophony, is an "accumulation" of letters that are remainders, litter, of "what was once spoken chant or dramatic procession."[3] The examination of the literary work as a collection of letters that are litter, remainders of the spoken word, leads Lacan to situate this work in the register of the real, beyond sense and representation. As object situated in the register of the real, the literary work as Lacan speaks of it in "Lituraterre" is isomorphic with the position of the analyst in the cure. The real, Lacan teaches, is the mainspring of the analytic act. The subject turns to analysis because of suffering that afflicts him. The cause of this suffering is a surplus of enjoyment that leaves no space for the desire of the subject, a desire precipitated by the object that is its cause. In an analysis, the analyst positions himself as semblance of this object cause. This is the Freudian lost object, which Lacan articulates as the *objet petit a*: the object that is at the foundation of the chain of representations or signifiers constituting the subject's unconscious but is itself extrinsic to the representations it makes possible. In the course of an analysis, Lacan explains in his eleventh seminar, the unconscious chain of signifiers propelled by the object cause emerges, but never in a linear sequence; the unconscious emerges in pulsations that are the remainders of conscious speech emanating from the ego.[4] The analyst's interventions starting from his position of a semblance of the object cause as real—the scansions of the subject's speech, the cuts of analytic sessions—are oriented, beyond the unconscious representations they make emerge, toward the isolation and extraction of the real object cause in the subject's life, an object that can be circumscribed as a logical consistency but never articulated.[5] The trajectory of an analysis too may thus be said to be an accumulation of remainders, be they fragments of the unconscious that are the litter of conscious speech or manifestations of the object cause that are remainders of these fragments.

For Lacan, the isomorphism between literature and psychoanalytic practice as accumulations of remainders is what justifies the intrusion of psychoanalysis into the literary domain, otherwise intrinsically heterogeneous to it, as a field from which it may learn something more about the enigmas which are its concern.[6] Visual art too teaches psychoanalysis something about these enigmas. As the previous chapter has shown, the genre of self-portraiture in painting, especially in those cases in which the constitutive cedability of the object is exposed, underscores the status of the artwork as detached object and the pervasive presence of the death drive in this genre in the phenomenon of repetition. As we have argued, as fragment detached from the body, the visual artwork acquires the status of an object remainder. Remainders of signification are part of the constitution of the literary artwork too, but differently. In the case of literature, the remainder appears not only as the object itself but also as a constituent of this object, the letter.

What, then, might psychoanalysis learn from literature, in particular autobiographical literature, about the relation between art and death, and between art and the death drive? If literature in general is, as Lacan teaches in "Lituraterre," an accumulation of remainders, discarded surpluses, what is the status of auto-biographical literature, wherein the accumulation of letters into readable graphism ostensibly aims to capture something of the author's *bios*?

In *L'acte photographique*, a meditation on the photographic medium which does not deny its psychoanalytical horizon, Philippe Dubois intriguingly theorizes photography as an art form that is inherently "thanatographic" because of the technique on which it is predicated, which because of its freezing of an image involves what Dubois calls a "medusation": the wrenching of an image from the flow of life and its petrification in a deathly temporality of total immobility.[7] The conception of autobiography implied by Lacan's position in "Lituraterre" may be said to be similarly thanatographic, implicated with death, and for reasons that have to do with properties inherent to the artistic medium (in the case of literature as conceived by Lacan, its status as an amalgam of letters as remainders). Autobiographical literature would thus seem to be, in Lacan's terms, the production of lit(t)eral body parts, that is, of the author's fabrication in writing of his body as cedable object, as corpse, an operation that in Dubois's terms could be labeled auto-thanato-graphic.

Jacques Derrida's *The Ear of the Other: Otobiography, Transference, Translation,* whose subtitle gestures toward one of the crucial components of psychoanalysis, also points to an inherent connection between autobiography and death which resonates with those implied by Dubois's *L'acte photographique* and Lacan's "Lituraterre." In both cases the connection has to do with a subtraction from linear temporality. Dubois speaks of photography's making a "cut in the continuity of the real,"[8] while Derrida points to autobiography's temporality as one which dislocates the tie of life and is verified only in or after the moment of "death's arrest."[9] As opposed to this morbid aspect of autobiography that Derrida, like Dubois, calls "thanatographic,"[10] Derrida proposes, via an analysis of Friedrich Nietzsche's autobiography *Ecce Homo*, another aspect of autobiography involving the "living language" of the feminine.[11] This living aspect of autobiography opened up within the mortifying "line of credit"[12] of paternal legacy, Derrida argues, has its roots and its ends in orifices structurally subtending man's relation to the Other. Grounded in one's omphalos, the primal corporeal connection to the maternal as the orifice that "gives rise to all the figure by losing [itself] in the background,"[13] autobiographical writing is, by virtue of this structuring figurality, what constitutively resonates in the "invaginated folds and involuted orificiality"[14] of the ear it reaches through stenography, although this ear "does not answer."[15] Between the omphalos as the life-giving orificial bond with the primordial Other which gives autobiography its background and shape and the anonymous ear of the Other to which autobiography is addressed, autobiography as Derrida theorizes it involves a "revitalization"[16] that always works against the deadening lines of paternal debt in which it expressly situates itself. Gesturing toward psychoanalytic categories, more the categories of sexual difference and of the orifices that are, in Freudian terms, the sources of the drive than the transference he mentions in the book's subtitle, Derrida insists on the possibility of an autobiographical writing that is revitalizing despite its constitutive verification by death and structuring by lines of symbolic debt.

In what follows, we too will attempt to show that an autobiographic literature that is revitalizing indeed exists but for reasons very different from those Derrida argues for in *The Ear of the Other.* Such autobiographical literature, we will claim, is neither the presentification of the author's body parts as remainders, the production not of the author's corpse in written form suggested by Lacan's "Lituraterre," nor the narrativization of events in her life often assumed in literary criticism, nor the effect of the structuring orificiality at the backdrop of every written life assumed by Derrida. If the drive is indeed constitutively intricated in auto-bio-graphical literature, as Derrida argues, it is less in its manifestation as source or orifice and more in its manifestation as object, which in the artistic domain, as we have shown in the previous two chapters, appears as style. Style, Lacan writes in an essay on André Gide, "is the object,"[17] that is to say, the subject's chosen form of enjoyment, of libidinal satisfaction, whether or not this involves the creation of art. What constitutes a style as a mode of enjoyment is what Lacan calls the "letter"—letter in the sense not of an alphabetical character but of a primal, unconscious imprint of trauma on the flesh. If we return to the case of the literary text, we might note its style neither generates its sense nor contributes to it; indeed, style undermines and punctures sense. Always working in dialectical tension with what Lacan calls the poetic text's "effect of sense," style is what causes a "hole effect" (*effet de trou*) that makes sense leak.[18] As such, style is a manifestation of the letter (imprint of jouissance) as situated in the domain of the object, outside representation, beyond the signifier. We will establish our claim regarding the hole effects distinctive of literary autobiography by scrutinizing two markedly different examples of what we consider auto-bio-graphical writing in modernist literature. One is the auto-bio-graphical writing of James Joyce, an author to whom Lacan dedicated an entire seminar; the other is the writing of Joyce's contemporary Virginia Woolf, often associated with Joyce's mainly because of her use of what is commonly known as the stream of consciousness technique. The examples of Joyce and Woolf enable us to demonstrate the operation of the letter as remainder in the domain of literary autobiography. The "letter" at stake in them is at once the material or empirical letter of which the literary text is made—the alphabetical character (and the products of its disintegration)—and the letter in the psychoanalytical sense as another name for the register of style, that dimension of the literary work constitutively exceeding signifier and sense and indexing the enjoyment of its author. In the two cases we examine, the style constituting the works as auto-thanato-graphical—writings of a life marked by an invigorating repetition beyond the death that structures them—generates aesthetic effects: irony and of splendor, both intricated with the death drive.

Both Joyce and Woolf wrote works partially or entirely based on events in their lives. Joyce's *Portrait of the Artist as a Young Man* and *Stephen Hero*, the earlier version of this novel published only posthumously, unfold narratives based on Joyce's difficult childhood and adolescence in Catholic schools and his choice to abandon religious life for an artistic vocation. Stephen Dedalus, the character portraying the younger Joyce, appears also in *Ulysses*, in episodes whose narrative backbone is based on Joyce's Dublin experiences.

Virginia Woolf left copious inscriptions of her life events, especially in the many volumes of the diary in which she wrote almost daily and in a few volumes of letters, and also in short works of prose such as "A Sketch of the Past" and

"Reminiscences."[19] These inscriptions also attest to the ways in which Woolf wove her life events into her fiction, for instance, the manner in which she constructed the characters of Mr. and Mrs. Ramsay in *To the Lighthouse* on the basis of childhood memories of her parents, or her characterization of Jacob in *Jacob's Room* on the basis of her memories of her brother Toby, who died at a young age.

Both Virginia Woolf and James Joyce are also famous for their radical innovations in literary style and narrative structure. For instance, in Joyce's last, monumental work, *Finnegans Wake*, the end folds into the beginning, generating a cyclical structure which almost completely annuls the vestiges of linear narrative. The last syntagm in the novel is an interrupted sentence whose continuation appears as the novel's famous beginning.[20] The conjoining of ending and beginning generates a narrative structure of a "recirculation" that never ends, always begins, which Lacan denominates a "false hole,"[21] and a sentence syntactically and grammatically correct yet largely senseless. Many of the other sentences populating the novel's several hundred pages too are syntactically correct but largely devoid of sense, compressed onto (and into) the rim of the false hole formed by the opening and closing syntagms and constantly subjecting its textual environs to what Lacan calls an "*effet de trou*" causing whatever little sense they generate to run or leak. On the level of the single word too, Joyce creates textual mechanisms that make the sense they generate leak to an extent more radical than had ever appeared in English letters, subjecting the customary patterns (in this case, of letters and sounds) of English to neologistic combinations that do not mean, and enabling Lacan to claim that in the wake of Joyce's writing, "the English language no longer exists."[22]

Woolf too invented new literary structures undermining the linear narrative of the classical novel. *The Waves* is a collage of pieces of the stream of consciousness of six characters disclosing their intertwining life stories from childhood to adulthood. These pieces are mounted onto the axis of the narrator's descriptions of the changing relations between waves and light in the course of a day, the lyrical interludes that can be said to constitute the novel's backbone. These descriptions follow the movement of the sun from its rise in the east[23] to its setting in the west[24] and the visual effects of this movement on the waves of the sea. The novel's last sentence, "The waves broke on the shore,"[25] points to the movement traced in the interludes as exceeding the lives of the characters depicted in the novel and persisting beyond its textual limit; points to this movement, that is, as an instance of repetition.

From a psychoanalytical perspective, the novel's structural backbone as manifest in the lyrical interludes tracing the motion of the sun in relation to the waves stages the motion of the drive from one point in the organism to another and back again. This motion, Freud writes in his essay on drives and their vicissitudes is one of constant work (*Konstantkraft*) which comes in waves.[26] Like Woolf in her construction of the backbone of *The Waves*, Freud in his conceptualization of the drives turns to the motion of waves to exemplify the structure of a cyclical movement persisting beyond individual life.

Like the compression of neologisms onto and into the loop of end folded into beginning in *Finnegans Wake*, *The Waves*' collage of fragments mounted onto the outline of a cyclical motion generates a false hole. In *The Waves*, what veils and indicates this hole is the novel's seventh character, Percival, who, while not represented directly, plays a central role in the lives of the other characters from whom we learn about his death in the prime of his life.

The complex structure of *The Waves* and of other works by Woolf can be explicated by means of topology as appropriated by Lacan for psychoanalysis. Topology is the study of shapes that do not follow the logic of Euclidian geometry upon its clear-cut distinction between inside and outside, such as the Moebius strip, a loop whose surface is continuous with its reverse; the Klein bottle, whose rim folds toward its outside; or the torus, a tire whose central hole functions as the external limit of its internality. The surfaces of all three shapes are not distinct from their interiority. In his later teaching, Lacan makes use of these shapes to underscore the way in which psychoanalysis destabilizes clear-cut dichotomies of inside and outside. Topologically speaking, Woolf's *The Waves*, like Joyce's *Finnegans Wake*, is toric in shape. But Woolf's torus differs from Joyce's in its phenomenality. While the surface of *Finnegans Wake* is a neologistic combinatory of letters in familiar patterns of English words and syntax, the surface of *The Waves* is a combinatory of fragments of the six characters' stream of consciousness. *The Waves*, that is, is a torus patched from fragments.

Woolf's experiments with topology were not limited to *The Waves* and reach their most dazzling form in her last novel, *Between the Acts*, during whose proofreading she took her own life by drowning. The narrator of *Between the Acts* repeatedly points to reverse evolution—the sliding of civilization into a primitive state.[27] Reverse evolution so dominant in the narratorial frame generates a temporality in which the diegetic present coincides with the most archaic past. The strange loop involved in this unique temporality is not only articulated thematically but mainly staged in the novel's linguistic and narrative structure. Woolf makes sophisticated use in this novel of the structure of quotation, which conventionally dictates the hierarchy of a fictional world in which a narrator quotes her characters. In *Between the Acts*, however, this hierarchy is tangled. Toward the end of the novel, Miss La Trobe, one of the characters, is busy planning her next play. According to the classical structure of quotation, Miss La Trobe's position in this play would be that of the playwright or narrator quoting the *dramatis personae*. The novel indeed ends with the diegesis of a theatrical drama: a description of a curtain rising over a stage. The play performed on this stage involves two characters, husband and wife, Isa and Giles, the two main characters in the plot of Woolf's novel. The novel's last sentence, "They spoke," is a frame of a quotation whose source is at once the narrator, and beyond her, Woolf as author, and the playwright, who is Woolf's literary creation.[28] And if the speakers are indeed Isa and Giles, could not what "they spoke," the content or inset of the quotation which appears as the last sentence of the novel, also be their speech (quoted by the narrator) on the novel's first page? In this case as in *Finnegans Wake*, published three years earlier, ending and beginning fold into one another; in *Between the Acts*, so do inset and frame of quotation, narrator and character.

Between the Acts generates a topological shape in which outside and inside, earlier and later, become paradoxically continuous.

The topological shape at stake in *Between the Acts* differs from that generated by *The Waves*. It is the cross cap, a sphere on whose envelope two polarized points converge, folding inside and outside into one another. In the case of *Between the Acts*, the topological fold is not only spatial (of inside and outside), but also temporal (of beginning and end, earlier and later). Furthermore, because of the recurrent references to inverted temporality, in this case the cross cap is in constant motion, rendering the text a vortex(t),[29] textual manifestation of the aquatic abyss into which Woolf threw herself as object remainder in the passage to the act which terminated her life. The remainders thrown into the vortex(t) that is *Between the Acts* are the litter not only of words but of letters, writing's lit(t)eral, senseless matter. These real, lit(t)eral fundaments of writing are exposed as the text folds back into itself, tearing the veils of sense—the plot and the relations between the characters which constitute its phantasmatic dimension—as it does so.

In *Between the Acts*, the lit(t)eral products of the text's vorticial motion are representatives of representation in a sense close to that developed by Freud in his discussion of repression.[30] Freud claims that repressed representations become manifest by means of the representatives that constitute their return—in symptoms or other formations of the unconscious.[31] But unlike in dreams or slips of the tongue where the representatives of representations are themselves representations (or in Lacan's terms, signifiers), in *Between the Acts* the representatives of the text's representations are not signifiers nor even letters but products of the letter's disintegration. These representatives of representation, remainders ejected by the motion of the textual vortex, are torn from the material fabric of the text and thrown into the hole at its center.

On the text's phantasmatic level, the level of its plot, the fragmentary remainders generated by its folding backward are often manifest in the many gaps in the characters' attempts to communicate, whose thematic context is the Second World War, the plot's historical backdrop.[32] On the register of style, these gaps are usually marked by the rhetorical form of ellipsis. On the graphic register, the material substrate of Woolf's written text, ellipsis usually appears as three points (. . .).[33] Semiotically speaking, these points are not even a letter, a graphic mark that while senseless in itself may be placed in a combinatory of letters geared to generate an effect of sense. Isolated or in combination, points are graphic marks that do not mean. In Woolf's novel, the points constituting the ellipses also occur precisely at those narrative junctures where the effect of sense generated by combinations of letters into words collapses. The many points punctuating the text of *Between the Acts* might thus be considered the literal products of the letter's disintegration. It is these lit(t)eral products of the disintegration of the letter that are cast into the vorticial structure generated by the text's folding backward. The topological structure of *Between the Acts*, then, is that of a senseless vortex, not text but vor-tex(t) into which the lit(t)eral foundations of words are cast. The graphic components of words, manifest in the text as points, constitute the real substrate of writing, which the sequence of the plot upon its narrative strategies veils in an attempt to generate an effect of sense these points continually puncture.

The topological structure of a vortex of points puncturing sense is indicated in the working title of the novel, whose early drafts bore the name of the country estate in which the plot takes place: Pointz Hall, homophonic with "points" and "all." The text as material object and narratological structure is the (H)all in which points swirl as litter of the letter, what falls from the word when it no longer functions as signifier in a chain and turns into a remainder whose status is real. As litter of letters, the points in the vortex are the products of the disintegration of constituents of the signifier. As such, they cannot even be situated as analogous to Woolf's falling body throwing itself into death. They are the analogues not of this body but of the products of the disintegration of this body caught in the vortex into which it threw itself in a last movement of a writing that engraves the trajectory of the death drive up to its terminal point.

Both in the case of Woolf and in the case of Joyce, then, one may distinguish between two kinds of writing related to autobiography. The first is a kind of writing whose dimension of sense is interlaced with autobiographic components, the narrativization or even fictionalization of conscious memories. Joyce's *Portrait of the Artist as a Young Man* and Woolf's "A Sketch of the Past" and narrative portrayal of Mr. and Mrs. Ramsay in *To the Lighthouse* belong to this category. The second is writing of another order: topological writing puncturing and decomposing the text's effects of sense. This writing too is autobiographical, but it is not in the registers of representation, the imaginary and symbolic registers, that it operates as such. This writing is autobiographical in the way in which something of the life of the author, and of his death, are vehicled in it as real. In the case of Joyce's *Finnegans Wake*, the textual component bearing something of the subjective real of life and death is the alphabetical letter as residue of the disintegration of the English language for the subject who writes. Woolf's *Between the Acts* is a more extreme case where the disintegration of language extends, for the subject, even beyond the letter.

Both in the case of Joyce and in the case of Woolf, the more conventionally autobiographical writing is the kind which has less to do with the inscription of the author's life as constitutively interlaced with something of the death drive. Nevertheless, following Lacan's "Lituraterre," it is possible to think even of such autobiographical writing as the author's production of his remainder, his corpse, in written form and hence as a kind of writing that does generate something of the order of death—of which the author cannot conceive even as unconscious. What this means in psychoanalytic terms is that conventional autobiographic writing as the inscription of conscious memories in effect veils not only repressed memory traces that are unconscious but also the author's death that it manifests as real object but that is not registered in the unconscious even as primal writing, what Freud calls *Niederschrift*.[34]

Freud distinguishes between three levels of memory in the psychic apparatus. Primal writing, *Niederschrift*, is the registration of an excitation that is not raised to the level of representation, that is, to the level of a repressed memory trace.

The second level of memory involves unconscious representations or memory traces. The third is the level of conscious memories, which, according to Freud, are the fragments of memory that remain in the subject's consciousness; screen memories veiling repressed unconscious events.[35] These conscious representations are actually not memories at all, since, as Freud states, "consciousness and memory are mutually exclusive."[36]

As representations of consciously remembered past events, conventional autobiographical writings such as exemplified by Woolf's "Moments of Being" or Joyce's *Portrait of the Artist as a Young Man* belong to the third level of memory described by Freud. In an early letter to Fliess, Freud calls this level the "official ego."[37] This ego as Lacan speaks of it is an imaginary and deceptive construct which is heterogeneous to the drive.[38] This construct does not register unconscious memories but empties them of cathexis and veils death, for which there is no unconscious representation. In other words, autobiography in the simple sense of the recording of the author's memories of his past is an imaginary description of his life events and as such is a deceptive screen to the real inscription of his life and his death.

The classically autobiographical writings of Joyce, Woolf and other authors, then, do not offer psychoanalysis a productive site for tracing the inscription of life as constitutively intricated with the death drive. This is why when scrutinizing the writing of Joyce, Lacan is suspicious of *Portrait of the Artist as a Young Man* as an autobiography. There is another reason for Lacan's suspicion. Lacan isolates two styles, or as he puts it, "slopes" (*versants*) in Joyce's writing: one characterized by the device Joyce calls epiphany, the other characterized by its neologistic style and its emptying out of sense.[39] Both these forms of writing—the epiphanic writing of *A Portrait of the Artist* and *Dubliners* and the writing outside sense of *Finnegans Wake*, pure combinatory of letters preserving the semblance of English grammar and word patterns—are exemplary of what Lacan calls a "sinthome": the subject's singular solution to the no less singular manner in which he is afflicted by language.[40]

The sinthome as an invention which makes it possible for the subject to bear life is constructed at the very points where the registers of the symbolic, and sometimes also of the imaginary, do not work for him, their failure afflicting him alongside the real he cannot bear. But Lacan treats the sinthome not only as a singular solution but also as a register of psychic life additional to the symbolic, imaginary and real. This fourth register is the effect of what might be described as a replication of the symbolic and the imaginary. This replication is not a specular doubling of the registers of representation in which something does not work for the subject and tortures him. Instead, the register of the sinthome as Lacan speaks of it may be described as a shadow projected by the symbolic and the imaginary and constituted by what in them fails for a given subject. It is from this register that the subject can draw the raw material for constructing a singular invention that would make it possible for him to go on living. It is to this singular invention, and not to the name that features on the cover or title page of a book, that Lacan grants the status of a proper name.

In the first lesson of Lacan's twenty-third seminar, only one of the two *versants* of Joyce's sinthomatic style, the neologistic style of *Finnegans Wake*, acquires the full status of a proper name.[41] Both the epiphanic style of Joyce's autobiographical writing in *Portrait of the Artist* and the neologistic style of *Finnegans Wake* are made of material from the same sinthomatic register of what does not work in language for Joyce. Both metabolize these materials into sinthomatic inventions treating points of error in the knotting of psychic registers that emerge in life as points of suffering. However, Lacan treats the epiphanic style as a weaker sinthome, which he calls, after a phrase in the novel referring to Irish self-government, "Sinthome rule."[42] The weaker sinthome involves something of the lie. One reason for this is that this sinthome is related to the fictionality of consciously remembered life events, the components of the ego, seat of identifications and misrecognitions. In the case of Joyce, the ego's function of endowing the subject with the foundation of his specular image is quite fragile. This is clearly evident from an episode in *Portrait of the Artist* in which Stephen, the character based on Joyce, is brutally beaten by his friends and describes a subsequent experience of self-disgust in which he senses "that some power was divesting him of that sudden-woven anger as easily as a fruit is divested of its soft ripe peel."[43] What Stephen is divested of, Lacan claims, is the "peel," very thin indeed in his case, of his specular image. The sense of disgust and nausea he describes is a product of his unmitigated encounter with the organism, the living tissue in itself. What accounts for the fragility of the ego in Joyce's case is a failure in the function Lacan calls the "Name of the Father." This function regulates the symbolic register, making it possible for the subject to generate definite sense in language and a coherent body image which might provide him with a semblance of self-identity. Both these functions are upheld by the quilting (*capitonnage*) of registers made possible by the Name of the Father. The failure in the paternal function affects Joyce's fragile body image, as is made evident in several episodes in *Portrait of the Artist* in which this image is shown to falter, giving way to an unbearable confrontation with living flesh unmediated by the calming lie of the mirror image.

Joyce's weakened sinthome is related to the lie for rhetorical reasons as well. Rhetorically speaking, the epiphanies constituting the weaker sinthome bind semantically distant signifiers by means of the similaic copula ("like," "as"), the same copula operating in the title of Joyce's autobiographic book, *Portrait of the Artist* as *a Young Man* (our emphasis). This copula, Lacan states, is a sign of a lie.[44] In Joyce's writing, the epiphanies can be understood as a somewhat failed attempt to tailor a prosthetic ego from shredded images of body parts similaically collated with fragments of images of natural objects. Joyce's aesthetics, which draw upon concepts from the philosophy of Thomas Aquinas, stress that the function of epiphanies is to produce an effect of beauty as splendor.[45] However, Lacan questions Joyce's ability to "find his bearing very well concerning . . . something he calls the Beautiful."[46] Indeed, the epiphanies' effect of beauty, if there is one, as well as the effect of awe that their new sense generates and that literary criticism amply comments upon, cannot hide what Joyce attempts to suture through the similaic copula structuring them: the inherent absence of relation between their components.

Where does Lacan believe that Joyce chooses to write his life in a manner that is not infected by something of the lie and is as real as writing could possibly be? In *Finnegans Wake*, where Joyce uses the material of the register of his sinthome, wherein the English language is decomposed down to the most fundamental components of the letter, without adding to the sinthome any phantasmatic veil of sense, as he does, for instance, in *Portrait of the Artist*. It should be noted that as for Lacan, the unconscious itself is a fiction veiling what cannot be said; the subject of the unconscious is constitutively sentenced to lie as he speaks the truth. How, then, does Joyce escape this lie? The Joyce of *Finnegans Wake*, Lacan shows, knots the idiosyncratic material of the register of his sinthome with components of the symbolic register of the English language of his time. Alongside meaningless neologisms such as "lissome," "larpnotes," "branewaill," combinations of letters in word patterns that sound like English words yet have no etymological or lexical context, the book is full of purely standard words from the English language and dozens of other languages, part of the symbolic of his epoch. The lacing or knotting of material from the symbolic with the material from the register of the sinthome peculiar to Joyce, Lacan says, is what constitutes Joyce's art in the novel. The result of this art is the production of a prosthesis not of the specular body, as in *Portrait of the Artist*, but of the split subject of the unconscious, the same unconscious, to which, Lacan states, the Joyce of *Finnegans Wake* "cancels his subscription."[47] In place of the split between ego and unconscious which characterizes the neurotic subject, who positions himself under the function of castration and the law of the Father, Joyce, whose father transmitted to him only a depleted legacy of the law and a phallus, Lacan says, that was "somewhat limp,"[48] constructs a substitutive split: between the symbolic register and the register of the sinthome. Instead of the lying truth of the unconscious, *Finnegans Wake* fashions a truth that is a product of art. This art of knotting the two registers of symbol and sinthome around a false hole so as to create a split that would make life bearable is Joyce's *savoir-faire* in this novel.

The artistic truth, which is also Joyce's singular proper name, is devoid of sense, or in other words, is located in an ironic position with respect to the Other. This ironic position can arouse anxiety in Joyce's academic readers, and subsequently lead them to engage, as Joyce predicted they would for at least three centuries, in injecting sense to an object which is constitutively outside sense because it is nothing but Joyce's singularity, his proper name. This proper name made it possible for him to live and extract satisfaction from a jouissance that is outside sense, what Lacan denominates "Other jouissance," throughout the decade in which he wrote *Finnegans Wake*.

Perhaps the height of irony is that the academic interpretation of Joyce misses what the writing of *Finnegans Wake* was for its author. Literary critics' refusal to wake from infinite and futile hermeneutic interpretations of Joyce is what makes it possible for a wake—that funerary rite that is part mourning, part celebration—to take place around the novel qua ceded object, literal remainder of Joyce's body.

If indeed the combinatory of letters from which the book is made functioned as a source of the Other jouissance Joyce extracted from his writing, then the academic preoccupation with Joyce functions as a preservative for the conditions of this enjoyment. Joyce's interpreters who busy themselves with words and fill libraries with exegeses believe that their work deciphers a writing that is complex. But in fact, as Lacan shows, *Finnegans Wake* is less complex than sense-less. As such, it is a nondecodable object, whose es-sence is the sinthomatic function it had for Joyce: producing a prosthetic split and extracting an enjoyment outside sense in the process of doing so. The academic attempt to interpret what is in essence noninterpretable thus does something utterly different from what it believes itself to be doing. It preserves in culture the book as a singular solution and a source of Other jouissance for Joyce.

Unlike literary critics, psychoanalyst Jacques Alain Miller locates in Joyce's writing in *Finnegans Wake* only what he calls "the formal envelope of the symptom," from which Joyce extracts Other jouissance.[49] This formal envelope is Joyce's literary style. In this style, alphabetical letters from Joyce's register of the sinthome function as part of the enjoying body he created for himself. That is why the wake, in the sense of the perpetual funerary rite academe conducts around Joyce's work, makes it possible for something of this body to remain hylozoically a-wake and to continue to enjoy long after Joyce ceased to exist as a living individual. This enjoyment that does not cease to return beyond Joyce's life, that operates like the molecules of organic matter that persist beyond an individual life but that is also kept alive by culture, is itself the manifestation of the death drive as principle of repetition that pulsates in Joyce's writing and invigorates it.

Style operates as site of the death drive also in the work of Virginia Woolf, but differently. For Woolf, enjoyment was unbearable; unbearable to such a degree that, in complete contrast to Joyce in *Finnegans Wake*, she did what she could so that nothing of her biological organism would remain. Nevertheless, in her work as in Joyce's, such traces do persist; they persist in the writing that is less related to the conscious representation of past events and that undermines the traditional structures of literary representation that might be termed auto-bio-graphic, or even better, "auto-thanato-graphic" on the register of the real. This is writing that inscribes not only life but also death, and that institutes a beyond in which the death drive as repetition continues to reverberate.

Woolf's particular relation to her biological existence evidently involves the mortifying aspect of the death drive. From a certain point in Woolf's life, the mortifying aspect of the death drive, which ultimately led to her suicide, became entangled with the death at a young age of her brother, Toby Stephen. It is common to consider one of Woolf's early novels, *Jacob's Room*, which narrates the childhood, coming-of-age, and death of a young intellectual, as a record and lament of her brother's life. That is, the status of *Jacob's Room* in Woolf's *oeuvre* is similar to the status of *A Portrait of the Artist* in Joyce's: the status of a writing whose content is seemingly (auto)biographical. Yet just as in *Portrait of the Artist* Joyce does not manage to furnish himself with more than a domesticated, weak solution to the suffering of too unmediated an encounter with the living flesh, stemming from the failure, in his case, of the paternal function, in *Jacob's Room* Woolf is unable to produce a satisfactory solution to the melancholy suffering involved in the death of her brother and to appropriately mourn, that is, decathect, an object that has been lost. In *The Waves*, the character of a young intellectual who dies at a young age returns in the form of Percival. However, Percival in *The Waves* is situated very differently from Jacob in *Jacob's Room*. Jacob is one of the novel's focalizers, from whose vantage point narrated events are transmitted. Even though he is not the narrator, a large proportion of narrated events are presented as if they were mediated by his consciousness. In *The Waves*, on the other hand, Percival, who like Jacob in *Jacob's Room* veils the hole of a lost love object that cannot be mourned, is the only one of the main characters who does not function as a focalizer, appearing instead only through his focalization by the six other consciousnesses.

Percival's place in *The Waves* is an empty place, the veil of a hole at the center of the patchwork torus that is the novel. The attraction of the six focalizing consciousnesses toward Percival indicates that this hole functions as a magnetic center centripetally drawing the other elements of the text into it—that is, functions as the center of a vortex(t). The patched torus of *The Waves*, pierced by the hole percival veils, is structured as a vortex into whose center the focalizing consciousnesses implode and their fragments are cast.

Woolf's last novel, *Between the Acts*, repeats the vortex(t) structure. In this novel, the intensity of the vortex(t)'s rotational movement is such that it draws into itself not fragments of focalizing consciousnesses but points that are letters' material remainders. Yet in *Between the Acts* the hole at the center of the vortex is not veiled by any name, any remnant of a conscious representation of events from the author's life; no attempt is made to attach a signifier, even a signifier with a special status such as a proper name, to a death that cannot be symbolized and cannot be mourned. In other words, in its topological vortex(t) structure, *Between the Acts* comes close to the structure of *The Waves* yet empties this structure of any vestiges of imaginary references to Woolf's life. It seems that this very act of emptying is what makes it possible for Woolf to complete in *Between the Acts* the trajectory of the desire already sketched in *Jacob's Room* and *The Waves*. This is a desire that is interlaced with the wish to find proper psychic burial for the lost love-object embodied in her dead brother, a desire that cannot be untangled from the death drive.

A desire of a woman seeking to find a proper burial place for a brother, a desire underlain by an unconquerable death drive—this is the structure emerging in different ways from *Between the Acts*, *The Waves* and *Jacob's Room*. Is not this structure congruent with that of Sophocles's *Antigone* as exposed by Lacan in his seventh seminar on the ethics of psychoanalysis? This is a structure of a dense medium between two deaths that is traversed by the desire of a woman that goes beyond the pleasure principle.[50] Desire, Lacan shows, for instance in his sixth seminar on desire and its interpretation, is not a wish that can be articulated but an empty place in the unconscious, a place not occupied by any signifier but opened up between signifiers. Any articulation of desire is hence an interpretation which necessarily veils it while allowing it to surface.[51] In the case of Antigone, desire surfaces through her desperate attempts to bring her brother to burial. As Lacan shows in his seventh seminar, not only is Antigone's desire not a desire for what she proclaims it is (as is the case with any desire); this desire is also propelled by the death drive.[52] Antigone moves in a trajectory of transgression: she resists any impediment the law of the State places in her path toward bringing her brother Polynices to proper burial, up to the point of the destruction of her own body. This trajectory of transgression, of moving beyond the limits of the law up to a nondialecticizable and insurpassable point, is isomorphic with the course of the Sadean drive as analyzed by Lacan, for instance in his seventh and tenth seminars. The hero in the writings of the Marquis de Sade aspires to investigate the body and the interior of the body of his objects up to the point wherein this body is no longer destructible. Both Antigone's traversal of the limits of the law up to the point of her real death and the Sadean hero's aspiration to locate the body that can no longer be destroyed within the body of his object exemplify the structure of the death drive as Freud conceptualizes it in "Beyond the Pleasure Principle": a drive that generates disturbances to homeostasis, such as the subject's compulsion to repeat precisely what he suffers from while aspiring to annihilate what it generates so as to reach a point of the absolute stasis of inanimate matter beyond organic life. Encountering obstacles they generate, insisting until they reach a point beyond dialectics, Antigone and the Sadean hero as analyzed by Lacan tread the trajectory of the death drive.

According to Lacan's reading in his seventh seminar, Antigone moves, in complete opposition to the law of the State, through her particular desire which is propelled by the death drive, not only toward her death as a represented event in a literary text, but also toward what cannot be represented, which surfaces as an effect of splendor beyond and through the representation of her death.[53]

What cannot be represented is none other than the Freudian "Thing." In his *Project for a Scientific Psychology*, Freud writes that the Thing is the remainder of excitations that escape the judgment of the pleasure principle.[54] According to Freud, both in the *Project* and in "Negation," this principle operates at the limits of psychic life, and in effect functions as the boundary between the series of representations that is the unconscious and the Thing that is beyond representation.[55] In other words, in Freudian meta-psychology, the only barrier between the series of representations that is the unconscious and what is cast out of the unconscious and receives the status of a Thing is the judgment of the pleasure principle, a literal judgment of taste, Freud writes, which determines, in terms of the most archaic of drives, the oral drive, whether or not a given excitation is good enough to take in.[56] The pleasure principle, that is, carries out a judgment of taste that unlike the Kantian judgment of the same appellation has to do not with the beautiful but with the good.

In what way might an object which cannot be represented, which cannot be reduced or dialecticized, an object of which the only thing that can be said is that it is the hole of the lost object or the Freudian Thing, appear within the framework of a literary work such as *Antigone*? The answer, Lacan suggests, has to do with an account of the structure of the text which supplements narratological description with the discernment of the motion of a desire.

In his seventh seminar, Lacan shows that Sophocles's tragedy is situated between two deaths, in a twilight zone beyond the pleasure principle. This structure makes it possible for the Thing to emerge as an effect of splendor. The liminal structure of the plot, in which the course of Antigone's particular desire is unfolded, makes the plot function as a crystal refracting a beam of light. The refraction of the beam in the crystal, of the trajectory of Antigone's desire in the liminal texture between her symbolic and her real deaths, generates an effect of splendor that is the effect of beauty of the character Antigone.

Antigone's beauty, then, is not related to an attribute assigned to the character on the text's level of sense; it is an effect created retroactively by the relation between the structure of the trajectory of desire and the structure of the liminal zone between two deaths that are two kernel events in the narrative. However, the effect of splendor that is Antigone's beauty may be considered not only from the standpoint of desire but also from the vantage point of the real. The splendor is generated not only by the movement of the literary persona of Antigone toward what she considers her particular good in a liminal space whose structure refracts this movement, but also from an encounter, in the beyond of this space, with the unrepresentable hole of the lost object or Thing. By analyzing the effect of beauty emerging from the movement of a desire propelled by the death drive in the liminal space between two deaths, Lacan follows in Freud's footsteps and extrapolates a meta-psychological principle. If for Freud the last barrier before the Thing is the judgment of the pleasure principle, a judgment of the good, Lacan posits another limit beyond the judgment of the good: the limit of the effect of beauty. In her insistence to bury her brother, Antigone moves beyond the Freudian pleasure principle, a principle Freud postulates as the last barrier, the barrier of what might be termed the judgment of good taste, between representations and the Thing. Beauty as an effect of splendor, which emerges as a result of this movement beyond the pleasure principle, makes it possible for Lacan to isolate the effect of beauty as an additional, more radical limit, between representation and the Thing. This is the *ultima Thule* of psychic life, the last barrier, Lacan says, in the face of the horror of the Thing.

Both *The Waves* and *Between the Acts* are traversed by a desire manifested in a wish to bury a brother, a desire propelled by the death drive. In both novels, this desire traverses a thick liminal space. Yet, in Woolf's novels, which unlike *Antigone* do not, on the level of sense, engage with the law and its transgression, this liminal space is the product not of narrative sequence but of narrative topology, not of the way in which the text unfolds between two deaths but of the crease that turns these texts into topological objects, torus in one case, cross cap in the other, vortices in which letters and other typographical signs swirl. Moreover, unlike in Sophocles's text, in *The Waves* and *Between the Acts*, the woman whose desire traverses the text is not a character in the plot but the one constructing it. In other words, what in Sophocles's text appears on the phantasmatic level, for Woolf becomes real. Unlike Sophocles, Woolf does not weave a phantasm which gravitates toward a woman whose insistence to bury her brother leads her to the nondialecticizable end point of the trajectory of the death drive; she *is* this woman. Furthermore, in the case of Woolf, the liminal space traversed by the desire of this woman is a product not of the represented events of the plot but of the text's linguistic structure.

In *The Waves* and *Between the Acts*, Woolf repeats in her writing the structure of the desire of the mourning sister which is intricated with the death drive, which made its literary debut in Sophocles's *Antigone*. But by positioning herself as an element in this structure rather than as the one who unfolds the necessarily phantasmatic narrative in which this structure becomes manifest, she tears away its veils of sense. What remains in *Between the Acts* is a pure structure of a vorticial medium traversed by a desire manifest in a wish to bury a brother, a desire stretched until it turns absolute death drive.

It is possible that the work of fashioning a vortex(t) without phantasmatic veil, an act of writing in and with the real without attenuating mediation, already enfolded the moment of Woolf's drowning. Woolf became another remainder cast, like the letters and the points of her texts, into the textual vortex she created. Yet for those willing to encounter Woolf's texts as acts of writing in the real, without the intervening screens of the phantasm, the effect of the refraction of the vector of desire by the vorticial medium they produce is more intense and powerful than it is in Sophocles's text, and subsequently, so is the splendor effected by this refraction. The encounter between the topological space Woolf writes in *The Waves* and especially in *Between the Acts* and the movement of Woolf's desire which traverses this liminal space has an aesthetic result more powerful than that of *Antigone*, a result that is not without relation to the manner in which Woolf inscribed her life (and her death)—that is, to her literary style. This result is the emergence of "Virginia Woolf," not as a collection of conscious, imaginary representations of fragments of a recorded life, and not even as a proper name such as that of Joyce in *Finnegans Wake*, that guarantees the return of jouissance even beyond the death of its creator as a manifestation of the death drive, but as an effect of beauty. The beauty or splendor that can emerge for those encountering Woolf's texts is not of the order of enjoyment. This beauty is the last barrier before the horror, one of whose imaginary names is "death"—a cruel and horrible beauty which is the result of Woolf's choice to cease not writing this horror and to manifest the death drive as what does not cease to be written through style.

Notes

1 In his eleventh seminar, Lacan speaks of the drive following a fragment by Heraclitus concerning the movement of a bow (in Greek *bios*), whose name is life (another sense of the Greek signifier *bios*) but whose work is death. Jacques Lacan, *The Seminar of Jacques Lacan, Book XI: The Four Fundamental Concepts of Psychoanalysis*, trans. Alan Sheridan (New York: W.W. Norton, 1981 [1964–1965]), p. 177.
2 Jacques Lacan, "Lituraterre," in *The Seminar of Jacques Lacan, Book XVIII: On a Discourse That Might Not Be a Semblance* (1970–1971), trans. Cormac Gallagher (unpublished manuscript), lesson of 12 May 1971.
3 Ibid.
4 Lacan, *Seminar XI*, p. 25.
5 The analyst's situating himself as semblance of the object cause means that in the Lacanian clinic, the analyst does not operate as the subject's interlocutor but is present through analytic interventions: scansions that return the subject's unconscious message to him in inverted form and cuts that terminate the session not according to predetermined duration but at a crucial point in the speech of the subject. This point is crucial not only because of its semantic content but also in its relation to the subject's object cause.
6 Lacan, *Seminar XVIII*, lesson of 12 May 1971.
7 Philippe Dubois, *L'acte photographique* (Paris: Nathan Labor, 1983), pp. 160–61.
8 Ibid., p. 160.
9 Jacques Derrida, *The Ear of the Other: Otobiography, Transference, Translation*, trans. Peggy Kamuf (San Francisco: Bison Books, 1984), p. 11.
10 Ibid., p. 19.
11 Ibid., p. 21.
12 Ibid., p. 19.
13 Ibid., p. 38.
14 Ibid., p. 36.
15 Ibid., p. 35.
16 Ibid., p. 26.
17 Jacques Lacan, "The Youth of Gide, or the Letter and Desire," in *Écrits: A Selection*, trans. Bruce Fink (New York: W.W. Norton, 2006 [1958]), pp. 623–44.
18 Jacques Lacan, *The Seminar of Jacques Lacan, Book XXIV: L'insu que sait de l'une-bévue s'aile à mourre* (1976–1977), trans. Cormac Gallagher (unpublished manuscript), lesson of 17 May 1977.
19 Virginia Woolf, "Reminiscences," in *Moments of Being*, ed. Jeanne Schulkind (London: Harcourt, Brace, Jovanovich, 1976 [1909]), pp. 25–60. Virginia Woolf, "A Sketch of the Past," in *Moments of Being*, ed. Jeanne Schulkind (London: Harcourt, Brace, Jovanovich, 1976 [1909]), pp. 61–138.
20 James Joyce, *Finnegans Wake* (Harmondsworth: Penguin, 2000 [1939]).
21 Jacques Lacan, *The Seminar of Jacques Lacan, Book XXIII: The Sinthome*, trans. A. R. Price (Cambridge: Polity, 2016 [1975–1976]), p. 15.
22 Ibid. The following sentence from *Finnegans Wake* exemplifies Lacan's argument: "The fall (bababadalgharaghtakamminarronnkonnbronntonnerronntuonnthunntro varrhounawnskawntoohoohoordenenthurnuk!) of a once wallstrait oldparr is retaled early in bed and later on life down through all christian minstrelsy." *Finnegans Wake*, p. 3.
23 "The sun had not yet risen. The sea was indistinguishable from the sky, except that the sea was slightly creased as if a cloth had wrinkles in it." Virginia Woolf, *The Waves* (New York: Oxford University Press, 2000 [1931]), p. 3.
24 "The sun was sinking. The hard stone of the day was cracked and light poured through its splinters. Red and gold shot through the waves, in rapid running arrows, feathered with darkness." Ibid., p. 173.
25 Ibid., p. 246.

26 Sigmund Freud, "Instincts and Their Vicissitudes," in *The Standard Edition of the Complete Psychological Works of Sigmund Freud, Vol. XIV*, trans. and ed. James Strachey (London: Hogarth Press, 1915), pp. 109–40.
27 On reverse evolution in *Between the Acts*, see Hana Wirth-Nesher, "Final Curtain on the War: Figure and Ground in Virginia Woolf's *Between the Acts*," *Style* 28, no. 2 (1994): 183–200.
28 Meir Sternberg, "Proteus in Quotation-Land: Mimesis and the Forms of Reported Discourse," *Poetics Today* 2, no. 2 (1982): 107–56.
29 On the concept of the vortex(t) in Woolf, see Shirley Sharon-Zisser, "'Some Little Language as Lovers Use': Virginia Woolf's Elemental Erotics of Simile," *American Imago* 58, no. 2 (2001), pp. 567–96.
30 Sigmund Freud, "Repression," in *The Standard Edition of the Complete Psychological Works of Sigmund Freud, Vol. XIV*, trans. and ed. James Strachey (London: Hogarth Press, 1915), pp. 141–58.
31 Freud's discussion of the representative of representation in the essay on "Repression" highlights an aspect different from the one emphasized in his discussion of the compulsion to repeat to which we referred in earlier chapters of this book.
32 "'So that each of us who has enjoyed this pageant has still an opp . . .' the word was cut in two. A zoom served it. Twelve aeroplanes in perfect formation like a flight of wild duck came overhead." Virginia Woolf, *Between the Acts* (Harmondsworth: Penguin, 2000 [1941]), p. 140.
33 "Isa dragged her chair across the gravel muttering: 'To what dark antre of the unvisited earth, or wind-brushed forest, shall we go now? Or spin from star to star and dance in the maze of the moon? Or . . .' she held her deck chair at the wrong angle." Ibid., p. 141. "[. . .] (they sang), hedging and ditching, we pass. . . . Summer and winter, autumn and spring return . . . All passes but we, all changes . . . but we remain forever the same . . . (the breeze blew gaps between their words)." Ibid., p. 103.
34 Sigmund Freud, "Extracts from the Fliess Papers: Letter 52," in *The Standard Edition of the Complete Psychological Works of Sigmund Freud, Vol. 1*, trans. and ed. James Strachey (London: Hogarth Press, 1960 [1896]), pp. 234–35.
35 Sigmund Freud, "Screen Memories," in *The Standard Edition of the Complete Psychological Works of Sigmund Freud, Vol. III*, trans. and ed. James Strachey (London: Hogarth Press, 1960 [1899]), pp. 299–322.
36 Freud, "Extracts: Letter 52."
37 Ibid.
38 Ibid.
39 "A girl stood before him in midstream, alone and still, gazing out to sea. She seemed like one whom magic had changed into the likeness of a strange and beautiful seabird. Her long slender bare legs were delicate as a crane's and pure save where an emerald trail of seaweed had fashioned itself as a sign upon the flesh . . . Heavenly God! Cried Stephen's soul, in an outburst of profane joy." James Joyce, *Portrait of the Artist as a Young Man* (Harmondsworth: Penguin, 1994 [1916]), p. 191.
40 The concept of the sinthome is developed by Lacan in his twenty-third seminar, of 1975–1976.
41 Lacan, *Seminar XXIII*, lesson of 18 November 1975.
42 Ibid.
43 Joyce, *Portrait of the Artist as a Young Man*, p. 89.
44 Ibid.
45 "The supreme quality of beauty being a light from some other world . . . The instant wherein that supreme quality of beauty, the clear radiance of the esthetic image, is apprehended luminously by the mind which has been arrested by its wholeness and fascinated by its harmony is the luminous silent stasis aesthetic pleasure." Joyce, *Portrait of the Artist as a Young Man*, p. 239.

46 Lacan, *Seminar XXIII*, lesson of 18 November 1975.
47 Ibid., lesson of 16 June 1976.
48 Ibid., lesson of 18 November 1975.
49 Jacques-Alain Miller, "Reflections on the Formal Envelope of the Symptom," *Lacanian Ink* 4 (1991 [1985]): 13–21. Though Miller in his title uses the signifier "symptom," the category he discusses in the article is "sinthome," as Lacan formulates it in his twenty-third seminar. It should also be noted that throughout the seminar, Lacan uses the terms "sinthome" and "symptom" interchangeably.
50 See Chapter 1.
51 Jacques Lacan, *The Seminar of Jacques Lacan, Book VI: Desire and Its Interpretation* (1958–1959), translated by Cormac Gallagher (unpublished manuscript).
52 Jacques Lacan, *The Seminar of Jacques Lacan, Book VII: The Ethics of Psychoanalysis*, trans. Dennis Porter (New York: W. W. Norton, 1986 [1959–1960]).
53 Ibid., p. 247.
54 Sigmund Freud, "Project for a Scientific Psychology," in *The Standard Edition of the Complete Psychological Works of Sigmund Freud, Vol. I,* trans. and ed. James Strachey (London: Hogarth Press, 1950 [1887–1902]). p. 333.
55 Sigmund Freud, "Negation," in *The Standard Edition of the Complete Works of Sigmund Freud, Vol. XI,* trans. and ed. James Strachey (London: Hogarth Press, 1925), pp. 233–40.
56 Ibid., p. 239.

5

THE ART OF INTERS(L)AYING

The inscription of death as stylistic form

Painting allows us to see things
that cannot otherwise be seen,
that cannot be shown.

—*Yitzhak Livneh, 2006*

Although Rembrandt's death did of course bring his self-portrait series to an end, as we have shown over the course of the last two chapters it is primarily as serial repetition on the level of the art object in its entirety or its components, not as theme, that death is made present in art. In the case of Rembrandt's self-portraits, death is present not in the progressively aging figure of the painter but in the status of these self-portraits as cedable objects. In the case of Woolf and Joyce, the death at stake in the artwork is not only the author's demise which is the horizon of any autobiography but a death drive manifesting itself primarily as jouissant repetition on the level of the letter as remainder or even of this remainder's deconstruction, which is the quintessence of a literary style. This chapter too will be concerned with modalities of repetition that are of the order of the death drive in specific stylistic forms, in this instance forms emerging from the visual artworks of Yitzhak Livneh: witticism in its Freudian inflection and the use of frames as stylistic dominant.

Livneh himself has more than once explicitly referred to cedability such as explored in this book's third chapter as foundational to an artwork. Livneh, that is, not only paints manifestations of the death drive; he also reflexively articulates the relation between death and art in his artwork and in his statements concerning it. In the case of Livneh, this reflection involves explicit allusions to myth, including Pliny the Elder's myth of the origin of painting. "I have learnt," Livneh says regarding the mythical invention of painting by the daughter of Butades, "that the invention of painting is connected to leave-taking . . . to separation from life."[1]

What Butades's daughter paints at the moment of separation is trace of what is not even the body of her beloved but a contour of this body's shadow. It is a trace of the material remainder of imaginary cohesion, of the ego as fictitious body image which Lacan delineates in his article on "The Mirror Stage."[2] The image of the body the infant sees in the mirror, Lacan says, is enchanting and captivating. It sharply contrasts with the infant's initial experience of bodily fragmentation. The unified body image is an ideal fiction, foreign to the heterogeneity of the partial drives. But it is this ideal fiction alone that can support the emergence of narcissistic love—the love of the ego's double appearing as a cohesive body which seems to reflect the very structure of the lover's own desire.[3] What this means is that what Butades's daughter tries to retain in the tracing the shadow of her beloved is ultimately none other than the fiction of her own unified body, the fundamental imaginary representation.

However, as Lacan shows at various points in his teaching, the act of representation constitutively exceeds any inscription of imaginary unity. Something invariably escapes the unity of the specular image, something which cannot be completely absorbed into it and is hence its material remainder.[4] Such a material remainder is what is left to another woman in another myth Livneh alludes to as a source of knowledge regarding the essence of art: the myth of Judith's beheading of Holofernes. In this historic myth, Livneh says, "a woman comes with the head of a man."[5] This statement suggests what is at stake for Livneh in the genre of portraiture, which plays a key role in his 2008 retrospective at the Tel-Aviv Museum of Art, *Astonishment*, whose unique stylistic dominants we will explore below.

The painting's material remainder, mythically embodied in the cut-off head of Holofernes, no longer has anything of the unique life upheld by a coherent image. But for Livneh it is precisely this material remainder of what is no longer a living individual nor even the living individual's unifying specular image which the portrait ostensibly doubles that embodies the very essence of portraiture. For Livneh, portrait painting and painting as such are real, material representatives of what is separate not only from the individual's cohesive image but also from the very organism the painting ostensibly represents. Livneh thus makes it possible to isolate another aspect of the relation between the art object's inherent cedability and the repetition inherent to the death drive. While the third chapter of this book isolated a signifier's insisting beyond the pleasure principle as a form of repetition in portraiture, Livneh's statements point to a repetition emerging by means not of a signifier but of a material remainder which continues to enjoy. Livneh's reflections on the relation between painting and death at the level of his artistic practice as well as his discourse concerning it teach something more about this repetition of the remainder and the aesthetics it engenders.

This is an aesthetics whose foundation is not what it seems. In Livneh's work the aesthetic basis of the death drive as repetition does not consist in the death-related content so frequent in his work, such as the skulls appearing in everyday scenes of home exercise or the images based on projected close-ups of the faces of dead soldiers. Instead, Livneh's artworks may be read as a theorization in practice of the act of painting. They comprise a theory they do not articulate but institute in their style, a theory of painting as libidinal inscription which, beyond the images and signifiers it engenders, makes present the constant motion of the death drive itself. The thematics of death appearing at the level of the image in Livneh's works, that is, are secondary to the manifestation of the death drive on the register of style—a style constituting this artist's unique way of formalizing the material remainder which is the foundation of the painting. In what follows we will explore two manifestations of this style: the visual witticism (*Witz*), and the generation of a cavernous space constituted by multiple frames.

Witticism and death

Witticism as visual structure appears in a number of Livneh's painting series from 2005 to 2006. The laughter-inducing effect of these series is the product of the contingent encounter between death as a theme in the painting and the representative of death in the material remainder from which the painting is made.

Quite a few of Livneh's works include the paradigmatic image of the *vanitas* paintings of the European Renaissance: the skull as *memento mori*, a reminder of the moment of death that awaits us all. Thus, for instance in *Michal I* (2004), a young woman holds a ball in her hand while tracing the outline of the shadow it casts on the wall. In *The Invention of Painting*, part of the same series, the ball is replaced by the image of death's head. The figure of the young woman is subtracted from the painting, as is its colorfulness.

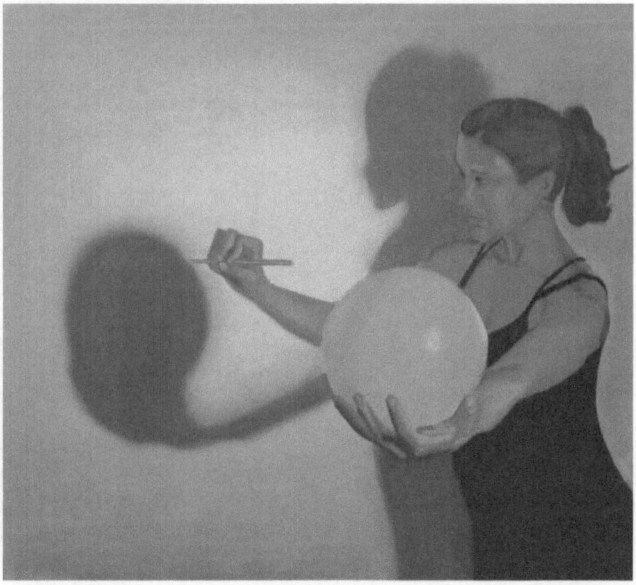

FIGURE 5.1 Yitzhak Livneh, *Michal I*, 2004. Image reproduced by courtesy of the artist.

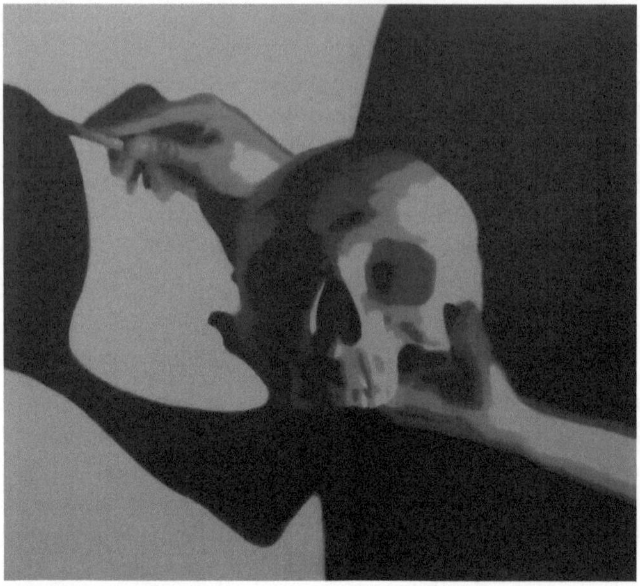

FIGURE 5.2 Yitzhak Livneh, *The Invention of Painting*, 2004. Image reproduced by courtesy of the artist.

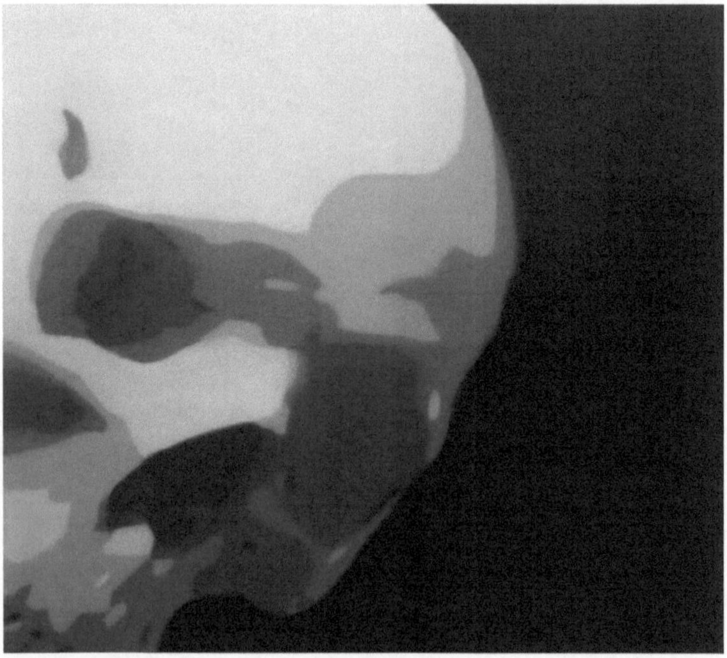

FIGURE 5.3 Yitzhak Livneh, *Goodnight*, 2004. Image reproduced by courtesy of the artist.

The following painting in the same series, *Goodnight*, is essentially a close-up of the skull, now magnified to the point of distortion and shifted from the center, appearing as a series of stains in various shades of gray against a black backdrop. In the *Astonishment* painting series of 2004–2006, too, a skull appears. The series depicts the scene of a ball shattering a glass window from various angles and degrees of proximity, yet always from the perspective of the person in whose direction the object is slammed. In this sequence too, what appears to be a ball in the first image is transformed into a skull seemingly thrown at the observer. A similar progression may be found in works from 2007, light and brightly colored perspective paintings of a woman doing Pilates exercises with a physiotherapy ball in her living room. As in the case of the ball shattering the glass, as in the case of the red ball held in the hands of a young woman, a modern version of the daughter of Butades, in the Pilates series the ball is transformed into a skull, in this case, a skull disproportionately large with respect to the body attempting to use it for exercise.

Unlike the grave and solemn images of death's heads in Renaissance *vanitas* paintings, the skull images in Livneh's series invoke laughter, particularly as they appear in the light-drenched Pilates paintings. What is the source of such laughter? Not the thematic tension between the semantic field unfolding from the toned female body and sophisticated interior design, formally subtended by the paintings' bright colors and the morose associations likely to arise from the skull as an ominous figure of the cruel fate awaiting every man. Nor is it the somewhat grotesque

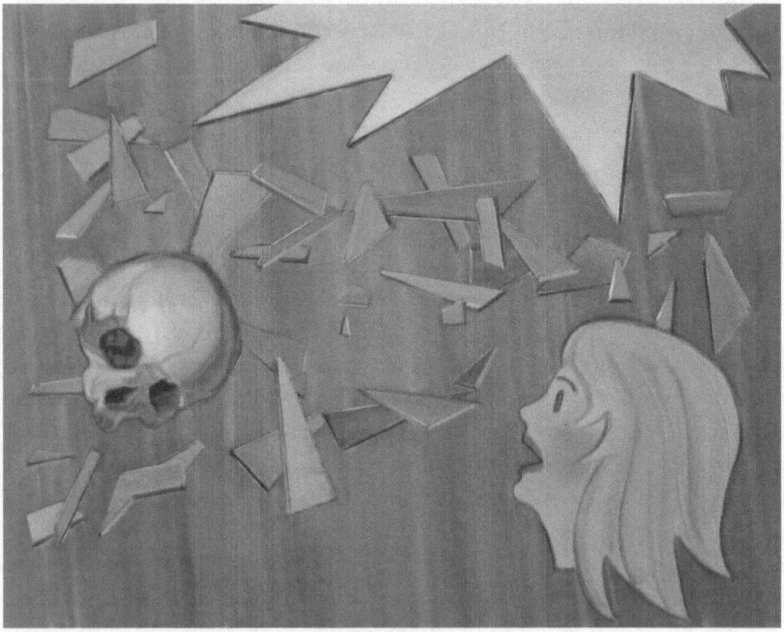

FIGURE 5.4 Yitzhak Livneh, *Astonishment*, 2004. Image reproduced by courtesy of the artist.

opposition between the dimensions of the skull in the Pilates sequence and the elements of the fictive reality depicted in the painting. What evokes laughter in these paintings, that is, is not the components of painting that are of the order of what Lacan calls the semblant, the knotting of the imaginary and the symbolic, of the specular and dyadic dimension of experience with its formulation in words.[6] The effect of laughter aroused by Livneh's skull images is caused in part by the way in which these images tear away the veil of the semblant of which they are a part. The material dimension of these paintings, a dimension exceeding the signifiers and images whereof the semblant is woven, is of the order of the real of writing. This material dimension empties the paintings of the sense it helps engender. The diluted layers of paint Livneh uses in the skull paintings, particularly in the Pilates sequence, and the light, almost random brushstrokes characterizing them, empty them of their ostensibly weighty subject matter, tearing the veil of morbid sense they themselves generate.[7]

As Lacan argues in his eighteenth seminar, the rending of semblant by a writing constituting the signifier's material foundation creates a hole in knowledge from which psychoanalysis may summon what is of the order of jouisssance, of the satisfaction of the drive.[8] In terms of Freudian metapsychology, the function of the signifying dimension or representation, essential to the semblant, is to bind libido or affect within the psychic apparatus. In other words, unconscious representations are not merely textual, but always bind an affect saturating them. Affect does not for the most part float in the psychic apparatus unbound. It is therefore for the most part accessible only indirectly, via the signifiers that bind it and that it saturates. Anxiety is an exception to this rule. Lacan states in seminar ten that anxiety is the only affect that does not deceive, for it is of the order of the real, that is, unconnected to any signifier whatsoever.[9]

What this means is that in Livneh's Pilates sequence, the tearing of semblant by letter, of the painting's thematics by the paradoxical presentification of the materiality ostensibly instituting this thematics, involves a release of affect from the signifier.[10] The affect released at the moment of the tearing of the semblant might be anxiety of which other affects (e.g., guilt, compassion) are veils. Such is the case also in Holbein's *The Ambassadors*, where the anamorphotic skull which comes into focus when the painting is viewed awry rends the veil of image and sense created by the perspectival representation of the two ambassadors against the backdrop of a panoply of trappings of humanist culture. This rending of the semblant occurs not only because the *vanitas* image of death's head confronts the subject with the ultimate castration of his own impending annihilation.[11] What arouses anxiety in the viewing of Holbein's painting is not the skull image's dimension of sense, but the manner in which the revealing of this image implicates the subject, entraps him, Lacan says, in a certain relation with respect to the desire to see.[12] Livneh's painting series in which death's head appears similarly trap the subject while tearing the semblant. But they do so in a manner that is different and whose affective product is not anxiety but another manifestation of the release of libido: laughter.

In *Jokes and Their Relation to the Unconscious*, Freud explains that the affective product of the joke, laughter—involving the release of an unconscious inhibition, that is, the discharge of affect bound to a repressed representation whose conscious formulation is prohibited by the pleasure principle—is made possible by a rhetorical technique functioning as a sophisticated smuggling mechanism. The technique is that of compression and condensation, also to be found at the basis of the linguistic form of metaphor: the condensation of two signifiers whose conscious expression is prohibited by the pleasure principle but which share a contingent resonance. Freud demonstrates this by means of a joke he borrows from Heinrich Heine, in which the protagonist boasts about his close ties to the Baron Rothschild, summarizing his sentiments as follows: "'I sat beside Salomon Rothschild and he treated me quite as his equal—quite famillionairely.'"[13] In this joke, the operation of condensation results in the omission of superfluous elements and a "substitute" or "composite word" ("*famillionär*") is formed, which though unintelligible in itself is immediately recognized as having meaning within the given context.[14] The composite word, says Freud, "is the vehicle of the joke's laughter-compelling effect."[15] Freud emphasizes that laughter induced by the joke, that same laughter attesting to the effect of witticism (*Witz*), is different from that evoked by the mechanism of the comic, which involves two figures alone: "a first who finds what is comic and a second in whom it is found."[16] The effect of witticism occurs when a third person, who is neither the teller of the joke nor its object (if one exists), affirms it by his laughter.[17] The *Witz* effect, then, emerges not in the dyadic or specular field, where two figures are locked in an imaginary struggle, but in a tertiary space—one that creates a community. The witticism is of the order of the unconscious and not that of the ego. This is not only because it is not situated on the imaginary axis, where the ego is formed and operates, but because it generates components of the Other: signifiers, which while appearing meaningless at first, are found to be part of a shared treasury, of an already existing Other, or in Freud's terms, of an Other scene.[18] One may say, then, that the *Witz* effect confirms something essential to the subject of the unconscious.

What, then, is affirmed by the *Witz* effect in Livneh's painting series where a ball is soon transformed into a death's head? And how is this effect created? The series are painted with a clarity which all but bares the *Witz* mechanism they generate. In each, the image of the ball—a red playing ball, a Pilates ball—is condensed into an image of a skull, giving rise to an amalgam which is of the order of the semblant weaving image and signifier. This amalgam is different from a skull such as those appearing in the still life paintings of the *vanitas* tradition, since it is marked by visual memories of ball images earlier in the series, yet it no longer is that ball. The massive skull on which the woman does her exercise routine in the Pilates series is no longer the colorful Pilates ball that appeared in the series' opening paintings, yet the outline of the Pilates ball, preserved in the circumference of the skull, remains in the painting as a memory trace of an image that persists under erasure.

Psychoanalyst Michèle Montrelay writes that the amalgam emerging from the *Witz* structure is in effect an instance of metaphor: one signifier is added to another, not as a reflection on it but precisely as what is alien or other to it.[19] What the otherness between the joke's two components introduces into the joke is the dimension of repression, wherein a conscious representation replaces an unconscious representation it veils.[20] The repression of the first representation—in Freudian terms, its failure to be translated to the conscious register—is in a sense a victory of the pleasure principle.[21] Montrelay emphasizes that the formation of metaphor, the substitution of one representation for another whose contours can be glimpsed beyond erasure, is accompanied by an eruption of pleasure. Unlike Freud, who argues that the effect of witticism is indicative of a lifting of inhibition, of a discharge of libidinal energy which had been bound in the repressed signifier, Montrelay asserts that this effect is conditional not upon repression's elimination but upon its creation, specifically by means of the introduction of a new representation which has a formative function in relation to other representations.[22] According to Montrelay, we laugh when we realize that words express a text that is other than what we thought they expressed—or, in terms of formalist literary theory, when they have an effect of defamiliarization.[23]

Transposed to the visual field in which Livneh's painting series operate, Montrelay's observations suggest that the metaphoric amalgam of the skull and ball that features in them induces laughter which is of the order not of the comic but of the *Witz*. Once this amalgam appears, the Pilates exercise scene is no longer itself. Nor is the skull exactly the death's head of the *vanitas* paintings, confronting the viewer with the inevitability of his demise.

There is something other in the laugher provoked by the amalgam image of the ball/skull in Livneh's paintings, something foreign even to the defamiliarizing effect of each of these images in itself. Following Montrelay, one might say that what arouses laughter is not the semantic shift defamiliarizing the images of skull and ball alike. What arouses laughter is that the very semantic shift in relation to the signifier "death" points to the manner in which this signifier, upon the (imaginary) semantic field it engenders, is itself shifted from a place that can never be included in the field of the signifier. Applying the defamiliarizing structure of witticism in the visual field to the semantics of death is particularly funny, as it reveals the *Witz* structure of this semantics itself. When it is death that is at stake, one invariably speaks about something other than what one appears to be speaking about, as death has no representation in the unconscious.

The *Witz* effect created by the appearance of the skull/ball amalgam in Livneh's painting series, then, partakes of a complex conceptual move of the painterly representation of the relation between death and representation. This effect points to the way in which death is present in painting not at the level of the image and the signifier, not at the level of what can be marked by a contour or a word. Death is present in the painting as what Livneh points toward in a meta-painterly statement, correlative to the raised finger of St. John the Baptist in Leonardo da Vinci's painting as Lacan describes it in the "Direction of Treatment." This finger points toward "the forsaken horizon of being," toward what can be neither spoken nor marked, toward the real.[24] In his similarly Leonardian statement, Livneh says that the act of painting aims to "show what cannot be shown; to show what is ruined."[25] The function of witticism in Livneh's paintings is to show death by means of the ludicrous effect of the metaphoric amalgam's excess visibility, to point (while saying nothing) to its semantic content as always already voided of any possibility of a thematics, to show death not as annihilation but as a repetition on the level of style whose very condition is an absence or loss.

Death and the maiden

A similar structure wherein death emerges not on the level of theme but as an effect of repetition on the register of style occurs in another of Livneh's painting series from 2006. This series comprises portraits of young women, their mouths wide open. The portraits are based on images from photos for a wig catalogue. The wide-open mouths, endowing the face with a look of wonder, astonishment, or horror, are clearly the portraits' most striking detail. Gaping mouths, however, appear elsewhere in Livneh's work as well, for instance, in the series of paintings of dying soldiers discussed in the introduction to this book, who seem to be either singing or emitting a frozen scream. A gaping mouth appears in the work *Medusa* of 2000 as well.

In *Nude over Mirror*, a work of the same year depicting a nude female figure standing astride over a mirror, another orifice gapes toward the viewer. In several of these instances, the gaping orifice dominating the painting is thematically related

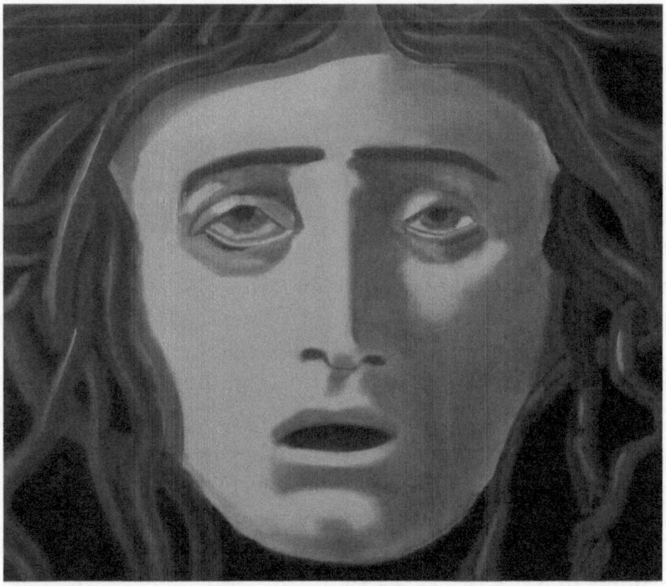

FIGURE 5.5 Yitzhak Livneh, *Medusa*, 2000. Image reproduced by courtesy of the artist.

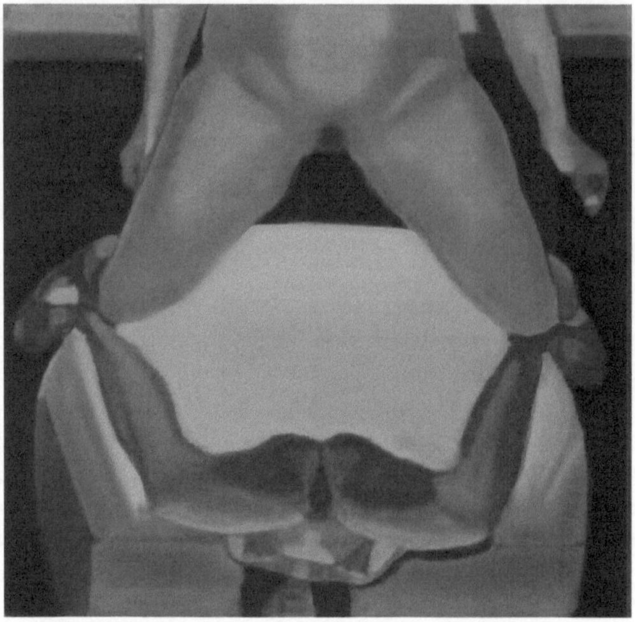

FIGURE 5.6 Yitzhak Livneh, *Nude over Mirror*, 2000. Image reproduced by courtesy of the artist.

to death. Medusa's gaze is one that petrifies and kills. The soldiers are painted at the moment their lives end. But what about the astonished women? In a conversation, Livneh mentioned Michael Powell's 1960 film *Peeping Tom* as a source of inspiration for this series. The film depicts the life of a serial killer targeting women who attaches a camera to the end of his murder weapon in order to document the terrified expression on his victims faces at the moment of their death. It is these women surprised by a serial killer, then, that haunt the astonished women of Livneh's series.

It is not the thematics of murder introduced through the allusion to *Peeping Tom*, however, that are constitutive of the series' relation to death. As in the case of the painted skulls in Livneh's various series, here the relation to death arises from repetition on the level of stylistic form. While in the skull series the repeated form was the visual manifestation of a Freudian *Witz*, in the *Astonishment* series what is repeated is a *mise en abyme* of frames within frames. The women's lips demarcate the gaping cavity of the mouth, a dark stain at the center of the work. This frame is located within the frame of the painted figure's face. The face, enveloped by hair, serves as a third frame, itself framed by the borders of the painting itself. The formal device of the *mise en abyme* appears more explicitly in earlier works by Livneh. Thus, for example in *Still Life with Mirror* of 1991, an empty picture frame appears within the painting itself. *Broken Mirror V* of 2003 depicts a mirror whose frame has multiple contours and which reflects another frame.

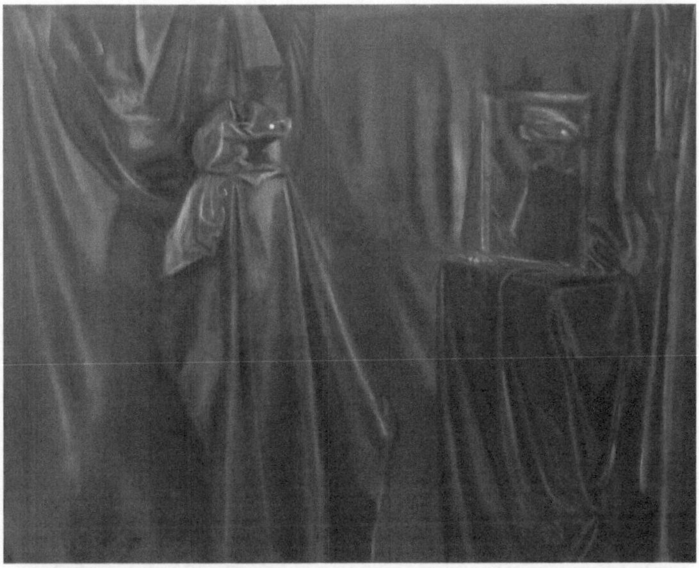

FIGURE 5.7 Yitzhak Livneh, *Still Life with Mirror*, 1991. Image reproduced by courtesy of the artist.

The *mise en abyme* as stylistic dominant generates a concentric pictorial space whose elements are related by inclusion and whose effect is double. First, the picture upon its multiple frames becomes a cavernous space whose limits are less than stable, in which images can slide from one frame to another, and which entices the observer to enter it. Second, the multiple frames constituting the painting undermine the painting's own status as a distinct framed object. The frame, in other words, does not function as what demarcates the picture plane as separate from the ground plane on which the viewer stands.

The effects of Livneh's *mise en abyme* paintings may be understood in terms of Lacan's topological analysis of what he calls "the visual structure of the subject" in the seminar on the object of psychoanalysis.[26] According to Lacan, it is topology which "allows us to formulate as giving, in an exact form, . . . what is involved in the relationship of the subject to extension."[27] In the topological structure generated by Livneh's multiple frames, ground plane and picture plane become continuous. Frames function not as limit but as contour of a cavernous void, enticing the viewer to enter it while allowing the images inhabiting it to slide out toward them. There is something anxiety inducing about this double movement, and not because of the instability it involves. Anxiety emerges upon the encounter with the *mise en abyme* structure of Livneh's *Astonishment* paintings because this encounter involves something that exceeds representation, for which the inset of the innermost frame, the dark stain of the woman's gaping mouth, is a veil.

This dark stain, sliding toward the observer it lures, is not a representation. It marks the point around which the pictorial space folds but which can never be

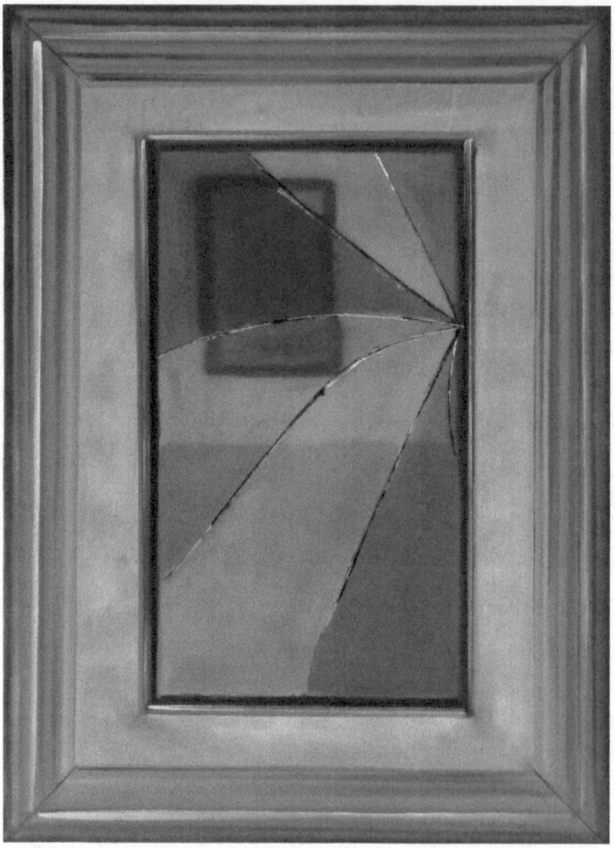

FIGURE 5.8 Yitzhak Livneh, *Broken Mirror V*, 2003. Image reproduced by courtesy of the artist.

represented within it. Like the navel of the dream around which the dream thoughts are tangled, it is the point at which interpretations open out into the unknown,[28] the many possible senses of the gaping mouth serving but to cover it. Like death, this folding point exceeds representation, has a value that, in Lacan's terms, is not symbolic but real. This point of folding of the concentric pictorial space of Livneh's *Astonishment* paintings, real and hence, as death, not representable, is the manner in which death is present in these paintings.

Notes

1 Ibid.
2 Jacques Lacan, "The Mirror Stage as Formative of the Function of the I as Revealed in Psychoanalytic Experience," in *Écrits: A Selection*, trans. Alan Sheridan (New York: W. W. Norton, 1977 [1949]).
3 Jacques Lacan, *The Seminar of Jacques Lacan, Book I: Freud's Papers on Technique*, trans. J. Forrester (New York: W. W. Norton, 1988 [1953–1954]), p. 142.

4 Jacques Lacan, *The Seminar of Jacques Lacan, Book XI: The Four Fundamental Concepts of Psychoanalysis*, trans. Alan Sheridan (New York: W. W. Norton, 1981 [1964–1965]), p. 73.
5 Yitzhak Livneh, from a lecture given at Gordon Gallery, Tel Aviv, 2006.
6 Jacques Lacan, *The Seminar of Jacques Lacan, Book XVIII: On a Discourse That Might Not Be a Semblance* (1970–1971), trans. Cormac Gallagher (unpublished manuscript), lesson of 13 January 1971.
7 Please see Efrat Biberman, "Splendor," in *Astonishment: Yitzhak Livneh* (Exhibition Catalogue, Tel Aviv: Tel Aviv Museum, 2008), pp. 120–30.
8 Lacan, *Seminar XVIII*, lesson of 12 May 1971.
9 Jacques Lacan, *The Seminar of Jacques Lacan, Book X: Anxiety* (1962–1963), trans. Cormac Gallagher (unpublished manuscript), lesson of 19 December 62.
10 Sigmund Freud, "The Unconscious," in *The Standard Edition of the Complete Psychological Works of Sigmund Freud, Vol. XIV*, trans. and ed. James Strachey (London: Hogarth Press), pp. 166–204.
11 Lacan, *Seminar XI*, p. 89.
12 Ibid., 92.
13 Sigmund Freud, "Jokes and Their Relation to the Unconscious," in *The Standard Edition of the Complete Psychological Works of Sigmund Freud, Vol. VIII*, trans. and ed. James Strachey (London: Hogarth Press, 1960 [1905]), p. 16.
14 Ibid., p. 20.
15 Ibid., p. 20.
16 Ibid., p. 181.
17 Ibid., pp. 181, 144.
18 Lacan differentiates between the "small other" and "big Other." The small other is the fellowman, another person in respect to whom the subject is situated in imaginary relations of rivalry or narcissistic identification. The big Other is a linguistic function operative on behalf of the subject, though it may manifest in the guise of a persona. Locus at once of the unconscious and of the general treasury of signifiers, the big Other is at once extremely intimate and utterly alien to the subject.
19 Michèle Montrelay, *L'ombre et le nom: sur la féminité* (Paris: Seuil, 1977), p. 76.
20 Ibid.
21 Failure in translation is the Freudian definition of repression, as evident in Freud's Letter 52 to Fliess: "A failure of translation—this is what is known clinically as 'repression.'" See Sigmund Freud, "Extracts from the Fliess Papers: Letter 52," in *The Standard Edition of the Complete Psychological Works of Sigmund Freud, Vol. 1*, trans. and ed. James Strachey (London: Hogarth Press, 1960 [1896]), p. 235.
22 Montrelay, *L'ombre et le nom*, p. 75.
23 Viktor Shklovsky, "Art as Technique," *Russian Formalist Criticism: Four Essays*, ed. Lee T. Lemon and Marion J. Reiss (Lincoln: University of Nebraska Press, 1965 [1917]), pp. 3–57.
24 Jacques Lacan, "The Direction of the Treatment and the Principles of Its Power," in *Écrits: A Selection*, trans. Bruce Fink (New York: W. W. Norton, 1999 [1958]), p. 536.
25 Yitzhak Livneh, lecture given at the Gordon Art Gallery, Tel Aviv, 2006.
26 Jacques Lacan, *The Seminar of Jacques Lacan, Book XIII: The Object of Psychoanalysis* (1965–1966), trans. Cormac Gallagher (unpublished manuscript), lesson of 4 May 1966.
27 Ibid.
28 Sigmund Freud, "The Interpretation of Dreams," in *The Standard Edition of the Complete Psychological Works of Sigmund Freud, Vol. IV*, trans. and ed. James Strachey (London: Hogarth Press, 2001 [1900]), p. 111.

6

BETWEEN TWO DEATHS

The case of photo-painting

> But are there any tombs that are not cenotaphs?
> And is there anything photographic without kenosis?
>
> —*Jacques Derrida, 2010 [2000], p. 19*

The previous three chapters examined, from a psychoanalytic perspective, the manifestation of death in the work of art in the two prevalent artistic mediums of painting and literature. This examination made it possible to point to the presence of death in the work of art not as a thematic occurrence but as the advent of a repetition which is the death drive itself. An examination of the manifestation of the death drive in yet another artistic medium, that of photography, will make it possible to point to another facet of the presence of the death drive in culture, one that is specific to this medium. In the last fifty years, we have been witness to a relatively new artistic phenomenon known as photo-painting. An analysis of photo-painting will allow for a discussion of the death drive's manifestation in art not only as unique to a specific medium or as traversing mediumal thought but also as subsisting in a liminal zone between two visual mediums whose connection amounts to a new artistic medium in its own right.

Our psychoanalytic conceptualization of subsistence in a liminal zone draws upon Lacan's treatment, in his seventh seminar, of Sophocles's Antigone as located in the zone between two deaths. It is from the traversal of this liminal zone, Lacan explains in this seminar, that Antigone's beauty emerges. In the case at hand, that of photo-painting, the liminal zone lies between the death drive in painting and the death drive in photography. What emerges from this liminal zone is a new mode of the manifestation of the death drive in art.

Between two deaths

In the *Ethics* seminar, Lacan theorizes the zone between two deaths in his analysis of Antigone in Sophocles's play, to which we have referred in different contexts in previous chapters of this book.[1] The two deaths in question are Antigone's symbolic death and her real death. The effect of the traversal of the zone between these two deaths is the emergence of splendor, a luminescence like that of a crystal refracting a ray of light. What functions as a ray of light penetrating the crystal in the play? For Lacan, it is Antigone's desire, a desire which goes beyond the pleasure principle. In Freudian terms, this is a desire which enters the realm of the death drive. The manifestation of this desire is Antigone's refusal to obey the law commanded by King Creon. Antigone's traversal of the threshold of the pleasure principle to its beyond leads her to a realm of infinite repetition. In the case of Antigone, the repetition at stake is of the destiny of her family.

In *Antigone*, then, the effect of splendor is the result of the traversal of the zone between two deaths by means of a particular desire, a traversal leading to the realm of the death drive as repetition. This effect, Lacan argues, is what enchants the play's audience in the character of Antigone. *Antigone*, Lacan says,

> reveals to us the line of sight that defines desire. This line of sight focuses on an image that possesses a mystery which up till now has never been articulated, since it forces you to close your eyes at the very moment you look at it. Yet that image is at the center of tragedy, since it is the fascinating image of Antigone herself. We know very well that over and beyond the dialogue, over and beyond the question of family and country, over and beyond the moralizing arguments, it is Antigone herself who fascinates us, Antigone in her unbearable splendor.[2]

Antigone's beauty is not a metaphor for her moral superiority. It is the result of her going beyond the pleasure principle whose ostensible function is to preserve her life. Antigone's beauty emerges exactly at the moment when real death approaches. This end does not consist only in annihilation, a conclusion after which nothing else follows. It makes possible the repetition of the mark of a destiny of transgression and death which Lacan, following Sophocles, terms *Até*.

Between concealment and hole: two mediumal means of the presence of the death drive in visual art

The phenomenon of traversing a zone whose poles are varying manifestations of death may be discerned in the field of the visual arts as well. In this case, the zone in question is that between painting and photography, mediums each of which has its unique way to presentify the death drive as repetition. This zone is traversed by those instances of art which combine elements from both mediums. In the third chapter, we noted one form in which the death drive emerges in painting:

the painting's status as cedable object. A different form of the presence of death in painting is clarified in the zone between painting and photography: this is the function of painting as concealment. In photography, by contrast, death is present as hole. This distinction between the forms of manifestation of death in painting and in photography may already be grasped at a verbal and obvious level. The action of painting involves covering one material by another: paper by pencil, canvas by paint. The action of photography, at least up until the digital age, involves several holes or perforations: the pupil of the eye, the eyepiece, the camera lens. Yet as we will show in what follows, the presence of death in painting as concealment and in photography as a hole involves more than these explicit modes.

To understand the function of painting in relation to death as covering or concealment, we turn to Lacan's treatment of the object of the phantasm in the thirteenth seminar.[3] As theorized by Lacan, the phantasm is a fictional narrative which is of the subject's own making and in which he is the primary protagonist. The subject is inscribed within this narrative in a very specific way. Psychoanalytic treatment in cases of neurosis is directed to the traversal of this phantasm so that the subject may position himself differently in relation to it. Lacan teaches that painting and phantasm are similar in structure. Both involve parallel plains upon which the subject is inscribed. The first is the picture plane while the second is the plane of observation, where the subject is situated. Lacan shows that the laws of geometric perspective essentially correspond to the structure of the phantasm. In perspective, a system of lines and projections allows the observer to construct a picture of a world that is ostensibly completely separate from him. However, as Lacan shows, in effect, in the perspective painting the observer is always already inscribed within what he sees without knowing anything about this.[4] In other words, the seen object is never distinct from the observer. Painting's phantasmatic aspect has to do with its ability to convince the viewer that he is looking through a window into a reality of which he is not a part. This ostensibly separate reality, however, in effect conceals the way, itself impossible to depict, in which the observer is inscribed in the painting, Regardless of the degree to which a painting is realistic, naturalistic, or answers to any other convention of representation, what is depicted in painting is invariably a concealment of what cannot be depicted. The phantasm too is a picture of a world covering something unrepresentable. What the phantasm conceals is not objective reality. From a psychoanalytic perspective, the phantasm itself is *the only* psychic reality. The phantasmatic covering serves to conceal those things that are unbearable for the subject, one of which is his own death. In painting too, death is an example of something that cannot be depicted but may emerge only via its concealments, as in cases of a still life bursting with ripeness, or the representation of a person sentenced to death extending his arms.

But Lacan shows how death as unrepresentable is nevertheless present in painting. In his eleventh seminar, two years before his discussion of the relation of painting and phantasm, Lacan turns his attention to Hans Holbein's *The Ambassadors*, discussed in the previous chapter. Alongside the perspectival mode in which the ambassador figures and their backdrop are painted, *The Ambassadors* involves another form of representation. This form appears by means of the skull placed at the bottom of the painting in anamorphic distortion. Lacan states that this painting shows how

> as subjects, we are literally called into the picture, and represented here as caught. For the secret of this picture, whose implications I have pointed out to you, the kinships with the *vanitas*, . . . is given at the moment when, moving slightly away, . . . we see what the magical floating object signifies. It reflects our own nothingness, in the figure of the death's head.[5]

In other words, what is unique to this painting is its comprising two covers manifesting two conflicting modes of vision. It is precisely the clash of these two modes that enables something of the unrepresentability of death to emerge. In the instance of perspective painting, death as present—or absent—is indicated by the very term "*vanishing* point," suggesting painting's infinite, condensing the unrepresentable in a point.

If death is presentified in painting as concealment, how is it registered in photography? According to the most prevalent theory, photography is indexical by nature, that is, maintains semiotic relations which, neither iconic nor symbolic, are an imprint of the represented thing. For this reason, in the past, photography, diminishing artistic intention in favor of clarity of expression, was perceived as weak in terms of intentionality.[6] If this is the case, photography can only register death in the sense of documenting an event. This event, however, is impossible to represent and escapes attempts to capture it in visual artworks.[7] It is perhaps such a train of thought that led Siegfried Kracauer to assert that photography differs from art because, in its rejecting any presence of death, it depicts an eternal present.[8] Nonetheless, quite a few major theorists link photography not with life but with death, offering varied ways of thinking about the presence of death in the photographic image.

Thus, for instance, Susan Sontag asserts in "Melancholy Objects" that the photograph is an object of visual art that is melancholic by its very nature because it functions as an "inventory of mortality": the registration of a transitory moment in life as it moves toward death.[9] Photography's ability to capture a moment, to collect "significant details, illuminated by a flash, fixed forever," writes Sontag, positions it in a special relation to temporality. Sontag suggests that photography is a kind of visual art that allows a stolen glimpse into the suspension of temporality, the likes of which are encountered only in human life at the limit of death.

Other art theorists share Sontag's fascination with the embalming qualities of the photographic act, focusing less on the thematic relations between these qualities and more on their structural, aesthetic and conceptual consequences. For instance, Paul Virilio in his *The Vision Machine* writes about the ability of the photographic act to freeze the flow of time. Quoting sculptor August Rodin, Virilio writes that as opposed to the act of sculpting, spread out over diachronic, chronological time, the photographic act is a flash, a fleeting instant capable of suspending time by creating an image of a frozen moment, shed from diachronic temporality like the moment of death.[10]

Philippe Dubois's *L'acte photographique* too deals extensively with the relation between photography and death. According to Dubois, photography is not what denies death but a means of writing death, what he terms "thanatography."[11] For Dubois, what makes photography a means of inscribing death is precisely the technology which Kracauer claims makes photography death-denying. Dubois claims that photographic technology isolates a moment from the flow of time and embalms it in the timeless dimension of the photographic image, replicating the structure of the transition between life and death.[12] "At the very moment the photograph is taken," Dubois writes, "the photographed object vanishes . . . banished for all time to the realm of shadows." Like Eurydice in the myth of Orpheus, Dubois adds, the photographed object becomes dead for the very fact of having been seen.[13] If so, the photographic act creates "a hole in time" in the diachronic continuum.[14] The frozen image, a fragment the photographic act carves out from diachronic time in what Dubois calls "photographic Medusation," situates itself in a dimension beyond time, enters the extra-temporality of death, the realm of shadows and stone.[15]

In *Camera Lucida*, an essay dealing with a childhood photograph of his late mother, Roland Barthes too interrogates the fundamental connection between photography and death. Barthes writes: "Ultimately, what I am seeking in the photograph taken of me (the "intention" according to which I look at it) is Death: Death is the *eidos* of that Photograph."[16] Further on he notes:

> [T]he photograph's immobility is somehow the result of a perverse confusion between two concepts: the Real and the Live: by attesting that the object has been real, the photograph surreptitiously induces belief that it is alive, because of that delusion which makes us attribute to Reality an absolutely superior, somehow eternal value; but by shifting this reality to the past ("this-has-been"), the photograph suggests that it is already dead.[17]

Toward the end of the book, Barthes argues that photography's singularity stems from the way in which it reveals the flatness of death's visibility. The photograph reflects death in its meaninglessness, in the inability to say anything about it. It bestows visibility on the corpse, but leaves death in many ways invisible, or perhaps exposes the death of every person photographed, whether living or dead.

In his article published two years prior to *Camera Lucida*, Thierry de Duve analyses the perception of time unique to photography, differentiating between two photographic practices: snapshot and time-exposure, and linking each with a different aspect of death.[18] De Duve argues that the snapshot is related to death in its pointing to the death of its referent, to the vanishing of the past, to the cessation of time. Time-exposure photography points to its beyond, where life goes on, time continues to flow, and the seemingly trapped object escapes. While "the snapshot stole a life it could not return, the time exposure expresses a life that it never received."[19] Unlike the snapshot, which refers to life as a developing process, time-exposure refers to an imaginary life, discontinuous and reversible, a life which takes place on the surface of the printed photograph alone. Whereas the snapshot is characterized by the death it shows on its surface, time-exposure relates to death as a state of what has already been: "the fixity and defection of time, its absolute zero."[20] As the article progresses, de Duve shows how his perception of photography offers a new category of time and space. The snapshot suggests a conjunction of "here and formerly" as opposed to time-exposure which conjoins "now and there." To qualify his assertion, de Duve compares two photographs: a photo of the execution of a Vietcong soldier taken by Eddie Adams and Julia Margaret Cameron's portrait of Thomas Carlyle.

De Duve shows that the photograph, irrespective of its content, demonstrates an impossible dimension of time. This emerges clearly in the photo of the soldier's execution with "the sudden vanishing of the present tense, splitting into

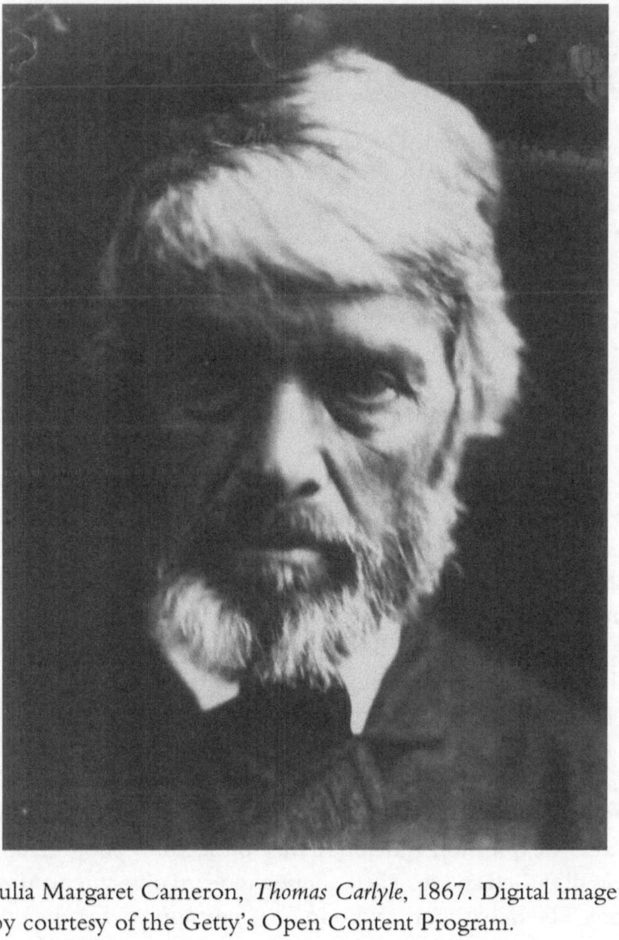

FIGURE 6.1 Julia Margaret Cameron, *Thomas Carlyle*, 1867. Digital image reproduced by courtesy of the Getty's Open Content Program.

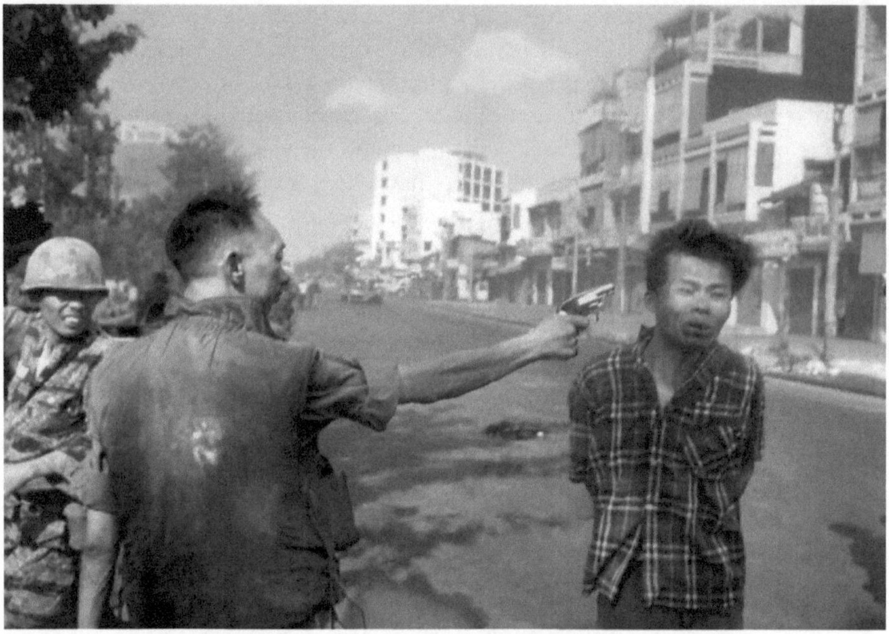

FIGURE 6.2 Eddie Adams, South Vietnamese National Police Chief Brig. Nguyen Ngoc Loan executes a Vietcong officer with a single pistol shot in the head, 1968. © Associated Press. Image reproduced by courtesy of AP Images.

the contradiction of being simultaneously too late and too early, that is properly unbearable."[21] According to de Duve, it is this paradox which forms the traumatic foundation of photography, irrespective of the image it depicts. Beyond the meaning of this image, it is this traumatic foundation that evokes horror at the moment of its being seen.

From a psychoanalytic perspective, the theories asserting a relation between photography and death we have examined so far are in effect themselves an instance of the death drive in culture whose manifestations we have been studying throughout this book. As is the case with any manifestation of repetition, psychoanalysis has little to learn from the very fact of the recurrence of the death drive in culture. It has much to learn, however, from the phenomenology of specific repetitions, that is to say, from the unique way in which each repetition is present at the level of artistic practice. From a psychoanalytic perspective, then, the question to be posed is what precisely distinguishes photographic manifestations of the death drive from manifestations of the death drive in painting. What we will claim is that photography has its own mode of presentifying the death drive, different from the modes of expression and appearance of death in photography delineated by the theorists discussed above. This unique mode involves the nature of the photograph as hole. The only theorist who in our view approaches the psychoanalytic perspective we will shortly propose is Barthes, whose view of the *punctum* is based, if only implicitly, on the teachings of Lacan.

In his study of photography, Barthes differentiates between two fundamental concepts: *studium* and *punctum*.[22] While the *studium* relates to "official" information derivable from the photographic image, the *punctum* is some photographic detail which pierces the coherent construction of reality established by the *studium* and consequently also wounds the viewer. Barthes writes that "these marks, these wounds are so many points. This second element which will disturb the *studium* I shall therefore call *punctum*; for *punctum* is also: sting, speck, cut, little hole—and also a cast of the dice. A photograph's *punctum* is that accident which pricks me (but also bruises me, is poignant to me)."[23]

In the second part of the book, Barthes meditates on a photograph of his late mother. The particularity of his meditation makes it possible to draw a theoretical conclusion concerning the temporality of the *punctum*. When a grieving Barthes looks through his mother's pictures, he discovers a childhood photo embodying something essential to her character: "that untenable paradox which she had nonetheless maintained all her life: the assertion of a gentleness."[24] In effect, this coherent description of the figure in the scene is of the order of what Barthes terms "*stadium*." However, later on, Barthes describes the influence looking at the picture had on him: a confrontation with his own death, which henceforth waits for him.[25] What this suggests is that the moment shortly after his mother's death when Barthes looks at the photo of his mother as a child constitutes the puncturing of the *studium* by the *punctum*, and that it is this moment which wounds Barthes. The mother's childhood photo presentifies Barthes's death as a future event, just as Alexander Gardner's photograph of the young man sentenced to death which Barthes discusses later in the book presentifies the handsome man's impending demise.[26] Barthes writes: "By giving me the absolute past of the pose (aorist), the photograph tells me death in the future. What pricks me is the discovery of this equivalence."[27] This is, of course, the *punctum* as Barthes theorizes it—the *punctum* which pierces, punctures, perforates—and the death to which Barthes refers is none other than the death of the photo's observer. What this means is that the *punctum*'s temporality exists in the gap between the moment of looking at the picture and the moment of the observer's death, which the picture elicits for him.

According to Barthes, then, death is present in the photograph by means of the temporal structure which necessarily assumes a gap between the time of photographic registration and the moment of the observer's death. What we wish to suggest is that in photography death emerges not between two events situated on the same temporal continuum, but in a different temporal structure which involves a tear in continuity, a hole which perforates the screen of complete and cohesive representation as well as the model of diachronic, linear time. It is thus that photography makes present an impossible moment which lies outside diachrony, a moment which cannot be registered within diachrony and therefore constitutes a hole in it. What is at stake here is not the freezing of a moment on the temporal continuum as suggested by theorists discussed above like Sontag, Virilio and

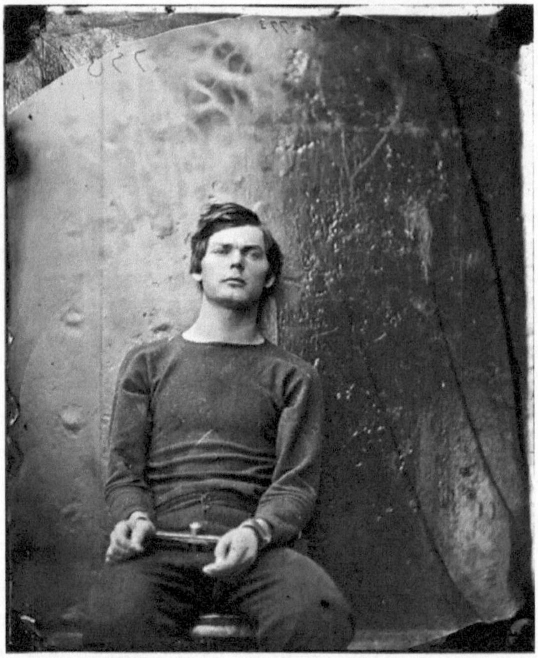

FIGURE 6.3 Alexander Gardner, *Portrait of Lewis Payne*, 1865. The digital image is in the public domain.

Dubois, but the rending of the continuum itself. This tear is what makes the continuum possible, just as the source of every representation is loss.

In psychoanalytic terms, painting may be conceived as covering or concealment and the photograph as hole. Both are cultural inventions for treating what manifests itself as the unbearable repetition of the death drive, saturated with jouissance. Painting deals with this repetition in its function as cover or means of concealment. It is precisely at this point in structure that photography tears open a hole.

Between painting and photography

If painting and photography each have their own means of making the death drive present in culture, what might be said, from a psychoanalytic perspective, as to the relation between those means? Theoretical discourse regarding the relation between painting and photography tends to present the connection between these mediums in two ways. One of these regards painting and photography as opposite poles while the other views them as situated on a spectrum. Something of the first type of theoretical discourse appears explicitly in the work of Benjamin, who points to certain characteristics of painting such as the halo and singularity that are absent from photography.[28] The understanding of photography but not painting as indexical discussed above is another example of this theoretical stance. Yet another involves the distinctions made between painting and photography with respect to intentionality. Photography seems less intentional than painting, as the camera documents reality regardless of the predominant intention of the person behind it. This is the claim made, for instance, by Michael Fried in his article on German photographer Thomas Demand.[29] Fried argues that Demand's uniqueness lies in his restoration of intentionality to photography by reconstructing historically and culturally intense sites from paper alone while granting meticulous attention to photographic quality. Kracauer similarly views painting and photography as dichotomous, in this instance regarding their relation to death and its representation. Kracauer argues that the work of art contains a monogram of history. In any given work of art, this monogram brings the knowledge of death to the most profound possible resolution, working against repression.[30] Photography, however, does not involve such a monogram of history. According to Kracauer, it blocks visibility by the very fact of posing a photographed image which provides an illusion of knowledge regarding the image's referent, which is precisely what the photograph conceals.[31]

The second view, according to which photography and painting are situated on the same axis, originates from those discussions which hold perspective painting to be the foundation of photography. A clear expression of this position may be found in an article by Peter Galasi, who argues that photography is an invention which is not disconnected from the history of art and should be viewed as part of a continuum of pictorial modes and forms of organization of pictorial space.[32]

From a psychoanalytic perspective, what matters is not arbitrating between these two schools of thought regarding the relation between photography and painting, but examining what occurs in the gap between them as two forms of the manifestation and treatment of jouissant repetition in culture. What emerges in this gap is a new artistic form combining photography and painting: photo-painting. How might the appearance of this practice between two forms of the death drive's manifestation in culture be considered in psychoanalytic terms? As we have shown, the field of art in Western culture is charged with repetition, pulsates with the death drive. From their very inception, art and the discourse concerning it have been connected to the moment of annihilation followed by reverberations whose condition is this annihilation itself. From a certain moment in culture, which we identified in Hegel's *Aesthetics*, this repetition rises to a higher power because it is reflected on, that is to say, in psychoanalytic terms, subjectivated. Henceforth, the relation of death to art assumes the form of repeated declarations of the death of art on the level of theory, while on the level of artistic practice repetition assumes the form of renewals of art spurred by the declarations of art's demise. It is precisely at such a moment of renewal that photo-painting emerges.

Thus, for instance, the rise of conceptual art toward the late 1960s and the 1970s ostensibly involved the death of painting—at least figurative painting. In the early 1980s, painting flourished once again, thanks to a group of Italian artists, among them Enzo Cucchi, Sandro Chia and Francesco Clemente. It was this same period that witnessed the rise of a group of German painters, the most prominent among them Gerhard Richter, Sigmar Polke, and Georg Baselitz. Painting also returns in the activities of various American artists, such as Erich Fischl, David Salle, and Robert Longo. Another wave of a renewal in painting took place at the turn of the millennium, after years when mediums such as installation, video and digital art had taken its place. One of the characteristics of some of these returns of painting was an increasing use of photography in the process of painterly production. Around the 1960s a new form of painting emerged, with photography at its backdrop, a form most explicitly formulated by Richter, who termed it photo-painting.

The preoccupation with painting on the basis of photography and with the relation between painting and photography it precipitates is well manifest in the curating of this new art form and in the writing about it. Photo-painting is a clear instance of repetition in artistic practice for which proclamations of death function as structural condition. What is unique about this repetition is that the materiality of its medium is liminal. Beyond its being yet another manifestation of the death drive in culture, photo-painting is located between two different material modes of repetition in the field of visual art. As Lacan suggests in his eleventh seminar, in the visual field, it is precisely in such an in-between that something of the real emerges.[33]

Lacan argues that "in our relation to things, in so far as this relation is constituted by the way of vision, and ordered in the figures of representation, something is transmitted, from stage to stage, and is always to some degree eluded in it—that is what we call the gaze."[34] If we consider painting and photography as two stages of representation, Lacan's statement can be read as pertaining to what occurs between them. The eye, according to Lacan, is an agent of a coherent, complete, and well-formulated vision ascribable to the imaginary order because of its compliance with the subject's ordered perception of reality. The gaze, for its part, is the object cause of desire, the object propelling the subject, as it appears in the visual field. The gaze is of the order of the real, and as such is subject to neither formulation nor representation, but it is nevertheless present in the picture. The presence of the gaze in the picture is predicated on modes of representation. It pertains to the gap between different stages of representation, and elides these stages of which it is a product. It is the presence of an absence, for the gaze is not a positive value susceptible to manifestation or representation but what emerges from their elision. Lacan later shows how the gaze is present in its absence precisely in those paintings where representational technique is present in all its glory, like those employing perspective or *trompe-l'oeil*. What is most significant for the discourse on art in Lacan's theorization of the gaze is his emphasizing that the gaze as the essential core granting painting its singularity and power emerges in the gap between different stages of representation. Photo-painting is a practice situated precisely in such a gap between two stages of representation in the visual field, as well as between two modes of confronting the real. It is therefore an intense cultural site where something of the real forcefully emerges. In what follows, we will discuss three instances of photo-painting: the works of Gerhard Richter, Yitzhak Livneh and Deganit Berest. The analysis of these cases will allow us to demonstrate that photo-painting is an intense cultural site where two artistic modes of treating death coalesce, enabling the death drive to appear as an invigorating repetition.

Photo-painting: the case of Gerhard Richter

From an early period, when he worked at a photo laboratory and was enchanted by the vast number of images to which he was exposed every day, Gerhard Richter always had a fondness for photography. When early on in his career he moved from his birthplace of Dresden in East Germany to Dusseldorf in the West, he began collecting photographs: amateur snapshots of family and friends, commercial photos from newspapers and advertisements, official portraits, and many more. Richter continues collecting photos, preserving and cataloging them, though not necessarily in chronological order. At some point, he turns some of these into paintings. This is a continuous and cumulative process, a project Richter calls *Atlas*. When Richter first presented the project as several sequences of photos arranged in groups on panels, he had more than three hundred panels. Today over eight hundred such panels are displayed on his website.

These photographs, which may be thought of as ready-mades, not only are used as preparation to painting but also constitute an inextricable element of Richter's *oeuvre*. It is also as such that they are displayed. Nevertheless, some of these photos do later become paintings, or as Richter calls them, photo-paintings: painted photos or paintings which bear their photographic origin within themselves. The transformation of a photograph into a painting necessarily changes the manner in which the visual object is encountered. Moreover, as Richter himself asserts, the purpose of his work on these visual objects is not to use photography as a means of painting but to use painting as a means of photography, although the final product is for all intents and purposes an oil painting in which traces of photography are perceptible only in features such as blurring, the black and white color, or the inclusion of text in the image.[35]

The signifier "death" appears in many ways on the iconographic level of Richter's photo-paintings and the varying images constituting the *Atlas* project. This is apparent in the skull and candle paintings alluding to the *vanitas* artworks of Dutch Baroque, or in the paintings of Allied airplanes bombing German cities. It is also apparent in paintings made from photographed portraits of young women from a nursing school who were later murdered. Death is iconographically present even more explicitly in Richter's painting cycle *18 October 1977*, which treats photographic images which accompanied the press coverage of the suicides of imprisoned members of the Baader-Meinhof group.[36] The motif of death appears, if only indirectly, in the series of gray photographs Richter exhibited at the Deutsche Guggenheim in Berlin in 2002. In his article for the exhibition catalog, Benjamin Buchloh shows that this series of abstract paintings was preceded by another work, commissioned for the Reichstag in Berlin. As is patently apparent from the preparatory work for this project, Richter initially intended to use photographs of concentration camp prisoners. It was only in the course of working on the project that Richter changed its direction, tilting it toward abstract painting.[37] Various interpretations of Richter's works have discussed their relation with death, firmly anchoring this connection in theory. After looking at two such theory-based interpretations, we will show that the connection to death as it emerges in Richter's work is not limited to artistic strategy and practice. Instead, what is at stake is a connection inherent to the very foundation of photo-painting. Richter's works clearly embody this foundation as what emerges in the gap between painting and photography.

Buchloh and Osborne on the representation of death in Richter's works

In an article from the late 1990s, Buchloh extensively examines Richter's *Atlas* project against the backdrop of similar historical precedents of collecting, cataloging, and arranging photographs.[38] The placement of *Atlas* alongside these precedents allows Buchloh to qualify and analyze this enigmatic project. Because Richter's project is constituted of panels on which various photos and images are fixed, it has a didactic appearance. Examining it against the backdrop of photographic works from the early twentieth century, like those of Kasimir Malevich and Hannah Hoch, makes it possible to explore the characteristics of the project's mode of display. Buchloh finds a further precedent for Richter's *Atlas* in the extensive project of art historian Aby Warburg, who in the 1920s placed various images, photographic and otherwise, on wooden panels covered with canvas, in a project named after the goddess of memory, the atlas of *Mnemosyne*.

Later in his article Buchloh claims that Warburg's project, which has been interpreted as an attempt to group and organize the collective memory of Western culture around the time of its destruction, serves as an inverted mirror image of Richter's *Atlas*, which is based on an attempt to reflect, after the fact, on the destructive effects Warburg anticipated from a position of denial and repression.[39]

Buchloh locates Richter's *Atlas* in an intermediary zone between two opposing perspectives on photography in relation to memory and its construction. One perspective is that of Kracauer, who maintains that photography involves an inundation with images which rather than aiding memory brings about its erasure. Kracauer claims that this attack of imagery is so overpowering it threatens to destroy the very awareness of things. The photographed image prevents its observers from seeing the represented world. Thus, although photography seems to inundate the viewer with information, what it actually brings about is an erasure of information.[40] Buchloh does, however, mention an opposite stance, that of Benjamin in *A Short History of Photography*. As opposed to Kracauer's pessimistic vision, Benjamin sees the promise inherent in these new artistic mediums.[41]

Posing Richter's *Atlas* project between these two opposing perspectives of photography in relation to the construction of memory becomes significant when one looks at the early *Atlas* panels. These panels include family photos and amateur snapshots, the likes of which interested theorists of photography from Kracauer through Benjamin to Barthes.[42] The panels which follow, on the other hand, include magazine photos and printed images. These panels were made after

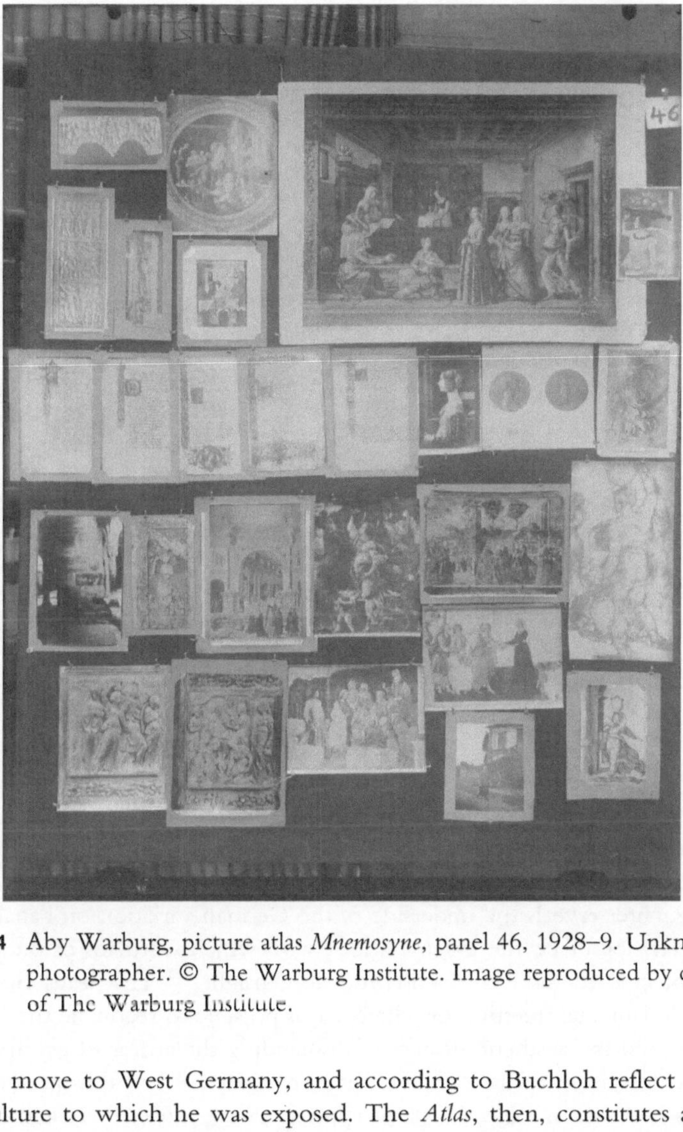

FIGURE 6.4 Aby Warburg, picture atlas *Mnemosyne*, panel 46, 1928–9. Unknown photographer. © The Warburg Institute. Image reproduced by courtesy of The Warburg Institute.

Richter's move to West Germany, and according to Buchloh reflect the consumer culture to which he was exposed. The *Atlas*, then, constitutes a kind of archaeology of pictorial and photographic registers, each of a distinct photographic form, each evoking a different emotional response, but all intersecting. Buchloh understands the shift in photographic subject matter, the movement from amateur family photos to those appearing in the later panels, and the intersection of all these types of photos in the panels, as constituting a complex sphere of disavowals and displacements, repressions and concealments, in which memory is forged by means of photographs. By constituting this sphere, Richter produces a system of signs and new languages which function outside conventional configurations of memory.[43]

Inundating the viewer with images enables Richter, then, to bridge the gap between seemingly contradictory models of photography in relation to memory:

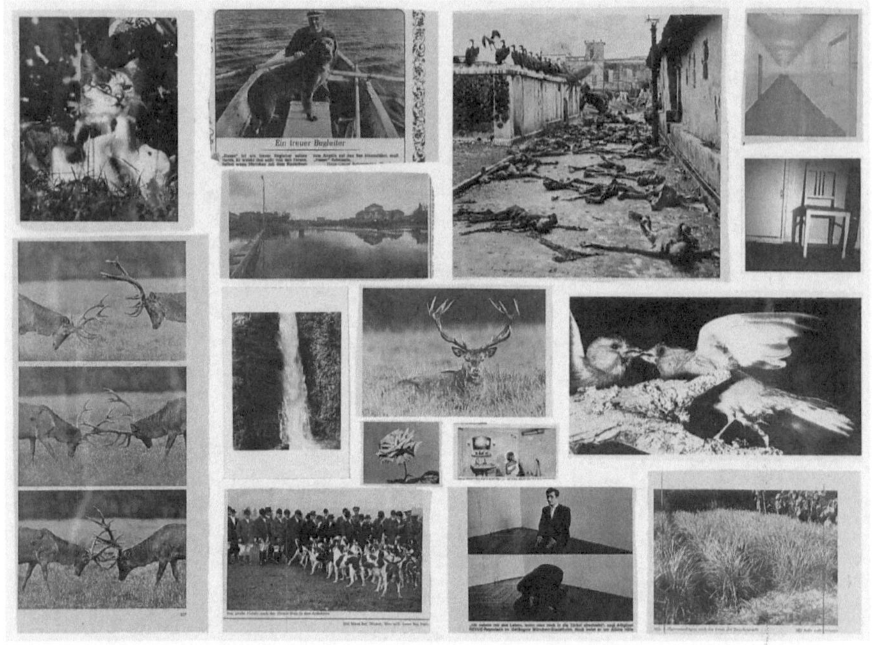

FIGURE 6.5 Gerhard Richter, *Newspaper Photos, Atlas Sheet 11*, 1963. © Gerhard Richter Images. Image reproduced by courtesy of the artist.

the model assuming that photography has an ability to organize and catalog, and the model assuming that photography itself, because of the inundation of imagery it generates, serves as an impediment to both memory and knowledge. In bridging this gap, Richter reveals the underside of the German variation on banality: "the collective lack of affect, the psychic armor with which Germans of the post-war period protected themselves against historical insight."[44] This leads Buchloh to pose the fundamental question of whether it is possible to reconcile the insistence on banality and the aesthetic project of dismantling the armor of psychic repression.[45] Buchloh believes that Richter at least partially answers this question in the first panels of *Atlas*. In *Panel 11*, dated approximately 1964–1965, landscapes and images of deer appear together with horrendous images from concentration camps, similar to those that appeared in the preparatory work for the Reichstag project.

Buchloh regards these images as instances of puncturing which locate the project at the heart of the dialectic of memory and amnesia. Pointing to a link between the image and its referent in an age saturated by empty imagery, they function as a sudden revelation. Paradoxically, Richter's *Atlas* functions as a pendulum swinging between "the death of reality in the photograph and the reality of death in the mnemonic image."[46]

For Buchloh, then, the *Atlas* project makes it possible to examine and analyze photography and photographic collection in their relation to memory, repression, forgetting and—by extension—death and obliteration. Yet Buchloh's argument is based on only one panel among the hundreds comprised in this project.

In another article extensively discussing Richter's photo-painting, Peter Osborne argues that the principal foundation at the base of this painting strategy is negation, a negation he links to the Hegelian concept of sublation (*Aufhebung*) and various proclamations of the death of art.[47] Osborne suggests constructing the logic of Richter's artistic operation as a double negation: the negation of painting by photography and the negation of photography by painting.[48] The perception of photography as a threat to painting is as old as photography itself. Although the many transformations in painting in the course of the twentieth century, such as the crisis of abstract art and its resolution, have to some extent alleviated this threat, it remains looming. Richter's response to the crises encountered by painting was an insistence on this medium. Photo-painting, Osborne argues, is an affirmation of photography by painting and of painting by photography. Although photography has declared itself the primal mode of producing naturalistic imagery and is generally preferred over painting for producing images, photo-painting is ultimately, for all intents and purposes, painting. If photo-painting, which is based on photographic forms, affirms the negation of painting by photography, it simultaneously negates this negation by demonstrating that painting is still valid after all.[49]

Osborne notes three precedents to this double negation. The first is a mathematical double negative, in which the second negation refutes its predecessor and thus cancels it, returning to a point of outset. This double negation is not adequate for describing Richter's artistic procedure as it involves an absolute canceling out the first negation, which in Richter's case is the negation of painting by photography. The second precedent Osborne mentions is the Hegelian double negation, that is to say, sublation. However, this double negation too is not adequate for describing Richter's work. Sublation implies raising to a higher level, which in this instance would be the victory of painting and its transcending itself while attaining a higher degree of artistic representation. Such a description, Osborne writes, does not fit Richter's work, characterized far more by restlessness and perpetual seeking than by any sense of triumph or complacency.[50] The third double negation Osborne considers is Theodor Adorno's negative dialectic. This is a negation which neither returns to its starting point nor rises to a higher level, but "dwells on the reciprocal negativity of the nonidentity of the two terms, and finds there, within the determinacy of their mutual negation, the utopian shadow of the reconciliation it is denied."[51] Osborne reads Richter's photo-paintings as a system of negatives: negatives of paintings, negatives of photographs—none of which supersedes the other. This is a kind of impasse which points—negatively—beyond itself. It is here that Osborne finds hope: Richter paints beyond the end of painting, conscious of the uncertain state of painting in such conditions. In painting the negation of painting, Richter paints another negation, the negation of the negation of painting. He does this not by elevating painting to a higher level, but while interrogating the double negations he encounters. To explain the significance of double negations as they appear in Richter's painting, Osborne turns to de Duve's discussion of the relation between painting and ready-made. According to de Duve, one of the radical consequences of ready-made is its marking a cut between art and craft. This is because the ready-made demonstrates that the art object may exist without it. Ready-made thus releases painting from its history, rendering it an object whose definition is unstable. This does not mean, however, that painting is negated. Painting after ready-made is redefined in terms that are unstable. From the very fact of its now being postconceptual painting, painting thus often needs to justify itself. Osborne concludes that Richter's photo-painting is located precisely in this sphere of painting after ready-made, and as such must reestablish a relation to the craft of painting. In other words, according to Osborne, the dialectic space between craft and conceptuality is precisely the realm of photo-painting.[52] The singularity of Richter's work lies not in its deviation from contemporary art but in its distancing of itself from contemporary art in the very process of contending with it. Richter, in other words, succeeds in being a contemporary artist precisely in the way in which he constructs his path while distancing himself from the field of contemporary art. Richter manages to operate within the impossibility of painting while fully aware of this impossibility. Thus he "render[s] determinate: a contradiction between the end of painting as a living form of collective representation and its continuation within the art institution on the basis of a serial ingenuity."[53]

Despite the many differences between Buchloh's and Osborne's approaches to Richter's work, both tie it to annihilation, impossibility and termination. Both also locate Richter's practice on a boundary, an uncertain liminal space. For Richter, this space is not an impasse but fertile ground precisely because it is an intermediary place impossible to settle and harmonize.

From a psychoanalytic perspective too, Richter's photo-painting is situated on a boundary or in a liminal space. The relation between this kind of painting and the death drive is neither thematic nor conceptual. This form of painting is itself a particular instance of the death drive in culture. The particularity of this manifestation lies in its traversal of the zone between two deaths, in the way that painting and photography—each in its own fashion—respond to the encounter with a real.

Photo-painting between two deaths

One of the most prominent features of Richter's photo-paintings is blurring. In effect, this is the hallmark of his works, which have the appearance of photographic images that have gone out of focus. But photo-painting retains its link to photography not only because of the photo at its basis or its use of blurring. It markedly alludes to photography also in its use of cropping, monochrome, or the combination of text and imagery. It is a form of painting that in almost every aspect makes present the photograph that engendered it—a photograph and not an image of reality.

As noted above, the relation to death emerges in Richter's paintings through their very means of production. Initially created as a figurative painting in every respect, and one that is fully in focus, the painting is blurred only later, acquiring photographic qualities that often have the appearance of disturbances in vision. By its way of coming into being, the painting points to the possibility of its utter obliteration. Richter creates the painting and then erases it, and while erasure is never complete, complete erasure is inevitably the painting's horizon. The observer is invited to extract the image from the painting, while the disturbance to vision only increases the desire to see.

If death is present in painting as covering or concealment, and in photography as hole, how is it present in photo-painting? Works of art that are of the order of photo-painting make a hole emerge by means of a cover. In order to demonstrate the result of this double negation, we will examine one of the paintings from *18 October 1977*: the work *Tote* (Dead), where Ulrike Meinhof is seen after having been taken down from the noose, whose marks are noticeable on her neck.

What does this painting cover? Not the lifeless corpse condemned to decay, but a moment extracted from continuity, an impossible moment torn from diachrony which a photograph seemingly managed to capture, leaving a hole in its wake. The repetition of this image by painting serves to intensify the presence of this hole which it also conceals. At the same time, the painterly reconstruction of photographic effects such as blurring and the use of black and white reinforces the hole's concealment.

As the tear in temporal continuity is a matter of structure that has no necessary connection to the contents of the image, it requires no demonstration by

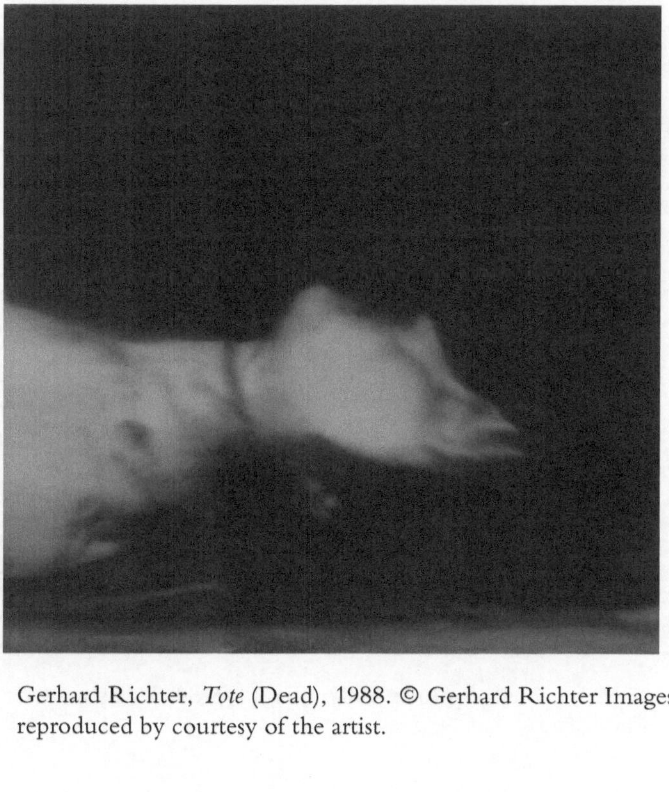

FIGURE 6.6 Gerhard Richter, *Tote* (Dead), 1988. © Gerhard Richter Images. Image reproduced by courtesy of the artist.

means of explicit images of death. It is presentified and embodied by the very use of photographic visibility and its translation into modes of painting. This may be demonstrated through the work of Israeli artists whose photo-paintings, like Richter's, make use of disturbances to visibility characteristic of photography: Yitzhak Livneh, who exaggerates color stains on photographic surfaces of light and shadow, and Deganit Berest, who dismantles images into digital units of information, pixels.

In the early 2000s, Livneh painted several series of works based on photographic images from various sources: ruins, architectonic environments in nocturnal lighting, flowers, or soldiers at the moment of their death. The works are painted in monochromatic colors, with tonal range and contrasting transitions from illuminated to shaded surfaces. They are painted after the original photographic image is projected onto the painting's canvas. Death as theme is present in Livneh's works from early on, as of the 1980s.[54] What makes Livneh's painting series of the 2000s unique is that they manifest death not in their theme but in their painterly means of production as well as their location in the zone between painting and photography. These paintings retain the photographic image in their background, but beyond this, retain something of photographic technique, specifically the way in which the camera processes transitions between light and shadow. Translated into painting, these transitions become nearly abstract color stains, from which an image emerges. The works are nevertheless painting in every sense of this term, in which

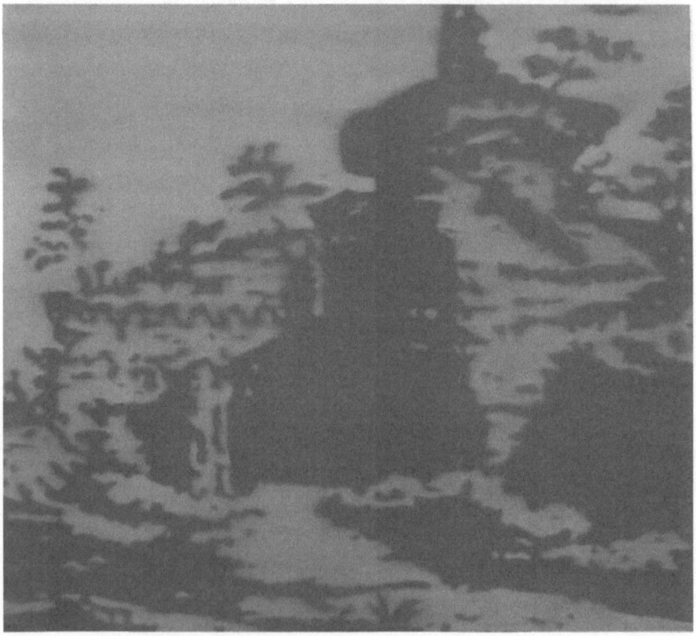

FIGURE 6.7 Yitzhak Livneh, *Big Ruin*, 2002. Image reproduced by courtesy of the artist.

the application of paint to canvas creates a radiant and warm effect. The intermingling of painting and photography confronts the viewer with an object whose status is not clear. These paintings appear in many respects as ghosts of painting, as images shining from the canvas after having been mysteriously inscribed in it by an imprinting or projection which continues to glow long after its source of light has been dimmed.

The painterly repetition of a photographic image which continues to appear through the painted canvas is in line with the process we described above, that of presentifying a hole by means of concealment. Whether the painting in question is of ruins, of an office in strange nocturnal lighting, or of the sculpted faces of fallen soldiers, its photographic source is evident in it. The painting processes this source, at once flattening the image and endowing it with materiality. It distils the photographic source into pure painterliness while preserving something of the moment of its tearing from temporal continuity, a moment that is of the very essence of photography. The result is a visual image which exists in the zone between these two modes of representation.

Another example may be found in the works of Deganit Berest. Berest's artistic work has explored painting, photography and the meeting point between them ever since she began working in the mid-1970s. Berest's preoccupation with the boundary between painting and photography is as prevalent as it is multifaceted. An early example is from the series *From the Atlas (The Dead Sea)* (1976), comprising

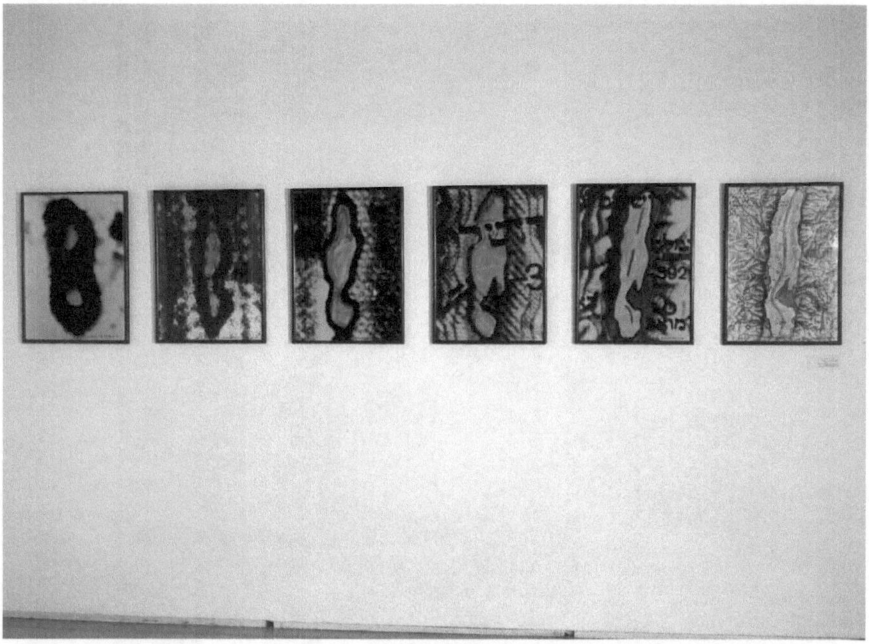

FIGURE 6.8 Deganit Berest, *From the Atlas (The Dead Sea)*, 1976. Image reproduced by courtesy of the artist.

six pieces, each of which includes a cartographic image of the Dead Sea as appearing in geographic maps of varying scales. The image is magnified and processed in watercolor, its momentous enlargement distorting its familiar form.

In Berest's later works, the relation between painting and photography even is more significantly present, as Berest treats photographic works by means of painting while dismantling the photographic image. In an article from 1996, Roee Rosen discusses the similarities and differences between Richter's *18 October 1977* series and Berest's 1992 work *M2*, where a photographic image of a masked figure is dismantled into vertical stripes which disrupt and distort it.[55]

According to Rosen, Richter's works clearly suggest political ambivalence, while Berest's masked figure, for all its political connotations, is appropriated into the artist's aesthetic world.[56] Rosen concludes: "[T]he viewer in Richter's work is confronted with a clearly defined problematic—ambivalence and helplessness in the face of a harsh political reality; the viewer of Berest's work must exert his eyes to return a no less harsh reality to itself, after it has been detached, isolated and veiled by the mechanism of art."[57] In other words, while Richter's artistic process heightens the ambivalence of the charged image it treats, in Berest's work the image is divested of its political charge to the benefit of its aesthetic properties.

Despite this difference, we wish to point out a common factor in the works of Richter and Berest. Their photo-paintings, each in its own way, reveal something

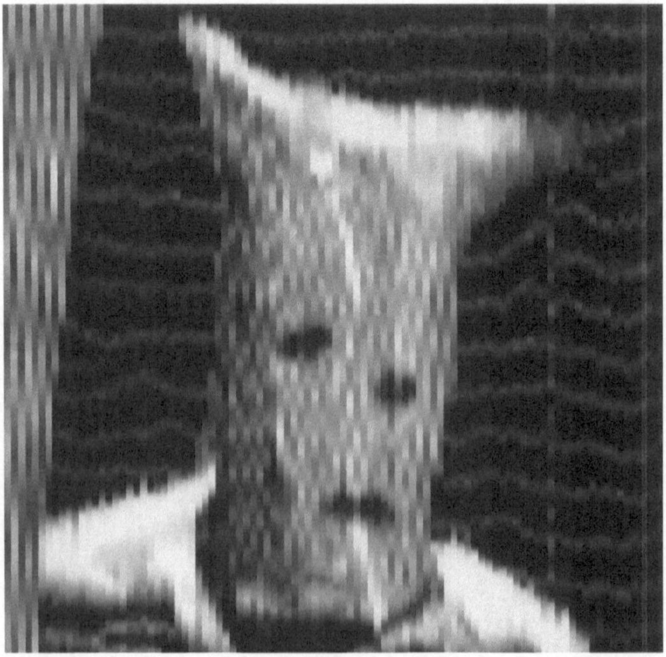

FIGURE 6.9 Deganit Berest, *M2*, 1992. Image reproduced by courtesy of the artist.

of the real—a remainder which escapes the order of the coherent and complete representation—in their very positioning in a zone between painting and photography. The presence of this remainder in Richter and Berest's photo-paintings is suggested also in Rosen's commentary, for instance, when he notes the helplessness of the observer of Richter's works, confronted with a harsh reality, and the effort of the viewer of Berest's work to return this harsh reality to the image which relinquished it in favor of artistic expression. The ambivalent position arising from Richter's works, and the need to unify the dislocation of content and artistic form precipitated by Berest's work, are, we wish to claim, two forms of veiling death's double presence (concealment and hole) in these works.

A text which accompanied a comprehensive exhibition of Berest's artwork at the Haifa Museum of Art in 2004 explicitly noted the preoccupation with death in several of the artist's series.[58] Tali Tamir writes: "[I]t would seem that what was not observed in Deganit Berest's work all these years is the allusion to the menacing presence of death, which appears also as the negative of creative power: the waiting for the moment of dawn, the moment in which all will become clear, burst into life, be delivered, distinguished by but a hair's breadth from the dimmed state, the stained, the 'Monstrous.'"[59] Unlike many art critics which regard Berest's work as preoccupied with an ironic presentation of scientific investigations, Tamir regards these works as dealing with another theme that is less conceptual and remote: "in this midlife exhibition, Berest talks through the image of the broken classical sculpture, about death that gnaws away at life, about illness that spoils beauty and about the foundation of the whole, the classical which was there in the very beginning."[60]

Tamir suggests an interpretation which shifts the discussion surrounding Berest's artwork from conceptual irony to the psychic realm. While not disagreeing with this point, we suggest that the subject of death in Berest's work is to be located neither as a figurative theme nor as what is diametrically opposed to life. Rather, death is an integral part of her artwork. Far from being a late addition derived from a hitherto untreated semantic realm, it is manifest in her work from its inception in its combination of painting and photography. In recent years, Berest's preoccupation with the transition between painting and photography as a structural site in which death appears is manifest in works where the photographic image is painted as dismantled into units of color, similar to pixels. One example of this type of work is the piece *Untitled* (2004), in which a pair of legs juts out from the ocean.

We wish to consider this work against the backdrop of another of Berest's pieces, *Icarus* (2004), which includes the very same image in photographic form. In the photographic image, which alludes to Peter Bruegel's *Landscape with the Fall of Icarus* (1558), the pair of legs, found almost at the center of the frame, are miniscule in comparison to their scale.

Despite the small size of the image, its centrality makes it prominent against the blue background of the ocean. The clear and unmistakable shape of the legs enhances the lack of clarity of other elements in the photo, such as the pair of

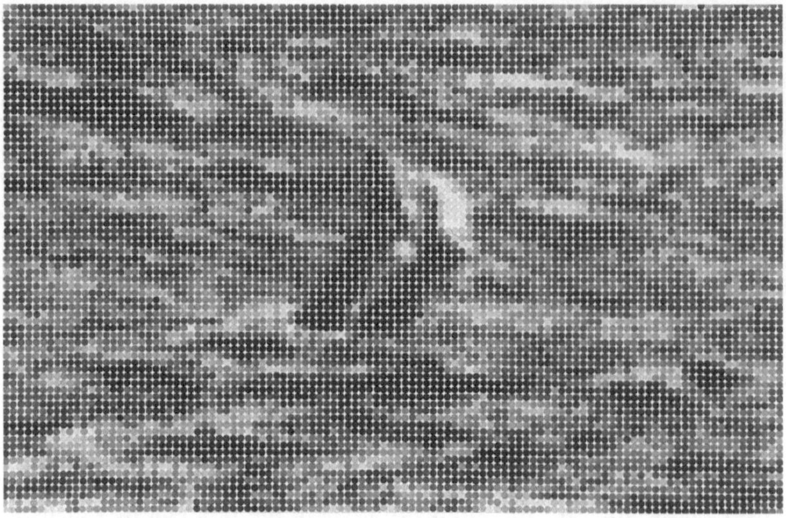

FIGURE 6.10 Deganit Berest, *Untitled*, 2004. Image reproduced by courtesy of the artist.

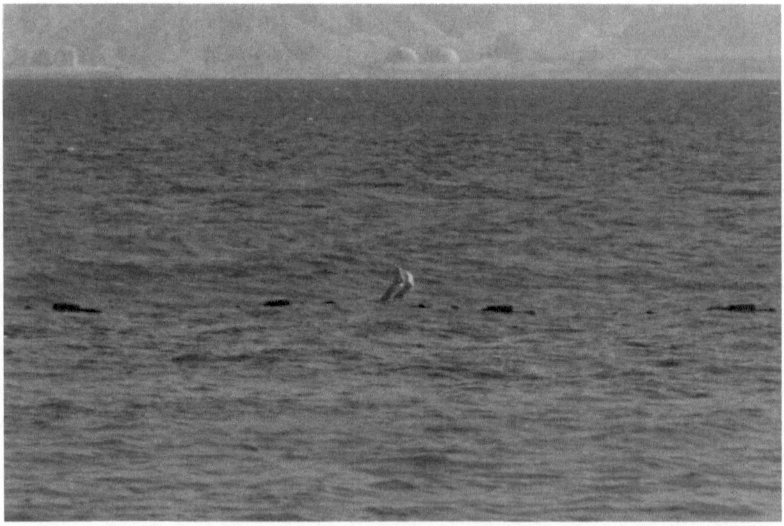

FIGURE 6.11 Deganit Berest, *Icarus*, 2004. Image reproduced by courtesy of the artist.

domelike buildings on the opposite shore, or the unidentified black stains floating on the same horizontal line as the legs. In the painted version, there is closer proximity to the legs, a kind of "zoom in" ostensibly intended to enhance and improve vision. In effect, however, the proximity and enlargement bring about the opposite effect: the image is dismantled into geometric clusters. Not only does the dismantling of the image not clarify its photographic counterpart; it shows that what we had believed to almost certainly identify as a pair of jutting-out legs is not necessarily what we imagined seeing.

As noted above, Richter does not perceive photography as a preparatory action to painting. Quite to the contrary, he regards photo-painting as related to photography. Berest takes this position to an extreme, blending the two mediums and pouring one into the other. Her photolike enlargements are accomplished by means of painting so as to sharpen and thus paradoxically blur the image. While photographic enlargement would obviously create a similar effect of blurring, or disrupted vision, the painting of the enlarged image effects a further turn in this complex process. The very reconstruction of a disturbance in vision, derived from the photographic technology of enlargement, by means of belabored painting emphasizes the multiple stages of the image's production and allows what is between painting and photography to emerge. In Lacanian terms, the gaze in this instance appears not on the level of the image but on the level of its mode of production, which involves making each medium present by means of the other. The photograph is made present because the painting traces it; painting is present through the photographic image at its foundation.

In another work from the 1990 series titled *The Bathers*, Berest uses watercolor to paint a photographic image of a boy paddling on a boat. This image, which first

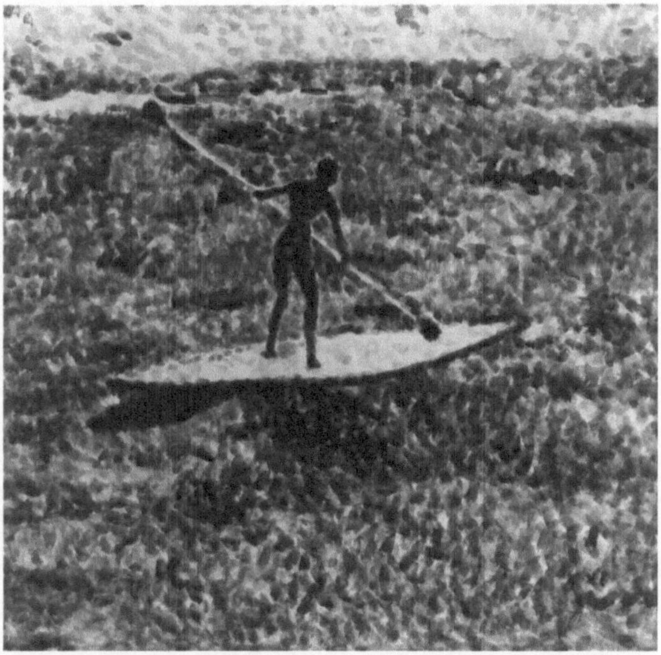

FIGURE 6.12 Deganit Berest, *Swimmer* from *The Bathers*, 1990. Image reproduced by courtesy of the artist.

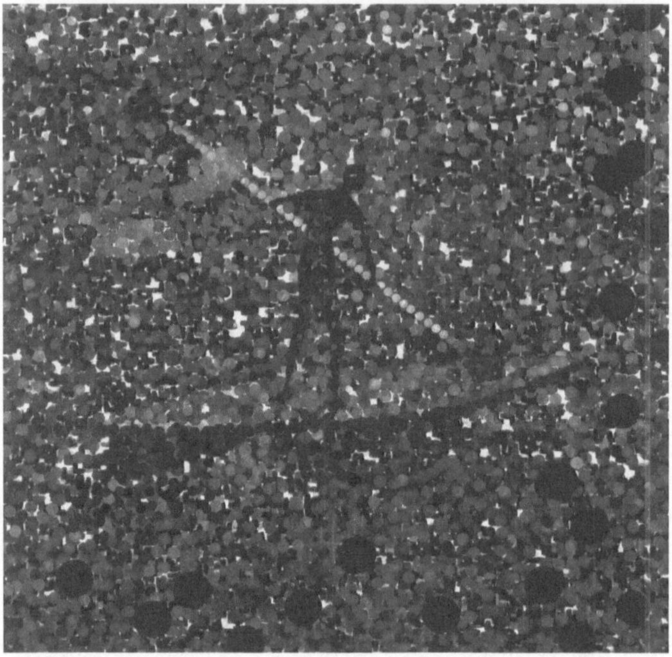

FIGURE 6.13 Deganit Berest, *Swimmer*, 1989. Image reproduced by courtesy of the artist.

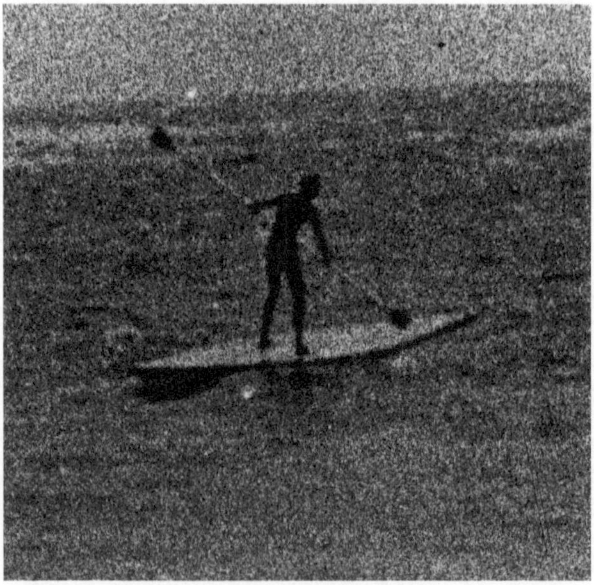

FIGURE 6.14 Deganit Berest, *Swimmer*, 1987. Image reproduced by courtesy of the artist.

appears in the *Loch Ness Investigations—The Photographs* (1987), also appears a year earlier, in a large oil painting where it is dismantled into circles.

The painting traces and even exaggerates photography's material graininess. The painted image flickers between the painting of a photograph and painting as such. These photo-paintings borrow the dismantling into units from the medium of photography, converting photography's mechanical graininess into time-consuming manual labor. The instance of the camera's operation is exchanged for the duration of slow and skillful work. This operation of exchange captures something which exists between the procedures of photography and of painting: a disturbance in duration, the ripping of a moment from continuity. Here, photography and painting—painting in all its photographic qualities and photography in all its picturesqueness—merge into one other.

These three instances of photo-painting, by Berest, Livneh and Richter, operate in the zone between two deaths. The traversal of the zone between the mode of the death drive's repetition in painting and the mode of its repetition in photography by means of the new medium of photo-painting allows something of the real—what is unbearable and impossible to represent—to emerge with full force. Lacan speaks of Antigone's beauty as flickering between two deaths: between the symbolic death of the king's violated edict and the bodily death which will take place after the food in her tomb runs out. Photo-painting works according to the same logic of between two deaths. However, while in *Antigone* what emerges between two deaths is the heroine's radiant beauty as the last barrier against the ultimate horror, in photo-painting, located between two forms of repetition of the death drive in culture, traversing the zone between them has the effect of tearing the veil, rending a gaping hole in the shield that art erects against the real.

Notes

1 Jacques Lacan, *The Seminar of Jacques Lacan, Book VII: The Ethics of Psychoanalysis* (1959–1960), trans. Dennis Porter (New York: W. W. Norton, 1986).
2 Ibid., p. 247.
3 Jacques Lacan, *The Seminar of Jacques Lacan, Book XIII: The Object of Psychoanalysis* (1965–1966), trans. by Cormac Gallagher (unpublished manuscript).
4 Ibid., lesson of 25 June 1966.
5 Jacques Lacan, *The Seminar of Jacques Lacan, Book XI: The Four Fundamental Concepts of Psychoanalysis*, trans. Alan Sheridan (New York: W. W. Norton, 1981 [1964–1965]), p. 92.
6 Michael Fried, *Why Photography Matters as Art as Never Before* (New Haven, CT: Yale University Press, 2008), p. 272.
7 In this context, one may mention the video works of artists such as Bill Viola or Sophie Calle, which deal with the documentation of the moment of death. Although in these works the image is continuous, not solitary, and although the moment of death is documented in them, it is nevertheless not present. In the case of Calle, although the camera does not leave the figure of the dying mother even for a moment, death escapes the image. The only way in which it emerges is the attempts to ascertain if there is still breathing.
8 Siegfried Kracauer, "Photography," trans. Thomas Y. Levin, *Critical Inquiry* 19, no. 3 (1933 [1927]): 433.

9 Susan Sontag, *On Photography* (New York: Dell Publishers, 1977), p. 71.
10 Paul Virilio, *La Machine de Vision*, 2nd ed. (Mayenne: Galilee, 1991 [1988]), pp. 14–15.
11 Philippe Dubois, *L'acte photographique* (Paris: Nathan Labor, 1983), p. 160.
12 Ibid., p. 160.
13 Ibid., p. 89.
14 Ibid., pp. 155–56.
15 Ibid., p. 160.
16 Roland Barthes, *Camera Lucida* (New York: Noonday Press, 1981), p. 15.
17 Ibid., p. 79.
18 Thierry de Duve, "Time Exposure and Snapshot: The Photograph as Paradox," *October* 5 (Summer 1978), 113–25.
19 Ibid., p. 116.
20 Ibid.
21 Ibid., p. 121.
22 Barthes, *Camera Lucida*, pp. 25–27.
23 Ibid., p. 27.
24 Ibid., p. 69.
25 Ibid., p. 93.
26 Ibid., p. 96.
27 Ibid.
28 Walter Benjamin, "The Work of Art in the Age of Mechanical Reproduction," in *Illuminations: Essays and Reflections*, trans. Harry Zohn (New York: Schocken Books). It should nevertheless be noted that a more careful reading of Benjamin reveals that the dichotomy is far from being this simple.
29 Michael Fried, "Without a Trace," *Artforum* 43, no. 7 (2005), pp. 198–203.
30 Kracauer, "Photography," p. 429.
31 Ibid., pp. 429–31.
32 Peter Galassi, *Before Photography: Painting and the Invention of Photography* (New York: The Museum of Modern Art, 1981).
33 Lacan, *Seminar XI*, p. 73.
34 Ibid., p. 73.
35 Peter Osborn, "Painting Negation: Gerhard Richter's Negatives," *October* 62 (1992), p. 107.
36 The "Red Army Faction" was active in Germany during the 1960s. Its leaders were Andreas Baader and Gudrun Ensslin. In the course of their activities, they were joined by the journalist Ulrike Meinhof. The group's members were accused of acts of violence, put on trial and imprisoned for long periods of time. On the evening of October 18, 1977, also known as "Death Night," four of the imprisoned members committed suicide. The circumstances of their death are highly disputed due to rumours that these were not suicides but murders. The story of the Baader-Meinhof group is to this day considered a national wound in postwar German society.
37 Benjamin H. D. Buchloh, *Gerhard Richter: Eight Gray* (Berlin: Deutsche Guggenheim, 2002), p. 28.
38 Benjamin H. D. Buchloh, "Gerhard Richter's *Atlas*: The Anomic Archive," *October* 88 (Spring 1999), pp. 117–45.
39 Ibid., p. 127.
40 Ibid., p. 134.
41 Ibid., p. 131.
42 Ibid.
43 Ibid., p. 140.
44 Ibid., p. 141.
45 Ibid., p. 142.
46 Ibid., p. 144.
47 Osborne, "Painting Negation."

48 Ibid., p. 104.
49 Ibid., p. 107.
50 Ibid., p. 108.
51 Ibid., p. 109.
52 Ibid., p. 111.
53 Ibid., p. 113.
54 For an extensive discussion on the relation of death and finality to Livneh's works, see Efrat Biberman, "Splendor," in *Astonishment: Yitzhak Livneh* (Exhibition Catalogue, Tel Aviv: Tel Aviv Museum, 2008), pp. 17–30.
55 Roee Rosen, "Mutation, Water, Sex, Place: Four Chapters on Deganit Berest," *Studio Art Magazine* 70 (March/April 1996), pp. 36–51. In Hebrew.
56 Ibid., p. 50.
57 Ibid.
58 Tali Tamir, "The Gondolier's Enunciation; or, The Moment of Dawning," trans. Dan Shorer, in *Deganit Berest: Four Chapters on Water*, curated by Daniella Talmor (Haifa: Haifa Museum of Art, 2004), pp. 95–106.
59 Ibid., p. 100.
60 Ibid., p. 95.

EPILOGUE

On painting and death

During the early 1990s, Yitzhak Livneh painted a series of paintings depicting mirrors which do not reflect. The paintings were based on auction-house catalogs exhibiting photographs of old murky mirrors. Unlike in well-known paintings of mirrors from the history of art, in Livneh's paintings mirrors are stripped of the outcome of their most prominent characteristic: the reflected object attesting to their specular power. Instead, what these painted mirrors foreground is the empty possibility of reflection itself. Although these paintings have an abstract quality, consisting as they do only of amorphous color stains on canvas, their appearance is definitely specular. Hence they can easily be regarded as instances of *trompe-l'oeil* which the naïve viewer might initially consider mirrors *per se*.

About two decades later, after having painted an abundance of themes in various styles, Livneh created a series of small paintings in which the word "EXIT" is inscribed from top to bottom, spread over most of the surface of a square canvas, invoking lit-up signs pointing the way out from a dark space such as a cinema hall. Text written in forceful brush strokes fills the square of the canvas, its bright and intensive colors illuminating the painting's surface. Like Livneh's mirror paintings, which allude to a long tradition of depicting specularity at the very same time as they are rooted in a tradition of abstract painting, his *EXIT* paintings rest on a double gesture. The paintings are instances at once of the modernist genre of text painting and of an earlier, formalist and modernist tradition of interrogating painting by means of its most prominent features, in this case, the format of the square crossed by painted strokes. The "all-overness" of the letters in the painting demonstrates the limits of the frame, alluding to Greenbergian assumptions regarding modernist painting's most prominent characteristics.[1] At the same time, disguising themselves as a familiar concrete object, the paintings flirt with the genre of *trompe-l'oeil*.

FIGURE E.1 Yitzhak Livneh, *Untitled*, 1990. Image reproduced by courtesy of the artist.

Interpreters and critics of Livneh's paintings produced over the last three decades agree that his art variously engages the theme of death. The paintings of the dead soldiers with which we opened this book and Livneh's *vanitas* paintings are characteristic examples of this thematic tendency—from which the mirror and *EXIT* paintings seemingly deviate. Nor do these two series seem to have anything else in common. Both, however, exemplify a link between painting and death inhering not in the painting's narrative or theme but in its structure and implication of the viewing or painting subject. Seemingly unrelated to each other or to death as theme, these two series exemplify the immanence of death in the very act of painting, as an inevitable horizon which

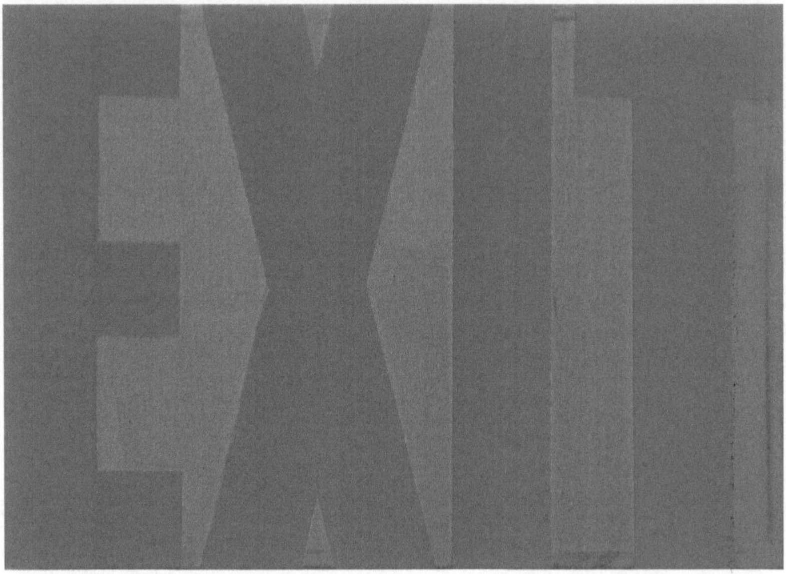

FIGURE E.2 Yitzhak Livneh, *EXIT*, 2007. Image reproduced by courtesy of the artist.

painting does not cease to challenge, hence justifying its existence no less than its ever-impending demise.

What is the common ground of these seemingly different series in Livneh's art? Both disguise painting as a concrete object, hence partaking of the long tradition of *trompe-l'oeil*. In the mirror series, the effect of deception is enhanced by the painting's wooden frame, an unusual occurrence in Livneh's art. In the *EXIT* series the effect of deception is the result of the resplendent color and dazzling appearance of the letters and of the artwork's measurements, which are close to those of actual exit signs.

Though the two series do share a *trompe-l'oeil* quality, it is in both cases but one aspect of the paintings, which take their place in the context of contemporary art. Focused on deceit and aiming at objectlike visibility, *trompe-l'oeil* paintings tend to share a common appearance immune to historical and stylistic changes. Seventeenth-century *trompe l'oeils* by Cornelius Gijsbrechts or Samuel Van Hoogstraten, for instance, strongly resemble in style the nineteenth-century instances of the genre by John Frederick Peto or William Harnett in their illusionistic depiction of an object. It is precisely from this largely uniform visuality that Livneh's *trompe-l'oeil* paintings manage to deviate, maintaining as they do a visuality rendering them clear instances of contemporary art.

What is more significant about Livneh's two series, however, and part of what makes them akin to one another, is their focus on an object suggesting an act it does not carry out or even contradicts. The two series involve a seen object whose visuality invites its viewer to do something more than merely contemplate it. In the case of the mirror paintings, the viewer is allegedly invited to see reflections in what seems to be a mirror, to enter into a realm of specular images. In the *EXIT* series, the viewer is lured to find his way out from a dark space where visibility is low. The ultimate example of such a space is the cinema hall, where the viewer sits in the dark enveloped by the illusory visuality emerging from projected images flickering on a screen and trying to find his way out once the images cease, replaced by darkness visible. But in Livneh's paintings the mirror turns out to reflect nothing and the exit sign leads nowhere, trapping the viewer by its bright colors instead.

Death seems to have nothing to do with these paintings, but its footprints soon become evident. It is the word that renders death prominently present in the *EXIT* paintings, which invoke the Latin *exitus*, metaphorical rendering of "death." The relation of mirrors to death is more indirect but no less salient. Mirrors, Pliny the Elder teaches, were commonly buried in sarcophagi next to the deceased alongside other objects, which would eventually turn to stone.[2] Another manifestation of specularity, the Claude glass, a black concave mirror used by landscape painters and travellers mainly during the eighteenth and nineteenth centuries, is intriguingly related to death as it emerges by means of specularity.[3] The Claude glass provided the viewer with a unified vision of the landscape, whose color range was limited by the dark shade of the glass. Because of its concave shape, the Claude glass functioned as a wide lens granting the reflected scene a pictorial quality. Travelers and painters equipped with Claude glasses, Arnault Maillet argues in his study of the device, were in effect engaged in "image hunting," which gave rise to the idiom "to shoot a picture" as a description of the act of photography.[4]

A more fundamental, and more troubling, relation of specularity and death has to do with the limits of vision and their transgression. Suffice it to mention the mourning custom in Judaism and other faiths of covering mirrors in the house of the deceased and of closing his eyes. The Jewish custom of shutting the eyelids of the dead has its origin in the Exodus verse "for no man can see Me and live" (33:20). Conventional interpretations of this verse suggest that while the living may not see God, the dead, who are not subject to this prohibition, may encounter God as an impossible to see, and their eyelids must remain shut.[5] The house of the dead, too, is believed to harbor an impossible sight, hence the custom of covering its mirrors. This belief, as it turns out, is not exclusively Jewish. Maillet describes a black mirror, used in ancient Greece, which was actually a hole in the wall through which one could ostensibly gaze out to the realm of the dead.[6] Another anecdote Maillet recounts concerns a black convex mirror which "enabled necromancers to conjure and to visualize the souls of the dead and thus to enter into communication with them."[7] In all these instances, mirrors are perceived as able to reflect something from life's beyond.

What the customs discussed by Maillet reveal concerning the relation of death and visuality is not unrelated to Lacan's discussion of the scopic dimension of melancholia in his seminar on anxiety. It is not by chance, Lacan says toward the end of that seminar, that when the melancholic commits suicide, he often does so by leaping out of a window, that is, by getting out of a picture, whose structure

Lacan identifies as isomorphic with that of the phantasm, the unconscious screen of visually represented scenes constituting the subject's psychic reality.[8] In the seminar on the object of psychoanalysis, Lacan reiterates that the structure of the phantasm is analogous to the structure of a figurative painting.[9] What this means is that the melancholic's defenestration is a literal traversal of this phantasm as picture plane.

Lacan's discussion of the split between the eye and the gaze in the seminar on the four fundamental concepts of psychoanalysis clarifies the visual structure of the phantasm.[10] What the eye sees is imaginary in nature, the product of a procedure in which the subject governs his field of vision. It is this imaginary procedure that is at work for the jubilant infant described by Lacan in his famous article on "The Mirror Stage," when he first recognizes his specular image.[11] This vision is predicated upon identification and involves narcissism. Even more significantly, it enables the subject to assume a visual field that is coherent and harmonious, one in which the visible world seems to be spread out in front of him, offering itself as what can be seen. In his seminar on anxiety, however, Lacan shows that there is more to this seemingly coherent and complete vision than suggested by so optimistic an account. What gives the subject satisfaction in the visual field is not only what is seen, but also what veils the option of confronting an impossible to see which may be qualified in Freudian terms as "uncanny." What this means is that specular reflection is so comforting not because it enables us to see but precisely because it prevents us from seeing what it does not include but which it nevertheless presentifies in the very act of veiling.

Alongside imaginary vision, Lacan describes another ocular procedure which is not its opposite but its counterpart. This is the gaze, a modality of vision involving something of the real, one that has to do less with what the subject sees and more with his being subjected to the gaze of the Other, who looks at him from an unexpected place. This Other is ultimately the unconscious scene of the subject himself, split as he is, for Lacan, between an imaginary ego (predicated on the vision of the eye) and the unconscious (in which the gaze can emerge, carrying something of the real). As the gaze pertains to the real as what cannot be represented, it is manifest in painting as what is presentified in it by means that are other than respresentational. In his seminar on the object of psychoanalysis, Lacan shows how the structure of looking at a painting is isomorphic with the structure of the phantasm. Freud had already theorized the phantasm as an unconscious script whose protagonist is the subject.[12] One may think of it, Lacan adds, in terms of frames from a film reel.[13] The phantasmatic script is particular to the subject, who unconsciously adopts it early on in his life as what would from that point on constitute his psychic reality. In his adult life the subject will continue to operate in accordance with that early script, while knowing nothing about this.

The formula of the phantasm according to Lacan consists of the split subject in all of his possible relations with the object cause of desire, the a object. The subject's position in the phantasm is structurally parallel to his position in front of a painting as articulated in terms of Alberti's geometrical perspective. As Lacan shows, although with the formulation of geometrical perspective Alberti sought to offer a precise and valid model of looking which would make it possible to measure the exact distance between viewer and picture, his model necessarily includes a blind spot. Lacan teaches that in contravention of the Albertian model which presupposes a subject who sees objectively and is in control of the visual field, the viewing subject is always already inscribed in the picture he is looking at, just as he is in the projected script that is his own phantasm.

Livneh's mirror series and *EXIT* series seem to exemplify Lacan's theorems concerning the imaginary and its embodiments in painting, and hence to be cases of an *experimentum mentis* as Regnault uses this term, cases to which psychoanalytic knowledge is applied. Their interest for psychoanalysis, however, lies not in their imaginary dimension, the dimension which makes it possible for them to illustrate theory, but in the very way in which they exceed this dimension. The unique structure of these paintings is inherent to the gap they tear open in the visual field: between the gesture of pointing at an exit and the materiality of the *EXIT* sign as a painted object, between specular image and painted canvas. What functions as a structural condition for this gap is the imaginary dimension of the painted image, just as the complete and coherent image of the mirror stage is what enables it to presentify what it does not include.

The two series ostensibly delineate two ways of looking at a painting. The mirror paintings seem to invite the viewer to meditative immersion in the image, the *EXIT* paintings to offer a way out to what lies beyond the canvas. Yet the mirror which does not reflect any image leaves the viewer only with the possibility of reflection, rendering impossible the experience of devoted contemplation of the represented object which it solicits. Instead of a reflection of his own visage, what the painting returns to the viewer is a visuality oscillating between abstract painting and *trompe-l'oeil*, leaving the viewer with the act of reflecting detached from any object that might attest to it. Similarly, the *EXIT* paintings seem to point at a way out yet in effect captivate the viewer with their saturated and dazzling colorfulness. In both cases, in effect, what the viewer receives from the painting he contemplates is his own act of looking.

In his seminar on the four fundamental concepts of psychoanalysis, Lacan teaches that figurative painting offers the viewer something for his sight to feed on, pacifying the unsettling presence of the gaze.[14] But Livneh does the viewer no such grace. He leaves the viewer with a reflection without an object or with the indication of a way out detached from any escape route. He leaves the viewer, that is, with painterliness in itself. This is Livneh's particular invention in the sphere of art, his way of articulating what is in effect an *experimentum crucis*.

If the melancholic who defenestrates himself tears the screen of representation, refusing the visually represented script of the phantasm that upheld his psychic reality and enabled him to make sense of experience and try to leap beyond it, Livneh's two series too gesture toward a beyond. This beyond, however, is not of the phantasm as an isomorph of painting but of the diapason of painting itself. Yet in the case of these two series, approaching a beyond spells not the extinction it risks but the stretching and pushing of the limits of painting while all the while continuing to paint. While the melancholic who commits suicide expunges any possibility of invention in his life or transformation in the phantasm he tears, isomorph of a painted scene, Livneh's move in these two series involves the reinvention of painting through proceeding beyond its familiar borders. It is here that the fundamental structural link between these paintings and the death drive becomes apparent, since the very thrust of painting, its impelling force, is to proceed toward the beyond of the limits of representation, courting these limits or attempting to break through them—as long as it still remains possible to go on painting.

Notes

1 Clement Greenberg, "Modernist Painting," in *Modern Art and Modernism: A Critical Anthology*, ed. Francis Frascina and Charles Harrison (London: Harper & Row, 1982 [1960]), pp. 5–10.
2 Pliny the Elder, *Natural History*, trans. H. Rackham (Cambridge, MA: Harvard University Press, 1991), p. 360.
3 Arnaud Maillet, *The Claude Glass: Use and Meaning of the Black Mirror in Western Art*, trans. Jeff Fort (San Francisco: Zone Books, 2009 [2004]).
4 Ibid., p. 167.
5 Abraham Isaac Sperling, *Reasons for Jewish Customs and Traditions* (New York: Bloch Publishing, 1968). We would like to thank David Ginton for this information.
6 Ibid., p. 69.
7 Maillet, *The Claude Glass*, p. 50.
8 Jacques Lacan, *The Seminar of Jacques Lacan, Book X: Anxiety*, trans. Adrian Price (Cambridge, MA: Polity Press, 2014 [1962–1963]), pp. 335–36.
9 Jacques Lacan, *The Seminar of Jacques Lacan, Book XIII: The Object of Psychoanalysis* (1965–1966), trans. Cormac Gallagher (unpublished manuscript), lesson of 4 May 1966.
10 Jacques Lacan, *The Seminar of Jacques Lacan, Book XI: The Four Fundamental Concepts of Psychoanalysis*, trans. Alan Sheridan (New York: W. W. Norton, 1981 [1964–1965]), pp. 67–78.
11 Jacques Lacan, "The Mirror Stage as Formative of the Function of the 'I' as Revealed in Psychoanalytic Experience," in *Écrits: A Selection*, trans. Bruce Fink (New York: W. W. Norton, 2006 [1949]), pp. 75–81.
12 Sigmund Freud, "A Child Is Being Beaten," in *The Standard Edition of the Complete Psychological Works of Sigmund Freud, Vol. XVII*, trans. and ed. James Strachey (London: Hogarth Press, 1955 [1919]), pp. 179–204.
13 Jacques Lacan, *The Seminar of Jacques Lacan, Book VI: Desire and Its Interpretation* (1958–1959), trans. Cormac Gallagher (unpublished manuscript), lesson of 26 November 1958, p. 6.
14 Lacan, *Seminar XI*, p. 101.

BIBLIOGRAPHY

Alberti, Leon Battista. 1966 [1435–1436]. *On Painting*. Trans. John R. Spencer. New Haven, CT: Yale University Press.

Alpers, Svetlana. 1988. *Rembrandt's Enterprise: The Studio and the Market*. Chicago: University of Chicago Press.

Badiou, Alain. 2005. *Handbook of Inaesthetics*. Trans. Alberto Toscano. Stanford: Stanford University Press.

Barthes, Rolan. 1981 [1980]. *Camera Lucida: Reflections on Photography*. New York: Noonday Press.

Bataille, George. 1989 [1961]. *The Tears of Eros*. Trans. Peter Connor. San Francisco: City Lights Books.

Belting, Hans. 1987 [1983]. *The End of History of Art?* Trans. Christopher S. Wood. Chicago: University of Chicago Press.

——. 1994 [1990]. *Likeness and Presence: A History of the Image before the Era of Art*. Trans. Edmund Jephcott. Chicago: University of Chicago Press.

Benjamin, Walter. 1969 [1942]. "The Work of Art in the Age of Mechanical Reproduction." In *Illuminations: Essays and Reflections*. Trans. Harry Zohn. New York: Schocken Books.

——. 1980 [1930]. *A Short History of Photography*. New Haven, CT: Leete's Island Books.

Biberman, Efrat. 2005. "Painted Theory or Theoretical Painting: Gabriel Orozco and the Psychoanalytic Discourse." In *Protocols in History and Theory, Vol. 1*. Jerusalem: Bezalel Academy of Art and Design. In Hebrew.

——. 2008. "Beyond the Painting Principles." *Machbar-Ot: The Journal of the Center of Lacanian Studies* 3: 69–78. In Hebrew.

——. 2008. "Of the Gaze as Topological Locus: Alberti and Lacan." *(Re)-Turn: A Journal of Lacanian Studies. The Gaze* 3 & 4 (Spring 2008): 135–49.

——. 2008. "Splendor." In *Astonishment: Yitshak Livneh*. Exhibition Catalogue. Tel Aviv: Tel Aviv Museum, pp. 17–30.

——. 2009. "Between Oblivion and Anxiety: The Duplicity of the Image in Sebald and Richter." In *Germany, Catastrophe and Representation: W. G. Sebald: Between Fiction and Testimony*. Ed. Galili Shahar and Michal Ben Horin. Jerusalem: European Forum at the Hebrew University of Jerusalem. In Hebrew.

——. 2009. *Visual Text(a)iles: Narrative and Gaze in Painting*. Ramat Gan: Bar-Ilan University Press. In Hebrew.
——. 2010. "The Iconography of the Unconscious." *Machbar-Ot: The Journal of the Center of Lacanian Studies* 4. In Hebrew.
Bryson, Norman. 1983. *Vision and Painting: The Logic of the Gaze*. New Haven, CT: Yale University Press.
Buchloh, Benjamin H. D. 1999. "Gerhard Richter's *Atlas*: The Anomic Archive." *October* 88 (Spring): 117–45.
——. 2002. *Gerhard Richter: Eight Gray*. Berlin: Deutsche Guggenheim.
Danto, Arthur C. 1986. "The End of Art." In *The Philosophical Disenfranchisement of Art*. New York: Columbia University Press.
——. 1997. *After the End of Art: Contemporary Art and the Pale of Modernism*. Princeton, NJ: Princeton University Press.
——. 1998. *The Wake of Art: Criticism, Philosophy, and the Ends of Taste*. Amsterdam: B+G Arts International.
de Duve, Thierry. 1978. "Time Exposure and Snapshot: The Photograph as Paradox." *October* 5 (Summer 1978): 113–25.
——. 1996. *Kant after Duchamp*. Cambridge, MA: MIT Press.
de Man, Paul. 1984. "Autobiography as De-Facement." In *The Rhetoric of Romanticism*. New York: Columbia University Press.
Derrida, Jacques. 1984. *The Ear of the Other: Otobiography, Transference, Translation*. Trans. Peggy Kamuf. San Francisco: Bison Books.
——. 1987. *The Truth in Painting*. Trans. Geoff Bennington and Ian McLoed. Chicago: University of Chicago Press.
——. 1993 [1990]. *Memoirs of the Blind*. Trans. Pascale-Anne Brault and Michael Naas. Chicago: Chicago University Press.
——. 2010 [2000]. *Copy, Archive, Signature: A Conversation on Photography*. Ed. Gerhard Richter, trans. Jeff Fort. Stanford: Stanford University Press.
Dubois, Philippe. 1983. *L'acte photographique*. Paris: Nathan Labor.
Freud, Sigmund. 1950 [1887–1902]. "Project for a Scientific Psychology." In *The Standard Edition of the Complete Psychological Works of Sigmund Freud, Vol. 1*. Trans. and ed. James Strachey. London: Hogarth Press, pp. 283–344.
——. 1955 [1920]. "Beyond the Pleasure Principle." In *The Standard Edition of the Complete Psychological Works of Sigmund Freud, Vol. XVIII*. Trans. and ed. James Strachey. London: Hogarth Press.
——. 1957 [1915]. "The Unconscious." In *The Standard Edition of the Complete Psychological Works of Sigmund Freud, Vol. XIV*. Trans. and ed. James Strachey. London: Hogarth Press, pp. 166–204.
——. 1960 [1896]. "Extracts from the Fliess Papers: Letter 52." In *The Standard Edition of the Complete Psychological Works of Sigmund Freud, Vol. 1*. Trans. and ed. James Strachey. London: Hogarth Press, pp. 233–39.
——. 1960 [1905]. "Jokes and Their Relation to the Unconscious." In *The Standard Edition of the Complete Psychological Works of Sigmund Freud, Vol. VIII*. Trans. and ed. James Strachey. London: Hogarth Press.
——. 1960 [1901]. "The Psychopathology of Everyday Life." In *The Standard Edition of the Complete Psychological Works of Sigmund Freud, Vol. VI*. Trans. and ed. James Strachey. London: Hogarth Press, pp. 1–7.
——. 1961 [1925]. "Negation." In *The Standard Edition of the Complete Psychological Works of Sigmund Freud, Vol. XIX*. Trans. and ed. James Strachey. London: Hogarth Press, pp. 233–40.

——. 1962 [1898]. "Screen Memories." In *The Standard Edition of the Complete Psychological Works of Sigmund Freud, Vol. III*. Trans. and ed. James Strachey. London: Hogarth Press, pp. 303–22.

——. 2001 [1915]. "Instincts and Their Vicissitudes." In *The Standard Edition of the Complete Psychological Works of Sigmund Freud, Vol. XIV*. Trans. and ed. James Strachey. London: Hogarth Press, pp. 117–40.

——. 2001 [1919]. "The Uncanny." In *The Standard Edition of the Complete Psychological Works of Sigmund Freud, Vol. XVII*. Trans. and ed. James Strachey. London: Hogarth Press, pp. 219–56.

Fried, Michael. 1992. *Courbet's Realism*. Chicago: University of Chicago Press.

——. 2005. "Without a Trace." *Artforum* 43, no. 7 (March 2005).

——. 2008. *Why Photography Matters as Art as Never Before*. New Haven, CT: Yale University Press.

Galassi, Peter. 1981. *Before Photography: Painting and the Invention of Photography*. New York: Museum of Modern Art.

Greenberg, Clement. 1982 [1960]. "Modernist Painting." In *Modern Art and Modernism: A Critical Anthology*. Ed. Francis Frascina and Charles Harrison. London: Harper & Row, pp. 5–10.

Hegel, G. W. F. 1988 [1835]. *Aesthetics: Lectures on Fine Art*. Trans. T. M. Knox. Oxford: Clarendon Press.

Homer. *Odyssey*. Trans. George Herbert Palmer. Mineola, NY: Dover.

Joyce, James. 1996 [1916]. *A Portrait of the Artist as a Young Man*. London: Penguin.

——. *Finnegans Wake*. 2000 [1939]. Harmondsworth: Penguin.

Kant, Immanuel. 1952 [1790]. *Critique of Judgment*. Trans. James Creed Meredith. Oxford: Oxford University Press.

Kenaan, Hagi. 2006. "Tracing Shadows: Reflections on the Origins of Painting." In *Pictorial Languages and Their Meaning*. Ed. G. Fishof and C. Versar. Tel Aviv: Tel Aviv University, Faculty of the Arts.

Kracauer, Seigfried. 1993 [1927]. "Photography." *Critical Inquiry* 19, no. 3 (Spring 1993).

Kristeva, Julia. 1989. *Black Sun: Depression and Melancholia*. Trans. Leon S. Roudiez. New York: Columbia University Press.

Lacan, Jacques. 1957–1958. *The Seminar of Jacques Lacan, Book V: Formations of the Unconscious*. Trans. Cormac Gallagher. Unpublished manuscript.

——. 1958–1959. *The Seminar of Jacques Lacan, Book VI: Desire and Its Interpretation*. Trans. Cormac Gallagher. Unpublished manuscript.

——. 1960–1961. *The Seminar of Jacques Lacan, Book VIII: The Transference*. Trans. Cormac Gallagher. Unpublished manuscript. Lesson of 16 November 1960, p. 46.

——. 1961–1962. *The Seminar of Jacques Lacan, Book IX: Identification*. Trans. Cormac Gallagher. Unpublished manuscript.

——. 1964–1965. *The Seminar of Jacques Lacan, Book XII: Crucial Problems of Psychoanalysis*. Trans. Cormac Gallagher. Unpublished manuscript.

——. 1965–1966. *The Seminar of Jacques Lacan, Book XIII: The Object of Psychoanalysis*. Trans. Cormac Gallagher. Unpublished manuscript.

——. 1969–1970. *The Seminar of Jacques Lacan, Book XVII: The Other Side of Psychoanalysis*. New York: W. W. Norton.

——. 1970–1971. *The Seminar of Jacques Lacan, Book XVIII: On a Discourse That Might Not Be a Semblance*. Trans. Cormac Gallagher. Unpublished manuscript.

——. 1974–1975. *The Seminar of Jacques Lacan, Book XXII: R.S.I.* Trans. Jack Stone. Unpublished manuscript.

——. 1977 [1953]. "The Function and Field of Speech and Language in Psychoanalysis." In *Écrits: A Selection*. Trans. Alan Sheridan. New York: W. W. Norton.

——. 1977 [1949]. "The Mirror Stage as Formative of the Function of the I as Revealed in Psychoanalytic Experience." In *Écrits: A Selection*. Trans. Alan Sheridan. New York: W. W. Norton.

——. 1981 [1964–1965]. *The Seminar of Jacques Lacan, Book XI: The Four Fundamental Concepts of Psychoanalysis*. Trans. Alan Sheridan. New York: W. W. Norton.

——. 1986. *The Seminar of Jacques Lacan, Book VII: The Ethics of Psychoanalysis* (1959–1960). Trans. Dennis Porter. New York: W. W. Norton.

——. 1988 [1953–1954]. *The Seminar of Jacques Lacan, Book I: Freud's Papers on Technique*. Trans. John Forrester. New York: W. W. Norton.

——. 1988. *The Seminar of Jacques Lacan, Book II: The Ego in Freud's Theory and in the Technique of Psychoanalysis* (1954–1955). Trans. Sylvana Tomaselli. New York: W. W. Norton.

——. 1999 [1958]. "The Direction of the Treatment and the Principles of Its Power." In *Écrits: A Selection*. Trans. Bruce Fink. New York: W. W. Norton.

——. 2014 [1962–1963]. *The Seminar of Jacques Lacan, Book X: Anxiety*. Trans. A. R. Price. Cambridge: Polity Press.

——. 2016 [1975–1976]. *The Seminar of Jacques Lacan, Book XXIII: The Sinthome*. Trans. A. R. Price. Cambridge: Polity Press.

Maillet, Arnaud. 2009. *The Claude Glass: Use and Meaning of the Black Mirror in Western Art*. Trans. Jeff Fort. New York: Zone Books.

Miller, Jacques-Alain. 1985. "Reflections on the Formal Envelope of the Symptom." *Lacanian Ink*, no. 4, 1991: 13–21.

——. 1997. "Extimité." In *Lacanian Theory of Discourse: Subject, Structure and Society*. Ed. Mark Bracher et al. New York: New York University Press.

Montrelay, Michele. 1977. *L'ombre et le nom: sur la feminite*. Paris: Seuil.

Nochlin, Linda. 1994. *The Body in Pieces: The Fragment as a Metaphor of Modernity*. New York: Thames and Hudson.

Osborne, Peter. 1992. "Painting Negation: Gerhard Richter's Negatives." *October* 62, Autumn, pp. 102–13.

Pliny the Elder. 1991. *Natural History*. Trans. H. Rackham. Cambridge, MA: Harvard University Press.

Regnault, François. 1991. "Lacan and Experience." In *Lacan and the Human Sciences*. Ed. Alexandre Leupin. Lincoln: University of Nebraska Press.

Rosen, Roee. 1996. "Mutation, Water, Sex, Place: Four Chapters on Deganit Berest." *Studio Art Magazine*, no. 70 (March/April): 36–51. In Hebrew.

Sharon-Zisser, Shirley. 2001. "Some Little Language Such as Lovers Use: Virginia Woolf's Elemental Erotics of Simile." *American Imago: Studies in Psychoanalysis and Culture* 58, no. 2 (Summer): 567–96.

——. 2006. "The Topological Mortography of the Palimpsest: Towards a Lacanian Aesthetics of the Writing of Death in the Photographic Act." In *Constructions of Death, Mourning, and Memory*. Ramsey, NJ: WAPACC.

——. 2009. "On the Suffering Body in Visual Art and Medicine." *Et Lacan: A Psychoanalytical Journal* 3: 65–82. In Hebrew.

Shkolvsky, Victor. "Art as Technique." In *Russian Formalist Criticism: Four Essays*. Ed. Lee T. Lemon and Marion J. Reis. Lincoln: University of Nebraska Press.

Sontag, Susan. 1977. *On Photography*. New York: Dell Publications.

Sternberg, Meir. 1982. "Proteus in Quotation-Land: Mimesis and the Forms of Reported Discourse." *Poetics Today* 3, no. 2 (Spring): 107–56.
Stevens, Wallace. 1990 [1923]. "Sunday Morning." In *The Collected Poems of Wallace Stevens*. New York: Vintage Books.
Stoichita, Victor I. 1997. *The Self-Aware Image: An Insight into Early Modern Meta-Painting*. Trans. Ann-Marie Glasheen. Cambridge: Cambridge University Press.
Storr, Robert. 2003. *Gerhard Richter: Doubt and Belief in Painting*. New York: Museum of Modern Art, Thames and Hudson.
Tamir, Tali. 2004. "The Gondolier's Enunciation; or, The Moment of Dawning." In *Deganit Berest: Four Chapters on Water*. Curated by Daniella Talmor. Haifa: Haifa Museum of Art.
——. 2008. "Beyond the Threshold of Beauty: A Conversation with Shosh Kormosh, 2001." In *Shosh Kormosh: Terms of Stillness, Works 1987–2001*. Tel Aviv: Open Museum of Photography, Tel-Hai Industrial Park and Gordon Gallery.
Vasari, Giorgio. 1996 [1550]. *The Lives of the Most Excellent Painters, Sculptors and Architects*. Trans. Gaston du C. de Vere. New York: Random House.
Vattimo, Gianni. 1988. "The Death or Decline of Art." In *The End of Modernity: Nihilism and Hermeneutics in Postmodern Culture*. Cambridge: Polity Press.
Viereck, George Sylvester. 1930. "Sigmund Freud Confronts the Sphinx." In *Glimpses of the Great*. London: Duckworth.
Virilio, Paul. 1991 [1988]. *La Machine de Vision*. 2nd edition. Mayenne: Galilee.
Woolf, Virginia. 1945. *Jacob's Room*. London: Hogarth Press.
——. 2000 [1941]. *Between the Acts*. Harmondsworth: Penguin.
——. 2000 [1931]. *The Waves*. Ware, Hertfordshire: Wordsworth Editions.

INDEX

(Page numbers for figures appear in *italics*.)